D0916893

ANALYTIC PHILOSOPHY AND PHENOMENOLOGY

AMERICAN UNIVERSITY PUBLICATIONS IN PHILOSOPHY

II

ANALYTIC PHILOSOPHY AND PHENOMENOLOGY

edited by

HAROLD A. DURFEE

ANALYTIC PHILOSOPHY AND PHENOMENOLOGY

edited by

HAROLD A. DURFEE

MARTINUS NIJHOFF - THE HAGUE - 1976

To

DORIS

for being the center of

my *Lebenswelt*

ISBN 90 247 1880 5

PRINTED IN BELGIUM

SERIES EDITOR'S PREFACE

This is the second volume in the series of American University Publications in Philosophy. It, like the first volume, moves significantly beyond what other books have done before it. The first volume's originality lay in its bringing together essays that explored important new directions in the explanation of behavior, language, and religion. The originality of the present volume lies in its collecting, for the first time in book form, essays at the interface between analytic philosophy and phenomenology. In this volume there are essays about a number of the most seminally influential philosophers among both the analysts and the phenomenologists.

Barry L. Blose, for the editors of
American University
Publications in Philosophy

EDITOR'S PREFACE

Philosophy inevitably creates divisions and this anthology deals with what is perhaps the central division in twentieth century Western philosophy. The collection, originally the foundation for a seminar in comparative philosophy which I offered at The American University in 1971 and 1974, was sufficiently suggestive to students of both traditions to lead me to initiate its publication. The future development of Western philosophy is far from clear, but I am convinced that it will inevitably involve a more open conversation between phenomenologists and analytic philosophers, between the current dominant orientations among both European and Anglo-Saxon philosophers. This volume of essays is offered as an attempt to stimulate that conversation.

I am grateful to the authors and publishers who cooperated in allowing these essays to be published, to the publishers of these series for both their interest and efficiency, and to the students in seminars, whose active participation evidence what higher education is all about. Special thanks are due to the editors of the American University Publications in Philosophy for including this volume in their series; to Barry L. Blose, whose advice throughout this project was frequently solicited and graciously offered; to Peter A. Durfee, whose suggestions offered welcomed improvements in the design of this volume; to Madaline K. Shoemaker, whose patience at the typewriter never failed; and to my wife, whose constant help made it possible.

H.A.D.
The American University, 1975

TABLE OF CONTENTS

AN EARLY EVALUATION

FOUNDATIONAL PHILOSOPHERS

META-PHILOSOPHICAL REFLECTIONS

INTRODUCTION

Philosophy is a discipline of fundamental diversities and extremely divergent modes of thought some of which occupy center stage in Western intellectual development. This book deals with such a central division. For centuries significant differences have developed between the philosophical reflections of the Western European (mainly French and German) and those of the Anglo-Saxon countries (especially Britain, Australia, Canada, and the United States). These differences extend at least as far back in history as the major epistemological division between the early modern rationalism of Descartes and Leibnitz and the British empiricism of Locke, Berkeley, and Hume. At certain periods there has been greater compatibility, as with the development of Hegelian Idealism in England and the United States or the development of Logical Empiricism in the Vienna Circle. In spite of such interesting exceptions, however, continental and Anglo-Saxon philosophers have frequently moved in different directions and have worked within different philosophical traditions, for example, the French tradition of Descartes and the Anglo-Saxon tradition of Hume.

The essays in this volume do not deal with historical or nationalistic themes, but rather with a contemporary manifestation of the traditional Anglo-Saxon/continental dichotomy. During the twentieth century continental philosophers have been developing the philosophical position which has become known as phenomenology, while at the same time Anglo-Saxon philosophers have been working out a position which has come to be called Analytic Philosophy, or Linguistic Analysis. The essays which follow do not describe the nature and history of these movements in themselves, but attempt rather to investigate at some depth the relationships and relative merits of these two positions.

It is dangerous to generalize about dominant philosophical tendencies on any continent or national scene, and alternative positions are usually well represented. Nevertheless, certain tendencies do seem to capture primary attention. Marxism, as well as phenomenology, obviously plays a significant role on the European continent, but it too is frequently in dialogue with the phenomenological movement, as in its dialogue with Jean-Paul Sartre or Maurice Merleau-Ponty. It should also be noted that there are significant centers of analytic thought in Europe, especially in Scandinavian countries. More recently European philosophers have taken increased interest in linguistic analysis and philosophy of language, but even when this occurs, as in the continental concern with hermeneutics, it carries on its reflection in a unique manner quite distinguishable from the concern with language in Anglo-Saxon circles.

It is also clear that non-analytic concerns are widely present in Anglo-Saxon countries. Pragmatic naturalism and the tradition of Whiteheadian process philosophy are major interests on the American scene. Nevertheless, in recent years linguistic analysis seemed to hold the forefront of attention, although there also has been a growing interest in phenomenological proposals. While analytic concerns have dominated British philosophy, more recently a society with interest in phenomenology has been formed, and the discussions of that group in the British setting already have furthered significantly the dialogue with which this volume is concerned.

It has been suggested that borderline or boundary situations may be the most fruitful position from which to view many intellectual phenomena. The essays which follow attempt to stand near such a boundary, although the authors may be patriots of either philosophical homeland. Both analytic and phenomenological positions, as one would expect, contain within themselves considerable diversity, yet they have been sufficiently established to allow both to look over their own boundaries. Consequently some philosophers are beginning to inquire as to the relationships between these two traditions : the fundamental roots of the divisions between them, what they might have in common, and where the inevitable differences remain. These essays explore those very questions.

Philosophy, although it may have its essential constants, participates itself in some way in the Heraclitian flux and seldom stands still. The present exercise in meta-philosophy as comparative philosophy will not necessarily bring about agreement, but one may be able to discover some common meeting ground, some frame of reference, some set of problems, some method or procedure which will make a genuine dialogue possible. By such comparisons one hopes to discover whatever rapprochement there may be between positions which have so divided contemporary thought, and also to achieve some clarity regarding that set of issues which appears central in the debate and integral to that very discipline of dialogue which is philosophy.

The philosophical air has been full of competing charges, and each side has attempted to settle matters with simplified categorization. One side or the other is accused of not doing philosophy, or of using ineffective methods, or concentrating upon inconsequential matters, or simply emoting, or speculating, or doing psychology, or pursuing linguistics rather than doing philosophy. To get beyond such castigations, which do little to enhance philosophical dialogue, the next step would seem to be to open the dialogue in order to discover where essential similarities and differences lie. Too frequently it appears that either side of this dialogue is barely familiar with the literature which the other side is producing. Thus the next step would seem to be to initiate the conversation. It has been said that " 'Dialogue' is surely the most wistful term of the times." [1] However wistful it may be, and while each position has its own internal development to foster and promote, the next period of philosophical reflection may require such dialogue, necessitating that we stand back from both movements and attempt to put them in some fruitful perspective. The essays which follow indicate the initial steps which have already been taken in such meta-philosophy.

It is not the function of the introductory essay to analyze the relationships between these two movements, the very purpose of the following essays. Nevertheless, some areas of inquiry, or limitations of too facile identification, could be indicated. Analytic philosophy is often identified with language analysis, and it obviously has proceeded through an analysis of language. It must not be assumed, however, that its concern is simply with the analysis of language, for non-linguistic factors are constantly present in this philosophizing. Consequently, any thorough clarification of the intention of this movement would need to indicate the relationships between language and thought, or language and facts. The oversimplication that analytic philosophy is confined to concern with language must, therefore, be carefully modified.

It is sometimes suggested that analytic philosophy is concerned with precision or "exact philosophy" and thereby with inconsequential minutae. It is true that analytic philosophers have been concerned with

[1] E. G. Ballard, *Philosophy at the Crossroads* (Baton Rouge : Louisiana State University, 1971) p. 286.

precision, but this concern would hardly seem confined to analytic philosophers, nor is the precision always as forthcoming from the analysts as one might wish. Surely Husserl's analysis of time-consciousness was a serious attempt at precision, as was Merleau-Ponty's analysis of perception. It is not important at the moment which analysis we prefer philosophically, but it is important to control the oversimplication of identifying analytic philosophy with precision as the factor which uniquely distinguishes it from phenomenology. Furthermore, one would frequently appreciate greater precision from the analysts rather than less. Clarity about clarity itself would help immensely, for there is little precision as to exactly what is called for by the beloved goal of "clarity," which hardly any philosopher would wish to disparage, even if some might conclude that it is not enough. Or, to take another example of desirable precision, to what extent is some version of the verification principle still valid? Clarity here would be most enlightening. Or, to what extent and in what sense do linguistic philosophers deal with non-linguistic entities? In many ways the request contemporary philosophy makes of analysts is for greater clarity and precision rather than less.

Furthermore, it does not seem satisfactory to charge analytic philosophy with dealing simply with inconsequential matters. It is true that it has not dealt with existential concerns as has existential phenomenology. Nevertheless, precisely how the logic of ethical judgments functions, while abstract, is not without consequence. If one wishes to understand the relationship of mathematics to experience, it is surely consequential to understand the analytic — synthetic relationship; and by now most thinkers have come to realize that the unique status of metaphysical propositions, while initially an analytic interest, has a strong element of existential concern and consequence. Although questions as to the meaning of life and death may be of paramount human concern, surely these are not the only issues of existential import, except by a most restrictive definition, nor are they the interest solely of phenomenologists.

It is equally unfortunate to dismiss phenomenology because of its supposed ambiguity and misuse of language. More often than not such claims are but proclamations of our own unwillingness to listen, even to those who have offered explication in language with which one may be more familiar. Phenomenology surely needs to clarify the extent to which it intends to maintain the tradition of a presuppositionless philosophy. It also desperately needs to relate its thought more directly to the realms of scientific inquiry which fascinate Anglo-Saxon philosophers. There are, however, sufficient common roots of both movements in the nineteenth century so that such sources might provide grounds of understanding even if not agreement.

I would suggest that it is too simplistic, therefore, to identify linguistic analysis with the analysis of language, or with the claim to exactness and precision, or with the concern for the inconsequential and non-existential. It is equally too simplistic to neglect the phenomenologists' concern for the phenomenon of language, or their concern for precision, or to reduce their philosophy to psychologism, or limit their concern to the relevant and consequential, the humane and existential. Contemporary philosophy must transcend such oversimplifications in order to understand the deeper structure of both movements and their inter-relationships.

Certain philosophical concerns deserve special attention in comparing and contrasting these two movements, and offering opportunities for looking beyond the current impass. Let me suggest, with greater brevity than they deserve, five areas of special concern upon which both of these movements throw light, which both have approached from differing directions, and where, so it seems to me, we may be able to make some philosophical progress by standing on the borderline of these two positions and creating a dialogue across such boundaries.

I. PHILOSOPHICAL METHOD : Analytic philosophy and Phenomenology have both been associated with special methodological commitments, but it may be the time for a reconsideration of philosophical methodology. The potentialities and limitations of each methodology have been proclaimed. Nevertheless, one still remains quite unclear as to the relationship of the method to the methodology of the sciences. The reduction of philosophical method to scientific method remains beset with difficulties, while transcendental methodologies need seemingly endless explication. Furthermore, the unique status of philosophical propositions themselves remains ambiguous. Their structure of great generality constantly tempts one to suggest that they have transcendental import even while discarding the methodological ladder upon which one has climbed.

Desirable clarity regarding method would have at least two distinct advantages. One advantage would be to clarify the empirical character of philosophy. British philosophy has worked in a tradition of empiricism leading to recent phenomenalism. Recent analytic philosophy, however, is not obviously empirical, and the extent to which empiricism is still the proper characterization of analytic philosophy is problematic. Even more important for comparative philosophical dialogue is the frequent suggestion that phenomenology is a new and radical empiricism. The methodology of description of that movement with its plea "back to the phenomena" suggests that the locus of empiricism itself is a matter of appropriate debate.

A second feature of methodology deserving notice is the remaining element of Kantianism in philosophical method. In spite of its many criticisms of Kant, phenomenology, with its plea for a science of the sciences, attempts to carry out in its own unique way the Kantian program for analyzing the conditions for experience or the foundation of the sciences. The Kantian elements and atmosphere of modern philosophy, however, are not confined to phenomenology, but are present as well in analytic circles. The attempt to find in ordinary language the grounds of philosophical abstractions may be a significant revision of Kantian interests, and the attempt to find the presuppositions of experience in linguistic structures also has its affinity with Kantian concerns. Furthermore, the presence of such Kantian a priori structures in both positions needs to be more clearly related to the proposed empirical interests of both movements. This is surely not the sole arena of Kantianism in the dialogue, but it is a central feature as far as philosophical method is concerned.

There is some validity to the suggestion that phenomenologists have offered excessive discussion of method and too few working instances of the method applied to philosophical perplexities so that one might watch it at work. At the same time, since Wittgenstein, analytic philosophers have been hesitant to analyze their meta-philosophical presuppositions. They have preferred to work on the detailed problems which seemed appropriate, employing their method with relatively little analysis and precise description of the method itself. There has been sufficient time for the Wittgensteinian methodology to have manifested itself so that renewed attention to what was valid in it, and what can be concluded methodologically from the experiment with language analysis might receive a new assessment. I would suggest that from one side more examples of phenomenology at work in philosophy, while from the other side an intensified attempt to state the method or methods of linguistic analysis at certain crucial points might allow for a fruitful meeting ground of both positions. In the essays which follow such considerations of methodology are especially analyzed by Ayer, Compton, Durfee, Gendlin, and Taylor.

II. MEANING: It has been suggested that the core of philosophical inquiry is the problem of meaning. Whether or not this is the case, at least it has been a central feature of both analytic philosophy and phenomenology. How narrowly one is to construe the analytic concern with language is a matter of considerable debate. Sometimes it appears that the analysts mean that there is nothing but language to talk about. With a slightly broader interpretation, however, the goal of the approach through language is to sketch the terrain of conceptual structures, or even arrive at the clarification of propositions which are certain. Propositions, however, are one of the most ambiguous features of the philosophical landscape, and surely are not to be reduced to noises from the larynx.

Related to the concern with propositions, concepts, and speech, the phenomenologists have proposed a complex doctrine of intentionality which transcends phenomenalism and involves a subtle doctrine of essence. Such essentialism seldom fares well in analytic circles, but nevertheless, we should be aware that the analytic concern with propositions may furnish an analogy to the doctrine of intentional meaning. To the extent that language refers to propositions, we may have even here an analytic doctrine of intentionality, and, to the extent that such propositions are central in analysis, and are neither linguistic nor empirical, we may have an interesting analogy to phenomenological essentialism. Furthermore, it should be remembered that the problem of word and object has been a central issue in analytic philosophy, and to the extent that object as well as word plays a featured role in analytic philosophy, this relationship may offer an interesting comparison with the doctrine of intentionality. Post-positivistic analysis has not been phenomenalistic, but the extent to which language is used in order to get to facts (Austin) is an unclarified feature of intentionality. Furthermore, even a doctrine of meaning as use, a central theme of recent analysis, seems to be implicitly intentional, for use presumably does not itself refer simply to further language but rather to something one may do in the world with the linguistic structure.

It is also to be remembered that if meaning is intentionally tied to language, as is often suggested, phenomenologists too have developed their theory of language. The hermeneutics of contemporary philosophy offers an arena of rapport between these two movements, directly within a philosophy of language.

Two further points are relevant. Within analysis there has developed a doctrine of the a priori (Warnock), and the charge that analysts, in looking for the use, are ultimately driven back to a renewed intuitionism. Whether this is in fact the case is problematic, but such a priori features are surely relevant to the question of the character of linguistic analysis as empirical or non-empirical, and also relevant to the question of the presence or absence of intentional meaning in analytic methodology and theory of meaning.

It should also be recognized that there is a realm of meaning where both movements might make helpful contributions and offer fruitful comparisons. This realm concerns questions about the meaning of life. Such queries may be put in a variety of ways, but in one way or another seem constantly to be of interest to the ordinary man. In raising such questions one obviously raises some of the large and metaphysical questions of which analysts have frequently been skeptical, but which at the same time have been a central concern of existential phenomenologists. Let me only suggest that if the analysts would begin to apply their razor sharp techniques to these, and related questions, even to clarifying what the questions might mean, we could be greatly enlightened, and at the same time would find a fruitful meeting point for these two movements. The following essays by Erickson, Morrison, Ryle and Solomon give special attention to the problem of meaning.

III. THE LEBENSWELT AND ORDINARY LANGUAGE: Modern philosophy has yet to arrive at the appropriate juxtaposition of two areas of concentration which have played leading roles in contemporary thought. Both movements have attempted to analyze the deep background out of which philosophical abstractions arise as a means of discovering roots for the philosophical difficulties with which we are beset. One movement finds this in the world of ordinary language, the proper understanding of which might eliminate or reduce our philosophical perplexities. This world of ordinary language may or may not be in good order, but the speech forms and life forms reflected there furnish the fundamental background of our philosophical abstractions. The other movement concentrates upon the pre-objective and pre-linguistic *lebenswelt.* If we could but understand, or at least approach that core of immediate and lived experience many of the philosophical dichotomies which have confounded human thought through the centuries would be illuminated if not resolved.

Both movements thereby attempt to analyze a pre-scientific stage of human life, which is the ground both of scientific activity and of philosophical reflection. Although the two movements are not doing precisely the same thing, the relationship between these two enterprises is close enough that it bears further investigation and offers a focus for conversation.

It is clear that the *lebenswelt* is a world of intentionality, which carries all of the difficulties of such a doctrine of consciousness. Regardless of its intentional status, however, it remains the ground of scientific and philosophical abstraction. Interestingly enough, both leading philosophical movements of our day have found it appropriate to look for the foundations of both science and philosophy in the immediate or everyday world in which we live and in which we speak. Is it not time to assess the results of these investigations into the deep ground of modern cultural achievements, and to investigate the relationships between these two somewhat parallel inquiries? While concentrating upon language analysis philosophers have done little to explore the world in which ordinary language is spoken and has its setting. Likewise, phenomenologists have done little to explore the lived speech of the *lebenswelt.* Both investigations would appear to provide profitable directions for philosophical conversation, and are considered by Erickson, Ihde, Ricoeur, and Wild.

IV. PERSONS, VALUES, AND HUMANE BEHAVIOR : The problem of the self has taken on special import in our day in both movements. The attempt to preserve the existing subject from being lost in the Hegelian absolute led certain phenomenologists to analyze in great detail what it is like to be an existing subject. Parallel to this development analytic philosophers were investigating anew the concept of a person, and the use of personal pronouns. It would seem an appropriate time to assess the results of these parallel inquiries.

I have used the phrase "humane behavior" in the heading of this section to point to a dilemma in relating the two movements. Within analytic circles a renewed interest in philosophy of mind has frequently been associated with versions of philosophical behaviorism. At the same time, the concept of the person has played a central role in the debate as to whether the person could be reduced to one's behavior, and frequently served to symbolize such irreducibility. Furthermore, the conflict between analytic philosophy and phenomenology has frequently been posed as a debate between behaviorism and a more humane or humanistic approach to the person and to philosophy itself. Consequently the possibility of analyzing the person simply in terms of behavior, and the further possibility of providing for humane existence, which itself perhaps ought not simply be explicated in terms of behavior, provides a prime arena for dialogue between these two movements. Even the philosophy of the social sciences debates the use of phenomenological foundations to provide a more humane concept of self as over against more behavioristic interpretation associated with analytic philosophy.

This realm of discussion extends even further, for the two movements in modern philosophy have each developed their own unique versions of what at one time would have been called philosophical psychology. The developments were evident in the philosophy of mind, as we have mentioned, but also appeared as renewed attention to a range of partially psychological phenomena such as the emotions, the will, and the status and nature of reason. Strangely enough, little conversation has occurred between the analytic concerns with such philosophical psychology, which is not always behavioristic, and the continental concerns with the emotions and the will. Phenomenology also has explored in some detail such features of human nature frequently using them as clues for ontological insight. The conversation between these versions of philosophical psychology is in need of exploration.

A closely related phenomenon is the recent development of a philosophy of action which offers another striking focus for cooperative discussions. The concept of action has served partially in analytic circles to draw attention to the person and the difficulties for a behavioristic reductionism. In phenomenological circles, action was crucial in the dialogues with Marxism and the problems of praxis, while, at the same time, *doing* was significantly distinguished from *being*, and action as the doing served to focus attention upon the I who was doing. This development made important impact upon the philosophy of mind and body, for it offered significant evidence that the person was an embodied self, and that the doing was someone doing. Thus the intimacy of the self and its embodiment, the fact that one was an incarnate self, became of major importance. Given the importance of the person and the fresh insight on the nature of action offered by both analytic philosophy and phenomenology, we have here one of the neglected opportunities for conversation.

A further consideration concerns philosophical psychology as related to interpretation of value. Attention to philosophical psychology offered not only new interpretations of the emotions, but also creative suggestions regarding the nature and status of both reason and the will. The relation of reason and will has a long philosophical history, but in our day the very nature or concept of reason has been an object of reinterpretation, while the relationship of man's willfulness to his reason was likewise reinterpreted. These relationships became especially important as it seemed necessary to understand what was meant by a rational will, and in view of the particular attention given to the phenomenon of freedom. At times, freedom was given a voluntaristic, and at other times a more rationalistic, interpretation. This problem pervaded both movements, and was crucial in ethics and value theory when attention was turned to reasons for and causes of actions. The attempt to distinguish between giving reasons and finding causes was intimately related to the rolls of freedom, the will, and the status of reason, as well as to behaviorism. The problem became even more important when it was suggested that one's moral stance was rooted in a *blick* for which there ultimately could be no rational justification. This complex of persons, values, and humane behavior forms a network of issues and proposals much too subtle for a simple introduction. Philosophers, however, have neglected the extent to which both philosophical positions gave attention to this network and have thereby neglected the extent to which it offered a primary locus for dialogue among those who wish to profit from the philosophical activity of the last fifty years. It becomes the special concern of Durfee and Hems in the following essays.

V. Ontology and the Critique of Classical Metaphysics: Although the similarity is seldom recognized, classical Western metaphysical analysis has come under severe attack from both analytic philosophy and phenomenology. The basis for the criticism differed significantly, while the outcome led each movement in different and ambiguous directions. The analytic assertion that metaphysical propositions were meaningless led to the neglect of metaphysics in some quarters, as well as a renewed discussion of meta-philosophy which attempted to clarify the status of metaphysical propositions in others. Metaphysics, however, dies a slow death, and seems to find resurrection in unexpected places. Consequently, there now appear numerous essays indicating analytic metaphysical proposals, and which describe the metaphysical positions of what supposedly were metaphysically barren analytic developments. Metaphysics may have been easy to kill, but it has been extremely difficult to bury, for its ghost seems to reappear in every graveyard, sometimes near a headstone reading "logic".

The phenomenological critique of metaphysics was frequently offered in opposition to the suggested subjectivism of Western metaphysical traditions, since phenomenological method offered as an epistemological position was intended to be without metaphysical presuppositions. Nevertheless, the method was frequently used to offer, if not a new metaphysics, at least a new ontology including an ontology of the *lebenswelt*. Consequently, while there may be some technical distinction between metaphysics and ontology, the phenomenological movement became the source of a new world view while at the same time offering a most serious critique of the metaphysical tradition. Meanwhile, across the English channel, others were developing another way of looking at the world, although seldom proclaimed as such, while also offering a serious critique of metaphysical propositions.

The situation becomes further complicated when one turns to philosophy of religion. Surely the Divine would seem to be a prime candiate for metaphysical or ontological status. While some analytic philosophy has confined itself to the analysis of the use or meaning of religious language and God-talk, other analysts have unashamedly offered an analysis of theism in such a way that the pretense to the elimination of metaphysics disappears. Although analytic philosophy was hardly the expected locus for the revival of natural theology, there is exactly where it has occurred. Leading phenomenologists have also remained ambiguous regarding philosophy of religion or religious realities, but at least the transcendental features of their philosophy were sufficiently evident that ontology, if not metaphysics or theism, was clearly evident. With this ambiguity regarding both the presence and absence of metaphysics, the critique of Western metaphysics would seem to have come full circle, so that even contemporary philosophy of science is beginning to discuss metaphysical issues. I would suggest that this ambiguity, this parallel although not identical critique of metaphysics, this seeming presence of ontology however hidden, and this renewed talk of God, all lead to an arena of fruitful dialogue about the very status of metaphysics after two quite different attempted revolutions in philosophy. Horgby is especially concerned with the problems of metaphysics.

The five areas of conversation mentioned do not exhaust the similarities and differences between the two movements, nor do such similarities suggest agreement. The proposed conversation should not be naively conceived as showing that phenomenologists are really doing linguistic analysis, or that analytic philosophers are in their innermost reflections phenomenologists. The dialogue is clearly between positions of great diversity and should not be expected to work miracles. One of the great difficulties with the discussion will be the differing philosophical languages which are used, for the languages themselves will be rooted in competing presuppositions, and may be reacted to as empty, or silly, or ambiguous, so that one must expect that great patience, but perhaps not another generation, will be required to sustain the conversation. Furthermore, the possibility of a dogmatism from either party, which is so sure of its basic orientation that it does not even desire conversation, and which will refuse to listen sympathetically, under the pretext that there is nothing illuminating to be heard, poses one of the most serious threats to the proposed dialogue. In the process of any successful conversation, both analytic philosophy and phenomenology may be changed and one can not forecast the forthcoming transformation; but the alternative to this conversation is such a thorough division of the philosophical world and of Western intellectual life that we ought not neglect the opportunity. In philosophy one does not expect peace, but one may expect honest, open, and genuine conversation. One may not expect that cultural differences which have allowed great peoples to present their most profound reflections differently for centuries will disappear, but one may hope that they can learn to talk with one another. If there is to be a meeting of East and West, there may also need to be a meeting within the West. A discipline so existentially related to dialogue as is the discipline of philosophy will only be enhanced by the stimulation of that conversation. The essays which follow have attempted the initiation of that dialogue.

AN EARLY EVALUATION

PHENOMENOLOGY

by

G. Ryle

I want to distinguish the question what Phenomenology is from certain special questions about certain special claims that are made for it.

I. *What Phenomenology is.*

Phenomenology is not specially concerned with phenomena in the sense of sense-data. Nor is it, unless *per accidens*, any sort of Phenomenalism.

The title (which is a misleading one) derives from the following historical source. Brentano, following Herbart, repudiated the psychologies which treated mental faculties as the ultimate terms of psychological analysis, and insisted instead that the ultimate date of psychology are the particular manifestations of consciousness. These he called "psychic phenomena," not as being appearances as opposed to noumena or things in themselves, but as being directly discernible manifestations of mental functioning as opposed to being inferred or constructed mental "powers." So "Phenomenology" only means, as it stands, the science of the manifestations of consciousness and might have been used — though it is not — as another name for psychology.

Brentano next distinguished between two radically different sorts of enquiry into mental functioning. One is empirical — or what he calls, oddly, "genetic" — psychology, which is inductive, experimental and statistical, and the conclusions of which are only probable generalizations. The other is the enquiry into the concepts or presuppositions of any such empirical psychology, namely, such enquiry as "What is it to be a case of remembering, judging, inferring, wishing, choosing, regretting, etc.?" It asks, what ultimate forms of mental functioning there are to be exemplified in particular instances, and so is not concerned, *e.g.*, with what it is that makes this or that man remember something, but with what it is for a mental act to be a case of remembering.

He got to this position, I gather, in this way. Convinced that the physiological and the associationist psychologies were radically false, he had to examine and reject their presuppositions — in particular, the presuppositions (1) that mental life is a mere avalanche of atomic "ideas" and (2) that these "ideas" are in no sense *of* anything. Instead, he argued, we can know *a priori* (1) that any case of consciousness of any form must be a case of consciousness *of* something and (2) that there are irreducibly different sorts of mental functioning, so that while "ideas" may be necessary ingredients in judging and wanting, judging and wanting cannot be analysed without residue into "ideas" or complexes of them.

Whatever his line of approach may have been, he and his pupils were always perfectly clear that the analysis of the root types of mental functioning is one thing and the experimental or statistical search for the natural laws governing the occurrence of mental acts and states was quite another. And I think that they were right.

Husserl uses the term "Phenomenology" to denote the analysis of the root types of mental functioning. And he tries to show (1) that Phenomenology is anyhow a part of philosophy; (2) that it is an enquiry which can become a rigorous *science*; (3) that it is *a priori*. (1) and (3) seem to me to be true; (2) seems to me to be either false or an awkward terminological innovation. For I don't think that philosophy or any part of philosophy is properly called a "science." Philosophical methods are neither scientific nor unscientific. But this is not a question which I want to deal directly with here.

It is not a new discovery or a new theory that at least a part and an important part of philosophy consists in the analytical investigation of types of mental functioning. Theories of knowledge, belief, opinion, perception, error, imagination, memory, inference, and abstraction, which can all be classed together as epistemology, have ever since Plato constituted at least an important part of philosophy. And anyhow a large part of Ethics has, since Plato and Aristotle, consisted in the analysis of the concepts of motive, impulse, desire, purpose, intention, choice, regret, shame, blame, approbation, and the like. And while parts of the treatments given by historical philosophers to these subjects have been not analytical, but speculative or hypothetical or dogmatic, other parts have always been strictly analytical and critical and have therefore been proper cases of what Husserl describes as the phenomenological method. So nothing much save a rather misleading title would have been secured by Husserl had he merely asserted that these and suchlike enquiries are all phenomenological enquiries, in that all are enquiries into the nature of more or less radical types of mental functioning.

He does, of course, go a good deal further than this. First of all he argues, in opposition, I take it, to special schools of positivists and experimental psychologists as well as to the whole associationist theory of psychology, that the way in which types of mental functioning are analysed by philosophers or phenomenologists when they know their business is quite different from the way in which empirical psychology enquires into the causal laws governing the occurrence of mental states, acts and dispositions in the life-history of actual persons in the world. For (1) the method of philosophy proper is *a priori*, whereas that of the others is inductive; and (2) the very questions raised by empirical psychology embody the concepts the analysis of which belongs to phenomenology. So that in two connected ways phenomenology is independent of empirical psychology : (1) that being *a priori* phenomenology cannot employ as its premises either the particular observations or the inductive generalizations of empirical psychology and (2) that being analytical or critical it enquires what any psychological proposition of this or that sort really means (whether it is true or false), and so throws light on and cannot derive light from the particular psychological propositions which psychologists put forward as true or probable.

This seems to me to be true and generalizable. Not only psychology, but all sciences and all sorts of search for knowledge or probable opinion aim at establishing particular or general propositions. But whether in any particular case such a proposition is true or false, the analysis of what it means, or of what would be the case if it were true, is different from and in principle prior to the discovery of what proves it or makes it probable. Thus, the philosophy of physics is indifferent to the answers that physicists give to the questions of physics, the philosophy of mathematics does not wait for the solution of all possible equations, and in ethics we must have some notion of desert, and one which we are already in principle ready to analyse, whether or not we are able to decide that a given defendant deserves a certain punishment.

No philosophical propositions are empirical either in the sense of being about this as distinct from that particular subject of attributes, or in the sense of implying as premises propositions which are so.

This does not, of course, involve that philosophical arguments should not contain references to particular cases as instances or examples. On the contrary, a good illustrative example is often of great utility. But an *exempli gratia* is not an *ergo* — as is shown by the fact that imaginary examples are often just as useful as actual ones, which would not be the case in a genuine inductive argument.

Husserl's apriorism is, perhaps, nothing very alarming. But, at the time of the last century, naturalism and empiricism were so fashionable that Husserl had to prosecute very difficult and painstaking logical enquiries in order to justify it. And we should first notice three cardinal points in his account of the *a priori* nature of philosophical propositions.

1. He does not hold that philosophers should or can construct deductive systems. Demonstration *ordine geometrico* belongs to mathematics and not to philosophy. For Husserl Spinoza's notion of philosophy as a sort of metaphysical geometry is a completely mistaken sort of apriorism. And I think Husserl is right.

2. Further, Husserl refuses to admit into phenomenology or, by implication, into philosophy in general, any sort of metaphysical system-building or speculative construction. Dogmatic metaphysics is put out of court by Husserl just as much as by Kant. (It is, however, arguable that some of Husserl's conclusions are of the nature of metaphysical constructions. His half solipsist and half monadological account of the experienced world is not at all what one would expect to find deriving from a purely analytical inquiry into the *summa genera* of the manifestations of mind.) But with his official view that the business of philosophy is not to give new information about the world, but to analyse the most general forms of what experience finds to be exemplified in the world I completely agree.

3. On the other hand Husserl's special account of the nature of *a priori* thinking seems to me to be wrong. Rather like Meinong he holds, or used to hold, that universals or essences as well as propositions, are objects of a higher order. And of these we can have a knowledge by acquaintance analogous to (though of a higher order than) our perceptual acquaintanceship with particulars like this tree and that man. We can, he holds, perceive or intuit essences in the same sort of way as we can perceive or intuit particulars, except that the direct intuition of an essence requires to be founded in the direct intuition of a particular instance of it (which may be real or imaginary). Philosophy is, accordingly, a sort of observational science (like geography); only the objects which it inspects are not spatiotemporal entities but semi-Platonic objects which are out of space and time. These are correlates to acts of conception and judgment, though whether it is essential to them to be so correlative or whether it is accidental, is left rather obscure in Husserl's writings. I fancy that Husserl used to think of them as independently subsisting and now regards them as intrinsically contents of possible acts of thinking.

I do not myself believe that phrases such as "being a so and so," "being such and such" and "that so and so is such and such" do denote objects or subjects of attributes. For I don't think that they are denoting expressions at all. Consequently, though I can know what it is for something to be a so and so, I think that this knowledge is wrongly described as an "intuition of an essence." For intuition, which I take to be a synonym for knowledge by acquaintance or perception, does seem to be or to involve a relation between two subjects of attributes, the perceiver and the thing perceived. And I do not think that what Husserl calls "essences" are subjects of attributes at all. However, I do not think that the whole notion of phenomenology hinges on this special theory, so I do not think that it need be discussed here. But we shall have to discuss later a more general question, which is connected with this one, concerning the theory of intentional objects.

So much for the general plan of phenomenology. It is that part, or those parts of philosophy in which the root types of mental functioning are distinguished and analysed. And most philosophers have talked phenomenology, as M. Jourdain talked prose. What Husserl has done so far is (*a*) to distinguish, as his predecessors had largely failed to do, between the philosophical and the psychological methods of investigating consciousness; (*b*) to make clear that anyhow this part of philosophy is analytical and not speculative or hypothetical; and (*c*) to name it with a rather unfortunate name.

II. Now for his main doctrines *in* phenomenology.

It is an "essential intuition", that is, it can be known *a priori* that all consciousness is consciousness of something. To wish is to wish for something, to regret is to regret something, to remember, expect, decide and choose are to remember something, expect something, decide something and choose something. To every piece of mental functioning there is intrinsically correlative something which is the "accusative" of that functioning. But though all consciousness is "intentional" or "transitive," it is not all intentional or transitive in the same way. The act of remembering may have the same object as one of regretting, but they are different sorts of acts and "have" their object in different manners. Moreover, some sorts of "consciousness of" demand others as their platform.

"Intentionality" has nothing special to do with intending in our sense of purposing. It is a revival of a scholastic term and is used only as a name for the fact that mental acts are *of* objects. I use the term "accusative" to render "gegenstand." "Object" is damagingly equivocal since it may mean "entity" or "subject of attributes" as well as meaning "object of..."

I cannot regret without remembering, though I can remember without regretting. And again, I cannot remember without having once directly perceived, but I can perceive without having to remember. And so on.

Next, all intentional experiences, whatever their "accusatives," must belong to an experiencing ego. *Cogito ergo sum* is a cardinal proposition in Husserl's phenomenology. "What is it to be an 'I'?" is perhaps, the most general way of formulating the question of phenomenology — indeed Husserl coins the unattractive alternative title for phenomenology of "descriptive transcendental egology."

These two marks of intentional experiences — namely, that in all of them there is a subject-pole and in all of them there is an object-pole — are not independent. They are intrinsically correlative. But the correlation can take as many different forms as there are different types of intentionality. For a type of intentionality is simply a not further analysable way in which an I may be about something.

On the other hand, the subject-pole is, for Husserl as for Descartes, something the reality of which is philosophically unimpugnable and presuppositionless, whereas any of its objects upon which it may from time to time be directed may have no other reality than that with which it is endowed by being what the self is dreaming, say, or expecting or believing in.

As we shall see, Husserl does, in fact, terminate in a subjectivist or egocentric philosophy, though he is at pains to argue that it is not a form of solipsism.

The Phenomenological Reduction

In our everyday frames of mind, and particularly in our scientific frame of mind, we treat the world and the things and happenings in it as independently existing. That is, we focus on their relationships to one another and ignore the fact that they all alike stand to us as pegs upon which we are hooking *our* interests, attentions, queries, emotions, decisions and volitions. They are — but we habitually fail to remember that they are — constituents of our variegated cognitive-*cum*-volitional-*cum*-emotional experiences. We think about things, but do not ordinarily notice that they are at least, whatever else they are, what we are thinking about.

Now, Husserl argues, of our experiences we can have direct and self-evident perception. Reflective inspection of our own *actus* of consciousness can give us knowledge in the strict sense of the term. I can know both that I am enacting an act of a certain description and what that description is. And he rather assumes than argues, following Descartes, that there is no other sort of self-evident (or knowing) inspection of particulars.

Let us, then, by a sort of Method of Doubt bracket out or shelve all that we accept in our everyday or scientific frames of mind over and above what reflective inspection can warrant. This will leave as one of our most important sets of data to be studied, such facts as that we accept the proposition that the sun is bigger than the moon, but will bracket out the fact (if it is one) that the sun *is* bigger than the moon. We are left with Erlebnisse, and that means that we are left with the whole experienced world. But what (if anything) exists or happens or is the case without being a constituent of experiences is not the theme of any phenomenological proposition.

What an "object" is now is nothing save what sort of an "accusative" it is to what sorts of intentional experiences. It is just that which constitutes particular mental functionings as the particular mental functions that they are. In a word, it is just the special character of an act or set of acts, or, to employ a misleading expression of which Husserl is fond, the object of an intentional experience, treated as such, is just the intrinsic meaning or sense of the experience.

We can now say that whatever may be the special objects of such studies and interests as physics, biology, astronomy, psychology, and the other natural sciences — history, sociology, economics and law, business, politics, and, in a word, of all intellectual, practical and emotional occupation, all alike have and have essentially the character of being constituents of experiences. They are the ways in which I or we function.

Consequently, Husserl argues, both the scientific search for the laws governing the existence of such things and the special philosophical analyses of the essences of them presuppose the philosophical analysis of the types of mental functioning in the several instances of which these objects present themselves as the specifying or individuating constituents.

So phenomenology is the first philosophy, or the science of sciences. It and it alone has for its topic the *summum genus* of the objects of all the other sciences and interests. It even has priority over logic.

It is therefore, for Husserl, part of the nature of all possible subjects of attributes to be constituents in the intentional experiences of an "I". But as persons in the ordinary sense of the term are only empirically discovered things in the world of objects, it is not empirical selves, but a pure or transcendental self whose "intentions" are the home of the being of objects. And Husserl accordingly develops a Kantian or neo-Kantian doctrine of a pure or absolute subject which is other than you or I for the reason that you and I are merely items in the list of the possible accusatives of intentional experiences.

I think myself that Husserl is (with Kant) confusing "I-ness" with a new I. Propositions about "Bewusstsein überhaupt" are really about what it is to be an I having experiences, and not about an I that has them. But I doubt if it would be profitable to let our discussion turn upon this question.

Husserl now seems to have reached the position that nothing exists — indeed, that it is nonsense to speak of anything existing — save, on the one hand, a pure subject of experiences, or several such subjects which exist in their own right, and, on the other hand, the entire realm of intentional objects, the being of which is their being "intended."

This conclusion seems to me to be false, and with it the consequential doctrine that phenomenology is logically prior to all other philosophical or scientific enquiries. Phenomenology seems to have turned in Husserl's hands into an egocentric metaphysic. But this seems to be the result of one or two false theories which need never and should never have trespassed into the analysis of types of mental functioning.

a. The Doctrine of Intentional Objects

It was an assumption rooted in the Cartesian and Lockean theories of mental life that what I am aware of when I am aware of something must always be an "idea." We need not bother our heads about the definition of "idea" (for nonentities are not necessarily definable), but at least it was held that an idea is a mental something and something existing or occurring inside the mind that is aware of it. The theory of intentionality is an attempt not to repudiate, but to modify, elaborate and reform the "idea" epistemology. The first modification was the distinction between the act and its object, the *ideatio* and the *ideatum*, e.g., in the idea of a circle, the circle is something with a centre but the ideating of it is not. But it was still supposed that the circle was really existing or occurring in the mind together with the act of which it was the "content." Similarly, the proposition which I judge and the desideratum which I desire, though distinguishable from the acts of judging and desiring, were still supposed to be actually resident where these resided.

Husserl, however, like Meinong in this respect, denies that what an act is "of" is essentially contained in or adjoined to the act. "Contents" are not real parts of mental functioning. Introspection cannot find them. (This is proved by the fact that two acts of different dates can have the same object.)

Nor can all possible "contents" be lodged in the actual world of space and time. For what fancies, false beliefs, wishes, expectations and conceptions are of, are nowhere to be found there. And as Husserl seems, anyhow latterly, to reject Platonic or Meinongian subsistence theories, it becomes very hard to see in what sense he holds that "intentional objects" really are genuine objects or subjects of attributes at all. He *should* hold (I believe) that what we miscall "the object or content of an act of consciousness" is really the specific character or nature of that act, so that the intentionality of an act is not a relation between it and something else, but merely a property of it so specific as to be a *differentia* or in some cases an individualizing description of it. He does in fact, however, continue to speak as if every intentional act is related, though related by an internal relation, to a genuine subject of attributes.

I would urge against this view (1) that it is erroneous in itself and (2) that it originates from an erroneous assumption that "consciousness of..." is a true *summum genus* of which the several forms of mental functioning (including knowing) are true homogeneous species.

1. It is certainly a convenient and popular idiom to speak of "the objects of" imagination, desire, belief, knowledge, etc., when we wish to refer to what some one imagines, desires, believes or knows. And as we often use "object" as a synonym for "thing," as when we call a Chippendale chair "a handsome" or "expensive object," we have anyhow this motive for supposing that some subject of attributes is being referred to when we speak of what Jones imagines or wants or believes or knows. But the supposition seems to be a mistake. For the phrase "the object of Jones' desire or fancy," *e.g.*, is not necessarily a referentially used "the"-phrase, any more than the "the"-phrase in "Poincaré is not the King of France." It is almost certainly a systematically misleading expression. For there is nothing of which we can say truly or even falsely "*that* is the object of Jones' desire or fancy." We can indeed state which attributes Jones is imagining something to be characterized by or what are the features of his situation, the absence or alteration of which Jones desiderates. But these statements will not require us to employ descriptive phrases referring to queer non-actual objects. Such references could not be made for they would be self-contradictory.

If, then, the doctrine of intentionality implies that to every case of mental functioning of whatever sort there must be correlative a special something describable as an "intentional object," then this doctrine seems to be false.

2. Husserl assumes that all forms of mental functioning are species or sub-species of a *summum genus* called "consciousness of..." And by "consciousness of..." he means to denote not *knowing*, but something of which knowing is, with believing, guessing, dreaming, craving, etc., only a species. From this, of course it has to follow that often I am "conscious of" something which is not a known reality and so is not real at all. (It is not possible to state this sort of view in an unobjectionable way.)

Now in my opinion Cook Wilson has shown in a strictly phenomenological manner that this whole assumption is vicious. Knowing is not one definable species of "consciousness of..." among others, it is something anyhow partly in terms of which believing, fancying, guessing, wanting and the rest have to be defined. Belief, *e.g.*, is a state of mind involving *ignorance* of such and such a *knowledge* of so and so : it involves more than that, but at least it involves this double reference to knowledge.

Consequently the "intentionality" of mental acts must be defined in terms not of "consciousness of..." but of "knowledge of..." And as it is, if not self-evident, anyhow plausible to say that what I know to be the case is so whether I know it or not, a phenomenology operating with this modified notion of intentionality would not be obviously bound to terminate in an egocentric metaphysic, or to claim a priority over all other branches of philosophy, such as logic or the philosophy of physics. For it would no longer be essential to any subject of attributes to be "accusative" to a mental act. Intentionality will not now be an internal relation.

b. Immanent versus Transcendent Perception

An important premiss in Husserl's argument which helps to involve him in his quasi-solipsistic conclusions is his theory of the self-evidence of immanent perception and the fallibility of transcendent perception.

By "immanent perception" he refers to the direct recognition or inspection that I can have of my own mental states and acts, when these are concurrent with the inspection of them. I take it that he is referring to what we call introspection. When, which is fairly infrequent, I introspect upon my present Erlebnis, I can *know* in the strict sense that I am enjoying this Erlebnis and what sort of an Erlebnis it is. Introspection tells the truth, the whole truth and nothing but the truth.

By "transcendent perception" he refers to the perception of physical things and events, the mental acts and states of others, and those mental acts and states of my own which are not contemporary with the inspection of them. This, Husserl maintains, can never be or give *knowledge.* It is never self-evident, and the possibility of delusion is always present. It follows that sciences of "the external world" cannot be or give knowledge, but that the science of the self can : and all that I can *know* about the world is what I can know about my fallible cognizings of the world and my resultant practical and emotional attitudes towards it. And if this were true, Husserl would, I think, have established some sort of primacy for phenomenology.

But (1), while I see no reason to doubt that we *can* inspect and recognize states and acts of our own minds, I think that this introspection is not really perception (save in an enlarged sense). I believe that introspection is merely remembrance controlled by a special interest. But whatever it is, it seems clear that we often make mistakes about our mental condition. Very likely these should not be attributed to "mistaken introspection," but are mistakes due to an unnoticed omission to introspect. But then the same indulgence should be allowed to what is very likely miscalled "mistaken perception" in the sphere of what Husserl calls "transcendent perception."

(2) I can see no *a priori* grounds for supposing that perception can only be knowledge where the object perceived and the perceiving of it are conjoined parts of one stream of experience. It seems to me just the old prejudice that the thing known should be in some way very near to the knowing of it.

So I see no grounds for denying universally that we can have knowledge by perception of physical things and events. Husserl's arguments on this point, which I have not expounded, seem to me only to show that particular perceptions don't tell the whole truth about their objects. But if they can tell us the truth and nothing but the truth, no conclusions damaging to the world seem to arise from the comparison of this sort of perception with introspection.

My conclusion is, then, this : (1) There is an important part of philosophy describable as the philosophy of psychology. It is, like any other part of philosophy, *a priori* in the sense that its methods are not inductive and that its objects are not this as distinct from that particular matter of fact. It is an inquiry into the forms of certain classes of facts, or, to put it in another way, it inquires what is really meant by such propositions as, "Jones knows or believes such and such," "Jones wanted this but chose that," "Jones took what he saw to be a so and so," "I am a such and such." And we can, if we like, call this part of philosophy "phenomenology."

(2) The fact that Husserl concludes that the world consists of nothing but bi-polar mental experiences, and consequently that phenomenology is "first philosophy" is the result of his acceptance of one or two theories which are not true and are not arrived at by genuine phenomenological analysis.

FOUNDATIONAL PHILOSOPHERS

SENSE AND ESSENCE: FREGE AND HUSSERL

by

ROBERT C. SOLOMON

> Pure or transcendental phenomenology will be established not as a science of facts, but as a science of essential being (as 'Eidetic' science); a science which aims exclusively at establishing "knowledge of essences" and absolutely no "facts."
>
> (*Ideen*, p. 40, Introduction)[1]

It is singularly unfortunate that Husserl, who conscientiously avoided use of terminology with long and varied philosophical histories, should choose the notion "essence" as a central concept in his philosophy. In the Introduction to *Ideen*, he comments that "its equivocations are harmless." But this is far from true regarding the disastrous effects of his own use of the notion. His talk of "essential Being" and "essences as objects of knowledge" has generated such antagonism among American philosophers that the formulation of an acceptable interpretation of Husserl's philosophy has become an almost thankless task. While most of his supporters remain content to give their endorsement to the insistence that philosophy must concern itself only with *essences* and the *Being of essences*, Husserl's detractors have not found it difficult to dismiss all talk of "essences" as an unwelcome remnant of a paradigm of philosophy long out-moded.

We find Husserl's philosophy thus dismissed in the dress of any number of doctrines not his own : the doctrine of essential Being is dismissed as a regression to Platonic "realism"; the notion that essences

[1] All references to *Ideen* are to the Gibson translation, *Ideas* (New York : Collier-Macmillan, 1962). Page numbers are included in parentheses in the texts or immediately following quotations, and followed by chapter number, section number.

"inhere in" facts is rejected as a hangover from scholasticism; the notion of "intuition of essences" is suspected to be an attempt to block all criticism; or, what is worse, it is thought to be a new variety of mysticism. This same notion of "intuition of essences," coupled with Husserl's own characterization of his philosophy as a "radical empiricism," has given critics cause to claim that Husserl attempted to give an empirical analysis of essences and essential truths. Other critics, focusing rather on Husserl's sharp separation of fact and essence, complain that Husserl is altogether opposed to factual science and causal explanations. All of these criticisms are misguided, but, to show this, we shall require an overall reevaluation of Husserl's doctrine of *essence* in much clearer analysis than Husserl ever affords us.

In this essay, I shall attempt to dislodge Husserl's notion of "essence" from "Platonic Ideas" and "Scholastic essences" as well as from the speculative metaphysics, the mysticism, and the too-radical empiricism with which it has been confused, and display it in the philosophical context in which it rightfully belongs. This context, I shall suggest, is one best defined by Husserl's contemporary and critic, Gottlob Frege. It has always appeared curious to me that Husserl and Frege are so often considered so very far apart, when the two men were, in fact, so similar in background, in interests, in the specific problems they encountered, and, I shall argue, some of the solutions they offered to these problems. Of course, the two very different movements these two thinkers set in motion explain our tendency to think of them as so markedly different. But if, as I shall argue, the differences between them is largely a matter of terminology and emphasis, there may be real hope for a sympathetic meeting between "analytic" and "phenomenological" philosophies as well.

Why should Husserl want to talk about "essences" at all, much less make such a problematic notion the central concern of his philosophy? Of course, Husserl might easily have coined a new term in place of "essence" (*Wesen*), but some such term is indispensable, we will argue, in just the same way that similar concepts are vital in the philosophy of Frege.

In the 1880's both Husserl and Frege were probing the foundations of mathematics, attempting to discover the source of validity of the basic principles of arithmetic. Frege's *Grundlagen der Arithmetik* (1884) [2] did not receive the attention it deserved, largely because it deviated so

[2] Henceforth *GA*.

markedly from the then fashionable "psychologistic" approach to this and other philosophical questions. Husserl's dissertation at Halle (1887) and his first book, *Philosophie der Arithmetik* (1891),[3] which did accept this approach, were much better received. Husserl had studied with Franz Brentano, and worked with Carl Stumpf, the leading proponents of Psychologism, a theory in which all necessary truths, including the basic principles of arithmetic, were reduced to empirical laws of psychology. Thus Husserl, in these early works, argued that the laws of arithmetic are nothing more than causal laws governing our experiences of *counting* and "collective association." Frege, at first ineffectively, argued against the psychologists that such treatment neglected the *necessity* of mathematical truths, and that psychologism was a confusion of two very different disciplines, a "building of dangerous inroads of psychology into logic." [4]

Frege published his more important *Grundgesetz der Arithmetik* in 1893, which began with a renewed attack on psychologism, and, in 1894, he attacked Husserl's *Philosophie der Arithmetik* specifically (in a review of the book in *Zeitschrift für Philosophie*). Again, Frege argued that there was a decisive difference between numbers and whatever ideas people might have about numbers. Arithmetic, he argued, gives us precise and necessary principles, while psychology can give us only imprecise and at best probable generalizations. Psychology is incapable of clarifying the most important notion of *necessity* which is so characteristic of mathematical truths, and so there can be no reduction of necessary principles of arithmetic to psychological principles governing our experiences of numbers.

Husserl's reaction to this onslaught was admirable. He cancelled the projected second volume of *Philosophie der Arithmetik*, and, seeing the validity of Frege's claims, utterly rejected his psychologistic approach to the philosophy of mathematics. In doing so, however, Husserl saw a general deficiency in the empirical methods he had learned from Brentano; they could not provide an analysis of necessary truth, and philosophy in general is concerned only with necessary truths. In his next work, the *Logische Untersuchungen* (1901),[5] Husserl joins with Frege in a relentless attack on psychologistic methods. He begins by quoting Goethe, "One is opposed to nothing more severely than to errors recently laid aside."

[3] Henceforth *PA*.

[4] *GA*, XIV.

[5] Henceforth *LU*.

After the traumatic encounter with Frege, Husserl's interest in philosophy turned to this newly discovered (very Kantian) problem — how is necessary truth possible? The introduction of the notion of "essence" is designed to solve this problem : "... and here is the place for the phenomenological analysis of *essence*, which however strange and unsympathetic it may sound to the naturalistic psychologist, can in no way be an empirical analysis." [6]

Husserl, like Frege, came to see that the account of necessary truth must reject any appeal to experience. In particular, such an account must reject any thesis which maintains that necessary truths are derivable by abstraction from particular experiences, using as its foundation some such notion as John Locke's "abstract ideas." In *PA* Husserl had employed just such a notion, and Frege had since convinced him that this consisted in a

> ... blurring of the distinction between image and concept, between imagination and thought ... The constituents of the thought, and *a fortiori* things themselves, must be distinguished from the images that accompany in some mind the act of grasping the thought-images that each man forms of things.[7]

Frege accuses Husserl of ignoring the distinction, which Husserl was later to adopt (and be given credit for), between empirical and essential generality : "It is surely clear that when anyone uses the sentence 'all men are mortal,' he does not want to assert something about some Chief Akpanya, of whom perhaps he has never heard." [8]

In the *LU*, Husserl turns to the notions of "meaning" (*Sinn*) to account for necessary truth. In *LU*, we are introduced to "meaning-structures" and "meaning-designation" and "constitution of meanings." "Meanings," we are told, "come from consciousness" and are "conferred on facts by consciousness." In the same context, we are introduced to "essences," which are also 'in consciousness' and are given in a "categorical intuition." It is quite evident, both in *LU* and *Ideen*, that "meaning" and "essence" are intimately related. (In *Ideen*, Husserl even employs the two jointly in a hyphenated expression, "meaning-essence.") Essences or meanings exist in a manner very different from the existence of *facts* : the "Being" and the Knowledge of essences or

[6] *Philosophy as a Rigorous Science*, trans. Q. Lauer (New York : Harper, 1965).

[7] From Frege's review of Husserl's *Philosophie der Arithmetik* in *Zeitschrift*, reprinted in Black and Geach, *Philosophical Writings of Frege* (Oxford : Blackwell, 1952), p. 79. Hereafter "Frege *BG*."

[8] *Ibid.*, p. 83.

meanings and the assertion of necessary truths are distinct from the "Being," or experiencing, of *facts* or "individuals":

> The positing of the essence ... does not imply any positing of individual existence whatsoever : pure essential truths do not make the slightest assertion concerning facts.[9]
>
> Knowledge of essences : independent of all knowledge of Facts.[10]
>
> It is a matter of indifference [with regard to the essence] whether such things have ever been given in actual experience.[11]

This independence of essences from actual existence or from facts illuminates a most important point about "essences" : the intuiting or the knowledge of essences is completely independent of any ontological commitment concerning the actual existence or actual experience of "individuals" who "have" that essence. Necessary truths are not "about" the world and are true independently of there being any individuals about which they are true. "All perfect circles are round," as a necessary truth, remains true although there might be no perfect circles. The fact that there are no perfect circles has nothing to do with the necessary truth.

The independence of "essence" and "fact" allows us to understand another thesis of central importance to Husserl's thought. In his earlier writings (*LU*), we intuit essences by concentrating on particular experiences of individuals : by *Ideen*, it is the role of *imagination* or *fancy* which occupies a central role in "grasping" essences. "The element which makes up the life of phenomenology as of all eidetic science is 'fiction,' that fiction is the source whence the knowledge of 'eternal truths' draws its sustenance." [12]

A geometer, who gives us necessary truths, and a physicist, who gives us empirical truths, can thus be distinguished by the role of "fancy" in their studies. A geometer, Husserl tells us, can prove his theorems on any figure he should like to employ : any triangle he imagines will suffice for a proof as well as any other. The physicist, however, must take into account only the results of actual experiments, not the possible results of any imaginable experiences. With geometric figures Husserl tells us, we "through direct analysis determine their immanent meaning." [13]

[9] *Ibid.*, p. 51, 1:4.
[10] *Ibid.*, section head, p. 50, 1:4.
[11] *Ibid.*, p. 51.
[12] *Ibid.*, p. 194, 7:70.
[13] *Ideen*, p. 85, 2:25.

For a physicist, "experiments conducted in imagination would be imagined experiments." [14]

The consideration of the role of imagination in "intuiting essences" allows us to understand yet another important Husserlian doctrine and shows us the way to a simple parallel in current analytic philosophy. Husserl tells us that, "... no essential intuition is possible without the free possibility of directing one's glance to an individual counterpart and of shaping an illustration." [15]

In other words, one intuits an essence (or, I suggest, 'understands a meaning') by considering all possible *examples* and *counter-examples*. One does not intuit an essence if he cannot think of a single example of an instance of that essence : again, one does not intuit an essence if he cannot distinguish a case that is not an instance of that essence from one that is.[16]

We can now begin to understand the significance of Husserl's characterization of "essence" in terms of " 'what' a thing is" : "At first 'essence' indicated that which in the intimate self-being of an individual discloses to us '*what*' it is." [17]

Husserl sometimes relates "essence" to the concept of a "concept" (e.g. *Ideen*, 1:10, 2:22) and tells us that an essence is a "body of essential predicables." This should afford us an easy interpretation of some of Husserl's more obscure comments on "essence." When he claims that "essences are repeatable," or that,

> ... whatever belongs to the essence of the individual can also belong to another individual, (47, 1:2).
> Essential intuition is the consciousness of something, of an "object" ... but which then can be "presented" in other acts ... (49, 1:3).

he is saying that an essence or meaning applies to indefinitely many particular instances of that essence or meaning. "Dog" *means* not just this dog or that dog, but *means*, or is the essence of, all possible dogs. As we shall see in a moment, Husserl's notion of *meaning* (*Sinn*) or essence is at least in this respect identical to Frege's notion of *Sinn*. In Frege's language, the *Sinn* of "dog" is such that "dog" can *refer* to any or every actual or possible dog.

[14] *Ibid.*, p. 85, 2:25.

[15] *Ibid.*, p. 50, 1:3.

[16] Certain qualifications have to be made here if we are talking about "formal" essences; to grasp the "essence" of the law of contradiction, we should not require that someone can imagine a case in which the law would not apply.

[17] *Ideen*, p. 48, 1:3.

When Husserl tells us that essences are "ideal," he is maintaining the essential difference between essences and facts, which are *real.* In other words, P is a fact only if the world (of our experience) is such that P is a state of affairs in the world (of our experience). But we can have an essence not manifest by any fact. This is to say, for Husserl, that essences have "their own mode of existence" : essences are ideal, or unreal (*irreal*) in the sense that they are not facts about the world, nor do they depend for their existence upon the existence of correlated facts.

We are also told that *essences* are "non-spatio-temporal" but yet not "Platonically independent." By the first, we understand that there is a difference between the sense in which an essence exists and the sense in which "real" individuals which instantiate that essence exist : only the latter have spatial location or can be said to occur in or endure through time. However, Husserl is forced (for obvious reasons) to continually defend himself against charges of "Platonism", a postulation of the existence of essences "somewhere" other than the "real" (spatio-temporal) would. It is thus necessary for him to persistently deny that essences are independent of all *possible* facts. Husserl insists that essences always demand the *possibility* of individual "counterparts," and that essences, like these individual counterparts, are given in intuition.

For a fuller understanding of this notion of "essence," I suggest we turn to the comparatively enviably clear writings of Gottlob Frege. Frege introduces a distinction between "*sense*" (*Sinn*) and "*reference*" (*Bedeutung*) of a *name* or a *sign*. A name or a sign is to be construed as a linguistic expression, a word, phrase, sentence, or set of sentences, whether written or spoken, or simply thought. We have already employed the distinction in our discussion of Husserl, and indicated the more-than-notational similarity between Husserl's notion of "*Sinn*" and Frege's notion of "*Sinn.*" "*Bedeutung*," however, is an expression used very differently by the two authors. For Husserl, "*Bedeutung*" will refer to a special kind of *meaning*, very close, in fact, to Frege's notion of "*Sinn.*" "*Bedeutung*" for Frege means *reference*, and the reference of a sign is an *object*. A sign "stands for" or "designates" or "denotes" (or, of course, "refers to") its referent. This object, however, need not be a material object, an "individual," but may be, for example, a number. Numbers are referred to by numerals (i.e. "1," "2," "3," ...) and numbers are therefore objects in the appropriate sense. Similarly, *concepts* or meanings can be referent objects of a sign, as when we speak of "the meaning of the word ..." or "the concept of man ..."

The sense or meaning (*Sinn*) of a sign must be distinguished from the reference of the sign. Frege allows that signs are usually used simply to *refer*, but there are cases in which they clearly do not. We can speak, for example, of unicorns, where "unicorn" has a sense but no reference. We can assert, "unicorns do not exist," and what we say can only be intelligible if we suppose that "unicorn" in this sentence has a sense independent of any referents. We usually *learn* the sense of signs through our familiarity with their referents, but our learning the sense through reference is irrelevant to this distinction. Because of their mutual opposition to psychologism, this separation of learning a sense and the sense itself is vital to both Frege and Husserl.

"A sign *expresses* its sense" (*BG* 61). Each and every [grammatically well-formed] sign in language has a sense, whether or not it has reference. However, each sense may have indefinitely many signs : "It is raining" and "it rains" are two different signs with the same sense, as are "it is raining" and "*Es regnet.*" There are as many signs for a single sense as there are intertranslatable expressions within any language and among all *possible* languages.

Because it is Frege's notion of "*Sinn*" which we intend to utilize in our analysis of Husserl's notion of "essence," we must further inquire into the nature of this. One might think that the *Sinn* of a sign can be distinguished from both the sign itself and from the reference of the sign by taking the *Sinn* to be an "image" that one associates with the sign (e.g. Locke's theory or Husserl in *PA*), or a "picture" (e.g. Wittgenstein, *Tractatus*, 2.1).[18] Frege categorizes all such 'associated images' as "Ideas."

> If the reference of the sign is an object perceivable by the senses, my idea of it is an internal image, arising from memories of sense impressions which I have had and acts, both internal and external, which I have performed. (BG 59)

Husserl's early analysis of "number" in terms of counting and ideas of "collective association" would neatly fit this notion of "Idea." However, Frege, as evidenced by his rejection of Husserl's *PA*, will have no part of this as an analysis of *Sinn*;

[18] I shall certainly not attempt to examine the very close connection between such "pictures" and sentences (*Satz*) in Wittgenstein. I simply work on the supposition that the "image-theory" which Wittgenstein later sets out to refute is not wholly distinct from the "picture-sentence" theory in the *Tractatus*.

The reference and sense of a sign are to be distinguished from the associated idea. (*BG* 59)

The same sense is not always connected even in the same man, with the same idea. The idea is subjective, one man's idea is not that of another. There results, as a matter of course, a variety of differences in the ideas associated with the same sense. A painter, a horseman, and a zoologist will probably connect different ideas with the name "Bucephalus." This constitutes an essential distinction between the idea and the sign's sense, which may be the common property of many and therefore is not a part of a mode of the individual mind. (*BG* 59)

For our comparison of Husserl and Frege, it is vitally important that we take special note of two very different employments of the English term "Idea." For Frege, the "idea" (*Vorstellung*) is the associated image : for Husserl, "Idea" (*Idee*) is closely allied with "essence." We shall therefore avoid use of this term as much as possible, and simply restrict outselves to a discussion of "images" and "essences."

"Image" for Frege, is contrasted with "thought" (*Gedanke*), and it is thoughts, not ideas, which constitute sense. Thoughts, unlike images, are *public*, not *private*. Images are "had" by one and by only one consciousness ("your images are 'yours' and my images are 'mine' "). In this sense of "image," it is logically impossible that you and I should "think the same thing." An image is not a property of a sign, it is a 'property' of individual men. However,

It is quite otherwise for thoughts; one and the same thought can be grasped by many men.[19]

For one can hardly deny that mankind has a common store of thoughts which is transmitted from one generation to another.[20]

With "thought," therefore, we can say that many men "think" the same "thought," or that you mean by "P" just what I mean by "P." [21]

This is clearly necessary for the sense of a sign — that it remain one and the same sense which is "expressed" by whoever employs that sign. A thought, therefore, is neither the object referred to by a sign, nor any image associated with the sign or arising from my perceptions or memories of the object, nor is it the sign itself, which only *expresses* the thought. The thought is the sense of a sign, and is independent of the particular employer of that sign, independent of any objects

[19] From Frege on Husserl's *PA*, *BG* 79.

[20] "On Sense and Reference," *BG* 59.

[21] E.g. we both learn *the* pythagorean theorem; I do not learn *my* pythagorean theorem : Frege, "The Thought," trans. Quinton, *Journal of Philosophy*, 65 (1956), 302.

referred to in the employment of that sign, and independent of the sign itself (any thought can be expressed by any number of signs).

The analysis of Frege's "sense" (*Sinn*) thus reduces to an analysis of the notion of "thought," or "The Thought." I hope that it is now becoming evident just how Frege's "sense (thought)" is remarkably similar to Husserl's "essence." Both clearly refer to "meaning" in some sense, and both philosophers are utilizing these notions of "meaning" as an approach to the analysis of necessary truth. We are now in a position to begin to bring these two authors together, and, in doing so, clarify some most puzzling passages in Husserl. "Essence" is to be distinguished from all objects that are instances of it, and from all signs which might "express" that essence (Husserl also utilizes this notion of "expression"); and, most importantly, an essence is to be distinguished from all 'psychological' ideas which we might have associated with it, i.e. all (sensory) experience and individual (factual) intuitions. The special or "ideal" mode of existence of essences is simply the independence of the essence from all "worldly" or "real" or "spatio-temporal" existence, the existence had by objects of reference (with necessary qualifications, e.g. when mathematical "objects" are referred to) and by signs themselves (which "exist" as markings or sounds). (I am not sure to what extent Husserl would want to count images as non-spatio-temporal; he certainly does insist that they are "natural," and "natural" for him seems to entail "existing spatio-temporally.")

We can now also begin to see how essences can yield necessary truths. Insofar as essences are senses or meanings, a statement about essences will be a statement which is non-empirical. To utilize one of Husserl's few examples, a statement about the essence of *sound* and the essence of *colour* to the effect that "The essence ... Colour is other than the essence ... Sound," [22] or, differently, "A colour in general is different from a sound in general" [23] will be essentially true, a statement of "essential generality." The latter is implicitly, as the former is explicitly, not a judgment about colour and sound but a judgment about the *essences* of colour and sound. In a different vernacular, these judgments are not "about the world" but "about the meanings of words," "the senses of signs." This would explain the necessity of truths which are about essences, and would explain the non-empirical nature and "independence of facts" of our "knowledge of essences."

[22] *Ideen*, p. 53, 1:5.
[23] *Ibid.*, p. 52, 1:5.

Our suggested equation between Husserl's notion of "essence" and Frege's notions of "*Sinn*" and "thought" thus begins to show us some reward. However, there are important differences between the two sets of concepts. We must ask ourselves, quite critically, to what extent this equivalence can be maintained, and to what degree "essence" and "sense" are markedly different. It is equally important to ask ourselves to what extent the differences between the two authors are not so much differences in the concepts of "essence," "sense-thought," but differences in their theories about essences and sense-thoughts. I shall argue that these concepts are equivalent, but that Husserl makes important claims about essences that Frege does not make about thoughts. Notably, Husserl claims that essences are to be "grasped" through *intuition* : Frege claims that thoughts are to be "grasped" through an examination of language.

It would certainly seem that the most important difference between Frege and Husserl, a difference more than sufficient to destroy our equivalence between Husserl's "essence" and Frege's "sense," lies in their very different attitudes towards language in their treatment of these two concepts. Frege is clearly a philosopher of language, and his analysis of "sense" is an analysis of the *sense of a sign*. Husserl, quite to the contrary, is dealing with essences *simpliciter*, not essences *of* verbal expressions. It would appear, therefore, that our attempted reduction of both "*Sinn*" and "*Wesen*" to some notion of "meaning" is most implausible.

The standard picture of Frege as a strictly "linguistic" philosopher and Husserl as an anti-linguistic philosopher is, however, an oversimplification in both directions. Frege is concerned with language, and his interest in *Sinn* is an interest in analyzing language, but the notion of "*Sinn*," as I shall attempt to argue, is not itself a purely "linguistic" notion. Moreover, Husserl is not so antagonistic to a philosophy of language as we are often led to suppose. Although Husserl has little to say about language, there is some reason to suppose that he would not have been willing to make any claim as harsh as the denial that essences were relevant to and even, in an important but puzzling way, dependent upon language. Thus, I shall argue that the alleged difference between the two philosophers *vis-à-vis* the importance of language for philosophy does not reflect a difference between their respective notions of "*Sinn*" and "*Wesen*."

We have already stressed Frege's insistence that the *sense* of a sign (the thought) must not be confused with the reference of that sign, any image associated with that sign, or most importantly, with the sign itself. The distinction between sense and sign can be demonstrated in many ways : a given sense can be "expressed" by many different signs — the sense of the word "cat" can be expressed by this inscription, or by my pronouncing a corresponding sequence of phonemes, or by appropriate inscriptions or pronouncements in any other language. Moreover, we can refer to a sense without expressing it with a sign at all; e.g. "Whatever that word means must be obscene in that context," and we can refer to a sense that could never be expressed at all; e.g. "There are inexpressible thoughts." Therefore, a sense of a sign is not the sign itself, nor is it equivalent to any combinations or sets of signs.

From Frege's characterization of the sense as the *thought*, it becomes clear that the sense thought is something quite apart from language and language users. But here we encounter a fascinating problem : what is this entity which Frege clearly claims is necessary for any adequate analysis of language (a necessity reclaimed by Russell, and more recently by Church [24]). But does the interpretation of the thought as an abstract entity necessary to do justice to an account of language give us the only possible approach to thoughts? Or, can one recognize and identify thoughts independently of their expressions in language? Unfortunately, we can say little more about Frege's own analysis of sense or thought, for he nowhere attempts to give us such a pre-linguistic analysis. His informal introduction in "On Sense and Reference," and his essay, "The Thought," are attempts to make clear several things a thought is *not* (e.g. "Thoughts are neither things of the outer world nor ideas,") [25] but Frege then leaves us, much as Husserl leaves us, with a statement to the effect that *thoughts* have their own "mode of Being."

From Frege's discussions of "sense," in the articles "The Thought," "On Sense and Reference," and "On Concept and Object," we begin to see that *thoughts* do not hold a unique position in his philosophy, but share with a number of such entities the peculiar status of being neither "an object in the world," nor "an image in someone's mind," nor a linguistic expression (a "sign"). Among these are *concepts, functions, truth* and *truth-values,* and perhaps *propositions.* Husserl also has a "system" of such entities :

[24] "The Need for Abstract Entities in Semantics" in *Structure of Language,* Katz and Fodor (Prentice-Hall, 1964).

[25] "*The Thought,*" p. 302.

Eidetic *judging*, eidetic *judgment* or eidetic *proposition*, eidetic *truth* (or true proposition) — these ideas manifestly belong to the same system. Connected with them is also the correlate of the third of these ideas : the plain eidetic *fact* ...[26]

These meaning-related entities become the center of philosophical activity for Frege, and his informal writings are considerably more taken up with discussion of "concept" and "truth" than with "meaning" itself, which is taken (as "thought") as a primitive for his studies. Husserl, on the other hand, concerns himself with the nature of essences and their being "grasped in intuition" and has relatively little to say about the *expression* [27] of essential insights or the *truth* of essential propositions as such.

Frege's "family" of entities presents special problems to the student of Frege. "Concept," for example, is surely a central notion in his philosophy, but, in "On Concept and Object" (*BG* 42-43), he tells us that "concept" is primitive and undefinable. Concepts are contrasted both with objects and signs and images; which leads one to reasonably suppose that concepts are very much like thoughts. Concepts, like thoughts, do not properly "exist," but may or may not be "*instantiated*," just as a thought may or may not be *true*. In *Grundlagen*, for example, Frege tells us that concepts are incomplete thoughts. But then we find a marked difference : "concepts are ... the reference of a grammatical predicate" (*BG* 43 including footnote), and we have seen that sense is not *referred to* by a predicate but is rather expressed by a sign. Yet Frege surely does not want to say that the concept is a standard *object* of reference. In most contexts, Frege uses "concept" as he uses "sense of a sign," but "concepts" seem to be the senses only of words or phrases, not of sentences.[28] But this fails to fully characterize some of what Frege says about his "concept" ("*Begriff*"). For example, he tells us that a concept is a special kind of *function* : "A concept is a function whose value is a truth value" (*BG* 30). However, Frege is insistent that truth-value alone is not sufficient to distinguish a concept. For example, two different concepts (*Man* : *Rational Animal*) may have the same *extension*, and so "to whatever object one applied, the other would

[26] *Ideen*, p. 53, 1:16.

[27] The only extensive discussion in Husserl concerning the relationship between meaning and its expression in language is in the "First Investigation" of *LU*.

[28] Church, for example, *op. cit.*, interprets Frege's "*Sinn*" as a "concept of the reference."

also." [29] Concepts are closely related to truth-values, but concepts have a *content* which truth-values cannot sufficiently determine.

This makes a concept look very much like a part of a thought ("part" in some sense relatable to the sense of a word or phrase being "part" of the sense of a sentence) and thus very much like a self-sufficient extra-linguistic meaning-unit, i.e. a sense. This interpretation is uncertain, however, for in some of Frege's own examples a concept looks very much like a "subject" : e.g. "What gives the result 10 when increased by 1." [30]

It is not clear, in this example, whether the concept is being *expressed* or *referred to*. Furthermore, the relationship of concepts to the objects *instantiating* them is unclear. Ferge's "extension of a concept" does not signify those "objects falling under it," but rather a set of arguments (functions) whose value is *true*. This is the general problem in understanding Frege's notion of *Begriff*; he introduces a notion of "concept" which plays an important but obscure role in the analysis of language but without being clearly related to "sense" or "reference," and with no independent characterization.

This same problem is repeated in a study of the notions of "truth" and "truth-value." On the one hand he offers us his famous analysis of Truth ("The Truth") and Falsity ("The False") as the *reference* of sentences. But this fares strangely with his pronouncements that

> Thought is true and false.[31]
> With every property of a thing is joined a property of thought, that is truth.[32]

(The characterization of the thought or the sentence as units of truth or falsity also raises problems for Frege's characterization of "concept" as "a function whose value is also a truth value.") But Frege also tells us that "truth" is a primitive concept in logic as well, and so he makes no attempt to clarify it for us.[33] (He denies, in the same article, that a "correspondence" theory of truth could make sense : but he does not give us, and tells us he cannot give us, an account of truth which does make sense.)

Similarly, "function" plays a peculiarly undefined role in Frege's extensive discussions of the foundations of arithmetic. Again, he care-

[29] *Grundlagen*, p. 108.
[30] "On Function and Concept," *BG* 33.
[31] "The Thought," p. 292.
[32] *Ibid.*, p. 293.
[33] *Ibid.*

fully tells us what a function is *not* (it is not a sign or a function of a sign, as the "Formalists" would have it) and it is to be distinguished from a "concept." But elsewhere we are told that a concept is a *kind* of function.[34] Taking his discussion of "function" from the employment of that term in mathematics, Frege, like Husserl, speaks of "unsaturated" functions, and of "concepts" as a type of "saturated" functions.

Thus these three concepts of "concept," "function," and "truth-value" (and, most important for subsequent philosophers, but little used by Frege, the concept of "proposition," as distinguished from "sentence"), are thus left with the uncomfortable negative characterization that they are not worldly objects, not mere "images," nor are they linguistic entities. Sometimes they are spoken of as "objects of reference" (truth is a reference of sentences : concepts are references of predicates), but most often they appear as ontological relatives of Frege's central notions of Thought and Sense. But in Frege, who was primarily interested in using these basic (for him "primitive") notions in an analysis of language and the necessary truths of mathematics, the ontology of these entities remains a considerable mystery.

My intention here is not to show that Frege and Husserl are similar in confused complexity, but simply to show that Frege generously populates his ontology with objects whose "Being" curiously parallels Husserl's talk of "essential Being" and its correlated notions. It might be helpful at this point if we were to digress slightly and note that this tendency to introduce non-worldly, non-"mental," non-linguistic entities was not in the least peculiar to Husserl and Frege. Although German philosophy-psychology was well served by philosophers who simply treated all entities as either "physical" or "psychical" (e.g. Brentano and Stumpf), at least two very prominent philosophers of the nineteenth century shared this concern for peculiar entities. In the early part of the century, Bolzano had introduced the notion of "proposition-in-itself" (*Satz-an-sich*) and like notions of "truth-in-itself" and "idea-in-itself" to refer to those entities which were asserted, questioned, believed to be true but which were themselves neither assertions (sentences or statements) questions, or beliefs. In the later part of the century, Alexius von Meinong, whose reputation in Anglo-American philosophy has largely been administered in the not-always-reliable historical criticism of Bertrand Russell, introduced a new "objective" "world" of entities to suit the same purpose. In his "Theory of Objects," Meinong presents

[34] "On Function and Concept,' *BG* 30.

us with a world of "objects" which have *Being*, but not *existence*, in order to explain how it is the case that we can talk about *non-existent* objects; e.g. in "Unicorns do not exist." Of special interest to us, however, is a special sort of non-worldly (i.e. non-existent) entity which Meinong refers to as an "objective." An "objective," like Bolzano's "proposition-in-itself," is that which is expressed in assertions, is believed, is doubted, and so on. The peculiar, ontological status of Frege's *sense* and Husserl's *essence* is a common problem in 1890; what is it that is *expressed* by assertions?

Of particular importance in our discussion of Husserl is our understanding that Bolzano and Meinong, as well as Husserl, were not exclusively concerned with language and its uses but with the nature of *mental acts*. Asserting is a verbal expression of a *Satz-an-sich* or an "objective," but it is also an *act* of asserting. This is not to say that it is an act which is clearly different from the act of assertively expressing the same *Satz-an-sich* or "objective" in language, nor is it even to say that it is possible to assert without asserting through language. Rather, asserting through language is but one very special instance of a huge number of mental acts, only some of which have any connection with linguistic expression. Husserl, we must emphasize, did not *deny* any role to language in mental acts; he simply did not concern himself *primarily* with linguistic acts.

Frege, however, also distinguished between mental acts and linguistic acts. We have insisted that the *thought* is not itself a linguistic entity, but rather, "itself immaterial, [it] clothes itself in the material garment of a sentence and thereby becomes comprehensible to us." [35]

Frege distinguishes :

1. the apprehension of a thought — (thinking)
2. the recognition of the truth of a thought — (judgment) [36]
3. the manifestation of this thought — (assertion) [37]

Thus, for Frege, assertion (while it is a necessarily linguistic act), is already two steps removed from the apprehension of a thought. The difference between Frege and Husserl would thus not seem to be Frege's employing a strictly linguistic notion of *Sinn* as opposed to Husserl's non-linguistic notion of "essence." The difference is rather one of em-

[35] "The Thought," p. 292.

[36] This use of "judgment" is at odds with a usage in "On Concept and Object." "Language presents the thought as a judgment" (*BG* 49).

[37] "The Thought," p. 300.

phasis; Frege concentrates his philosophical genius on the analysis of *assertion*, an essentially linguistic activity, and on an analysis of *judgments*, in which the truth-value of sentences (more properly of senses which sentences express) is recognized. Frege has little interest in the analysis of thinking itself, the prelinguistic mental act in which one has not yet attempted to evaluate the truth of a thought or its possible expression in language. Yet this is just what interests Husserl, who is not interested particularly in either judgments or assertions. Husserl and Frege differ not in their analysis of *thought*, but in their interest in it. Husserl is interested in the nature of thought *before* it gets captured in language. He is also interested in thoughts before they are recognized as true or false; this latter form of judgments "reduced" to unevaluated thoughts is the significance of Husserl's famous *epoche*, or "bracketing of existence." In phenomenology, he is interested only in the thoughts, i.e. the essences, themselves, barring any possible questions concerning the valuc of that thought or essence, as a model of the "real" world.

I do not wish to leave an impression that Husserl maintained, much less argued, that the grasping of essences can dispense with any consideration of language in which thoughts are expressed. Rather, his position on this matter seems to be ambivalent (not to say confused) concerning the rule of language in the essences to be examined. In his early essay, "Philosophy as a Rigorous Science," he tells us : "The phenomenologist ... derives no judgments at all from word concepts, but rather looks into the phenomena *that language occasions by means of the words in question.*" [38]

In *Ideas*, Husserl tells us again that "essences are distinguished from their verbal expression," but that verbal expressions, "relate to the essence and the essential connections which they *once fixated* and now express." [39]

This would seem to indicate that language has a role in "fixing" essences (i.e. "we can learn to think [employ concepts] only by learning a language"); but Husserl pays no head to the *origins* of our knowledge of essences, and so this claim is never investigated.

Husserl's views on language become yet more complex when we attempt to investigate further our reduction of both Frege's "sense-thought" and Husserl's "essence" to a notion of "meaning", as we did in the beginning of this essay. Husserl gives us three distinct notions of "meaning," making our attempted reduction too ambitious. Husserl

[38] *PRS*, p. 95, trans. Q. Lauer. Italics added.

[39] *Ideen*, p. 179, 7:67. Italics added.

notes that these different notions are used as equivalents in ordinary speech, but must, for purposes of philosophy be distinguished. They are :

(a) *Sinn*, "Sence of Meaning *simpliciter*," or Sense in its most general meaning.
(b) *Bedeutung*, "meaning at the conceptual level," "logical," or "expressing meaning."
(c) *Meinen*, "meaning as a functional act," or simply "intentionality."

It is only (b) in which we are interested. The sense of "sense" (*Sinn*) (a) encompasses Frege's "reference" as well as "sense" and it would also cover a notion of "significance," (e.g. "His answer made sense but was insignificant or meaningless"). *Sinn* also covers a special sense of *meaning* in which "the object perceived as such" or "thing-itself" is the *meaning* of an act of consciousness. (c) *Meinung* is a very general term of intentionality and would go far beyond the "sense" of a sign to whatever a person might *mean* (intend) in any act of consciousness. In this sense, every act of perception, imagination, becoming angry, falling in love, being hungry, or trying to insult someone would have a *meaning*. Again, this sense of meaning is much broader than the concept of "essence."

What Husserl says about (b) is perplexing. He says, "... originally these words (*Bedeutung*, *bedeuten*) relate only to the sphere of speech, that of 'expression.' " [40] But then he immediately suggests we extend their meanings to all acts, "whether these are interwoven with expression acts or not." [41] But later in the same section, he tells us that when we "grasp a meaning,"

> This process makes no call whatsoever on "expression," neither on expression in the sense of verbal sound nor on the like as verbal meaning, and here the latter can also be present independently of the verbal sound.

and then,

> Every meaning (*Meinung*) of any act can be expressed conceptually (*durch Bedeutungen*) ... Logical meaning is an expression.

and then,

> The verbal sound can be referred to as expression only because the meaning which belongs to it expresses : it is in it that the expressing originally lies.[42]

[40] *Ideen*, p. 319.
[41] *Ibid.*, p. 319.
[42] *Ibid.*, p. 320.

These passages indicate that Husserl clearly takes "expressing," including "conceptual expression" to be prelinguistic ("pre-verbal") notions. The expression of "meaning" (*Bedeutung*) is an act of consciousness which is distinct from and precedes "verbal expression" (Frege's "assertion"). We can express the meaning (*Meinung*) of every act of consciousness as conceptual meaning (*Bedeutung*) and can, in turn, express every such conceptual meaning in some linguistic expression. Husserl would thus make a claim for language that is more ambitious than many "linguistic" philosophers would assent to : there is nothing that can be thought that cannot be expressed in language.

What I have argued thus far in this essay is what I believe to be a most important correspondence between the philosophies of two supposedly very different philosophers. Granted that Husserl benefits far more from this statement of resemblance than Frege, I should not like to leave the merits of Husserl's doctrine of *essence* wholly dependent on his similarity to Frege. To a certain extent, Husserl does repeat more obscurely and less systematically, some of Frege's central positions. However, the difference in emphasis we have discussed is of considerably more than historical interest, for it holds a key, not only to the major breach between analysis and phenomenology, but also to some important disputes in contemporary analytic philosophy of language.

Neither the notion of "essence" nor the notions of "sense" and "thought" play as large a role in contemporary philosophy as they once did. However, current philosophy is quite occupied with notions derivative of these : we have already noted how "concept" is such a notion, and the ontological status of *concepts* remains as large a question for contemporary philosophers of the analytic tradition as the status of *essence* continued to be for Husserl. Of equal importance in current discussions is the problematic notion of a "proposition." Frege occasionally used "*Satz*" to refer to that entity which was not a physical sentence (also "*Satz*"; which meaning is determinable in context), but which was expressed by a sentence. Thus, in Frege, we can suggest a third concept like "sense" and "thought," and we can draw a further equivalence between Husserl's "essence" and "proposition." However, we must understand that this use of "proposition" is foreign to Husserl (for whom "proposition" and "judgment" are equivalent [quote on page 43 of this article]), and rare in Frege. This modern use is due to Russell and Wittgenstein, not Frege and Husserl. Of importance to us is the remarkable similarity between the functions of propositions, senses, thoughts, and essences in these various philosophies. Today, "proposition" is the most acceptable name for that peculiar entity which "has meaning," is "expressed" by a sentence, is true or false, but which is distinct from worldly objects, expressing sentences, and any "mental" occurrences (intentions, images) of persons who "hold" that proposition. In other words, "proposition" is the new name for Husserl's "essence," Frege's "sense" or "thought" : "It is clear that by "thought" expressed by a declarative, he [Frege] means what other philosophers call a "proposition." [43]

The status of propositions is not an isolated problem in the philosophy of language, however; it has rather become the (often-unrecognized) fulcrum of a wide-spread debate between what F. P. Ramsey called several *paradigms of philosophy*. The acceptance or rejection of these special entities, under whatever name, determines an entire philosophical outlook. I take the attitude toward the ontological status of *propositions* (*thoughts, essences*) to be the key point of departure of Husserl's phenomenology from analytic philosophy, as I take it to be the key factor in what at present is probably the largest single split among analytic philosophers.

The rejection of Russell's theory of descriptions by Strawson has often been interpreted, notably by Strawson himself, as a rejection of a single theory concerning referring expressions within a mutually accepted philosophical framework. In fact, however, the problem of referring is only a focal point for a most general problem in philosophy, namely, the subject matter of philosophical investigation. According to Bertrand Russell (and the "early" Wittgenstein, and most practitioners of "philosophical analysis") the subject matter of philosophy was the structure of *propositions*, an examination of which would show us the structure of "the world." Russell's philosophical analysis is an analysis of "propositions and their constituents"; the problem of philosophy must be the clarification of these. What are these? In his famous article "On Denoting," Russell sometimes indicates that the constituents of propositions are *words*, but that cannot be right, since the proposition and its parts are clearly to be distinguished from the language that expressed them. Elsewhere he mentions "single propositions of which the thing itself (i.e. the referent) is a constituent," [44] but that cannot be right either, for the proposition is to be distinguished from the things

[43] L. Linsky, *Referring* (London : Routledge, Kegan Paul, 1967), p. 25.

[44] E.g. in Feigl and Sellars' reprint of "On Denoting," in *Readings in Philosophical Analysis* (New York : Appleton-Century-Crofts, 1949), p. 115.

referred to. But the status of propositions and their constituents remains a problem unilluminated by Russell. Wittgenstein gave the problem its due attention, and his attitude, most representative of that to which Husserl is a viable alternative, is that "I don't know *what* the constituents of a thought are, but I know that it must have such constituents which correspond to the words of language." [45]

In this view, confusedly indicated by Russell, and expressly argued by Church (*op. cit.*), propositions (thoughts, essences) are entities which are expressed in language, which we can get to know *through* an analysis of language, but whose nature ultimately must remain a mystery. Wittgenstein, for example, adopts the same ploy used by Frege, and takes "thought" to bc a logical "primitive," inexplicable apart from its necessary functions in language.

The alternatives to this mystical concept of *proposition* (*essence*, *thought*) lie in two very different directions. First, there is the rejection of the notion of *propositions* and a simple appeal to the *use* of language. Thus, for Strawson, J. L. Austin, and the "later" Wittgenstein, philosophy studies not propositions but *sentences* and the *uses of sentences*. Through this examination, we discover the "structures of the world," presumably the same world explored earlier by Russel and the "early" Wittgenstein. Strawson's own attack seemed to be quite unaware of the nature of the disagreement between the two philosophers. Strawson attacks Russell's analysis on the basis of its failure as an analysis of our everyday uses of statements, while Russell's analysis was of a very different nature — an analysis of the propositions which are expressed by (but exist independently of) our ordinary uses of language. Strawson's conclusion to his article "On Referring" is symptomatic of the misdirection of the entire attack on Russel : "Ordinary language has no exact logic." But Russel's concern was with propositions, which are true or false, while Strawson's concern was with our use of statements in ordinary language "to make true or false assertions." Russell's criterion for the success of his analysis was to capture the structure of those entities which were expressed in language; Strawson's criterion for success was to satisfy the "purposes for which we ordinarily use language." In short, the dispute between Russell and Strawson was not over an analysis of certain referring expressions; it was "whether in our everyday discourse we speak in statements or in propositions?" [46]

[45] Wittgenstein, *Notebooks*, 1914, 1916, trans. Anscombe (Oxford : Blackwell, 1961), p. 129.

[46] Linsky, *op. cit.*, p. 99.

But this, according to Husserl, Frege, and Russell, is not the problem of philosophy, which is concerned with truth, meaning, reference, and so on, but a matter which may be described as *empirical*. (If we all learned language from Russell's philosophy, we should speak in propositions.) The problem of philosophy, as characterized by Frege and Husserl at least, are not the empirical problems of how people do *in fact* use their language, but matters of *essence* (*thought and logic*). The problems raised by Russell's theory about propositions are no more vulnerable to ordinary language criticism than our proofs of geometry are vulnerable to empirical refutation.

But despite the misplaced battle between Russell and Strawson, the underlying dispute is of momentous importance. The rejection of the role of propositions (thought, essences) in discussions of philosophy has been best expressed by the unique philosopher who was prominent as a defender of both views. In his later writings, Wittgenstein looked back at his almost mystical analysis of propositions, and complained that, "We don't get free of the idea that the sense of a sentence accompanies the sentence, is there alongside it." [47]

The "innocent" claim that the *thought* is "primitive" and has no extra-linguistic characterization is, Wittgenstein now argues, "the decisive movement in the conjuring trick," [48] a "myth of our symbolism." Philosophy must forget about this "occult sphere" of propositions and thoughts (and essences) and restrict itself to looking at "the given," which is, for Wittgenstein, our uses of language to *do* things.

But when one gives up the notion of propositions, all sorts of old taboos are broken, and with troublesome results. Once again, philosophy seems to become an *empirical* study of how persons (we) use language. But this leaves open an old Fregean-Husserlian wound, what justification can this seemingly *empirical* search provide us for the sorts of philosophical, i.e. *necessary* truths that we seek?

Why should we accept or not accept the existence of propositions? One reason for not accepting them, from what we have seen above, is the sort of serious problems we encounter in attempting to say what these entities are. Furthermore, as evidenced (but not made fully explicit) in the Russell-Strawson dispute, the introduction of propositions can generate problems of its own. But most important is the question of

[47] Wittgenstein, *Zettel*, No. 139, trans., ed., Anscombe and Von Wright (Oxford : Blackwell, 1967), p. 25 (e).

[48] *Philosophical Investigations*, No. 308, trans. Anscombe and Von Wright (Oxford : Blackwell, 1967), p. 56 (e).

whether these entities are *necessary* for adequate explanation of the behavior of language, and, in particular an account of truth, meaning and necessary truth, in order to compensate for the disadvantages of adding mysterious entities to our ontology and generating new problems. Church has recently argued that such entities *are* necessary for the purpose of explanation of language.[49] All of those who reject propositions, or all of those who accept the procedures of ordinary language analysis (whether or not they have questioned the existence of propositions), do not accept this necessity.

However, the standard dispute covered in the preceding paragraph bases itself on a supposition about the nature of propositions (thoughts, essences) which has not been questioned sufficiently in analytic circles (just as the analytic suppositions here involved have not been sufficiently examined by phenomenologists). All of these considerations assume that the only way to approach these peculiar entities is through an analysis of language, and the dispute between the two analytic camps thus rests upon a common ground — the assumption that, if propositions are anything at all, they must be entities which can *only* be expressed in language but not independently characterized in any way :

> There is, I think, a discoverable relation between the structure of sentences and the structure of the occurrences to which the sentences refer. I do not think the structure of non-verbal facts wholly unknowable, and I believe that, with sufficient caution, the properties of language may help us to understand the structure of the world.[50]

Husserl and phenomenology make an important claim : they maintain that the peculiar entities we have been discussing do allow themselves to be expressed in language by sentences, but that they can be characterized without such appeal to their expression in language through a direct reflection upon "intuition." Because we can investigate essences (propositions, thoughts) without appeal to language, it is therefore possible to reestablish the role of propositions in the examination of language, but on a different basis than their necessity for an adequate accounting for language. If we could show that intuition itself provides us with the data which make necessary truths necessarily true, which give us the prelinguistic structures of languages and the structure of thought, then philosophy would have to accept a very different paradigm indeed.

[49] *Op. cit.*

[50] Russell, *Inquiry into Meaning and Truth* (London : Allen and Unwin, 1940), p. 341.

One turns to "use"-theory in philosophy precisely because of the seeming impossibility of getting an adequate grasp on propositions (essences, thoughts). Husserl and Frege would both find this approach abhorrent to their vision of philosophy; the alternative would be to turn to the direct examination of the "things themselves" or the "given" — in other words, the propositions, thoughts, or essences rather than what expresses these propositions, thoughts, or essences. The business of philosophy is to provide and practice a technique for "reducing" our intuitions to those "eidetic" elements about which philosophers have been talking in so many ways. It is the function of Husserl's "eidetic reduction" to display for us these "pure essences" (or propositions). If Husserl is correct, then philosophers need not grapple with inaccessible "abstract" linguistic-related entities, nor need they look at how people *in fact* use language. Rather, philosophy would consist of a *theory of intuition* and a method for extracting *essential structures* from intuition.

The problem with all this, of course, is that it has not clearly been done. Husserl's own stylistic paraplegia makes his doctrine most unwelcome reading, and, for those who do master his exposition of his method in *Ideen*, there is the disappointment, I believe, of discovering that the endless distinctions there are based upon an obscure foundation, if not an insecure one. But phenomenology has had few articulate spokesmen in this country, and very few who have allowed themselves to become sympathetic to the goals of analytic philosophers. In this essay, I have attempted to make some sense out of one of Husserl's most obscure and most central concepts. As a result, I hope that I have indicated the direction which philosophers of both sides of the analysis-phenomenology breach must follow if there is to be a serious meeting of philosophical cultures. I suggest that the problems confronting analytic and phenomenological philosophers are identical : what has yet to be proved, even to those of us who are hopeful about the possible fruits of Husserl's method, is that the phenomenological approach is a fruitful one.

HUSSERL AND/OR WITTGENSTEIN

by

JOHN M. HEMS

> Of course, even scholastic ontologism is guided by language (by which I am not saying that all scholastic research was ontologistic) but *it loses itself by deriving analytical judgments from word meanings, in the belief that it has thereby gained knowledge of facts.* Is the phenomenological analyst to be branded scholastic too, because he derives no judgments at all from word concepts but rather looks into the phenomena that language occasions by means of the words in question...? In the ἐποχή of vigorous reaction against Scholasticism the war cry was : "*Away with empty word analyses*! We must question things themselves. Back to experience, to seeing, which alone can give to our words sense and rational justification." *Very much to the point*! (Husserl, *Philosophy as a Rigorous Science*; my italics).

The desire for unity is almost ineradicable in human nature, and a recent manifestation of this characteristic is to be found in the attempt to associate Wittgenstein with Husserl, or conscript Wittgenstein into the Husserlian camp or vice versa.[1] Not quite so hilarious as turning

[1] Robert Sokolowski, *The Formation of Husserl's Concept of Constitution* (The Hague : Nijhoff, 1965); T. N. Munson, "Wittgenstein's Phenomenology," *Phil. and Phenomenological Research*, 23 (1962-63), 37-50; C. A. Van Peursen, "Edmund Husserl and Ludwig Wittgenstein," *ibid.*, 20 (1959-60), 181-97; J. N. Mohanty, *Husserl's Theory of Meaning* (The Hague : Nijhoff, 1966); M. Dufrenne, *Jalons* (The Hague : Nijhoff, 1966); Emanuele Riverso, *Il pensiero di Ludovico Wittgenstein* (Napoli :

Kierkegaard into a linguistic philosopher, it nevertheless has its interest for those of us whose darling occupation it is to draw distinctions. It certainly cannot be gainsaid that there are points of resemblance between Husserl and Wittgenstein, but in my opinion these are of a superficial nature, whereas the differences between the two philosophers are quite radical. However, let us consider what they have in common.

Both Husserl and Wittgenstein (at least in the *Philosophical Investigations*) reject the image or "mental picture" theory of meaning. Wittgenstein also comes close to denying the notion of a criterion of meaning, a notion utterly rejected by Husserl; that is, both philosophers are agreed that philosophy is not competent to act as the legislator of what is or is not meaningful. (In this connection it is possible that Wittgenstein would have disapproved of those of his followers who wish to advance proposals as to how the word "meaningful" should be used.) Language is to be accepted for what it is, and the philosopher's task is not to alter it but describe it. "Philosophy simply puts everything before us, and neither explains nor deduces anything," says Wittgenstein (*P.I.*, p. 50), and similarly for Husserl the philosophical task with regard to language is purely descriptive. The philosopher is to describe, not decide, what is meaningful. Both drew inspiration from Frege and concerned themselves with the problems of Hume. As far back as 1900 (in the *Logische Untersuchungen*) Husserl is concerned with *Sachverhalt*, the term which in Wittgenstein's "Tractatus" is translated into English as "atomic fact," and there is also a parallel in the development of both philosophers as they move away from the notion of an ideal language towards, on the one hand, Husserl's *Lebenswelt* and, on the other, Wittgenstein's "everyday language." That Wittgenstein's interests are in some sense phenomenological might be argued from direct textual evidence. Consider the following remarks in a Joint Session Paper : "We can only arrive at a correct analysis by what might be called the logical investigation of the phenomena themselves." "Definite rules of syntax ... cannot be laid down until we have actually reached the ultimate analysis of the phenomena in question." [2] Even Wittgenstein's *criticisms*

Libreria Scientifica, 1964); J. N. Findlay, art. "Phenomenology" in *Encyclopedia Britannica*, 1964; Heinz Hulsman, *Zur Theorie der Sprache bei Edmund Husserl.*

There have also been rumblings of dissent. When Merleau-Ponty suggested to Gilbert Ryle that they were engaged in a common enterprise, the latter replied, "I hope not!" (*Quatrième Colloque de Royaumont*, 1962).

[2] *Proceedings of Aristotelian Society*, 29 (1928-29), 163, 141. Husserl's *Formal and Transcendental Logic* was also published in this year.

of psychological "meaning" — criticisms which seem *ipso facto* to alienate him from Husserl's thought — may be taken rather as expressing an agnostic disinterestedness, based upon his conviction that little of value can be said about such matters, than as a confrontation of Husserl's diagnostic interest with the denial of the very existence of psychological aspects of meaning. However, from these bits and pieces of correspondence let us turn to consider our philosophers at greater depth.

In the *Tractatus* the world is defined as a syntactical function, and yet running side by side with such linguistic accounts there are apparently ontological assertions (e.g. "The world is everything that happens.") It is this juxtaposition of logical with ontological elements which makes the book so puzzling to the uninitiated and which led to the not entirely satisfactory interpretation put out by Carnap wherein material language was replaced by formal (not entirely satisfactory because it tended to *obscure* the point that language says what *is*, and what *may be* arising out of what is). However, it is clear that in the *Tractatus* Wittgenstein's main interest is to consider the problem of the "truth" of language in the sense of the relation of thought to the world, and from the beginning he identifies thought with language, although not coextensively (since it is possible to say things that cannot be thought). A thought is a meaningful proposition. This position enables him to avoid considering thought in itself and to escape the temptations of psychologism. Language is the totality of propositions which extends throughout the *entirety* of logical space, and is *the logos*, i.e. the soul of meaning. *Principia Mathematica*, in Wittgenstein's opinion, furnishes us, at least approximately, with the incarnation of this soul. The soul of language, then, is a formal, logical system, or a language which expresses the logos immanent in all discourse.

Even from the beginning Husserl does not grant such a central position to logical considerations as Wittgenstein, but like the latter he understands logic as logos, the soul of theory and the theory of all possible theories. In his *Formal and Transcendental Logic* (1929) he is concerned with a logic not merely of consequence but of truth. He formulates a theory of the object in general, i.e. of a formal object which is the form of any object whatever. According to Mikel Dufrenne, Husserl's genetic phenomenology is echoed by Wittgenstein in the *Investigations*.[3]

[3] See *Jalons*, *op. cit.* in n. 1. Although I disagree with his conclusions, I am beholden to this author for some valuable exegesis.

For Wittgenstein, logic explicates the true language, and this true language must refer to the world and be the logic of the world. At this stage Wittgenstein had not yet renounced the "mental picture" approach. He maintains that we make pictures of facts which are a transposition of reality. But of course Wittgenstein is not offering us a version of intentionality. Instead of a theory of constitutive subjectivity Wittgenstein offers us a theory of language — but of language endowed with truth. This approach might be described as a linguistic version of the traditional correspondence theory of truth. What, may we ask, becomes of *a priori* truth in such a "picture" theory? What of logic itself? Here there emerges the tautological version of truth, with its almost violent sundering of the formal from the material, the analytic from the synthetic — later adopted by logical positivism. Necessity belongs to the realm of logic alone, and yet nevertheless language depicts the world, and it is impossible even to say what an illogical world would be. Hence logic is an ontology; not simply a theory, but an image reflecting the world. Logic must be transcendental, telling us the necessary conditions for speaking about the world : propositions represent, names signify, for the logos is common to both language and the world. The syntax of language is the syntax of reality. The logical form of objects consists in their ability to function as subjects or predicates, and "the logic of the world which is shown in tautologies by the propositions of logic, is shown in equations by mathematics." Language is ontological. Logical propositions await content and thus indicate the logical form of the world, or the world possibility.

Husserl came to a similar conclusion via a different route. Taking into account the nature of logic and the intentions of the logician, Husserl saw logic as at once concerned with judgments and objects, and he considered that logic must first of all refer to the individual object if it is latterly to refer to the object in general. The mere consideration of such priority could never arise for Wittgenstein, according to whom the logos is from the first common to language and reality, and the limits of the subject's language are the limits of his world. Yet if this is the case the world must be subordinate to a subject which is not *in* the world — in short, a subject reminiscent of Husserl's "transcendental ego" ("The subject does not belong to the world : rather, it is a limit of the world" (5.632)) rather than Kant's mundane subject. The transcendental subject is for Husserl creative subjectivity : for Wittgenstein it is the logos, i.e. *my* language, "that language which alone I understand" (5.62). The introduction of the "my" will perhaps oblige both philosophers to renounce the notion of a subject as pure correlate or unextended point and bring them back to the *Lebenswelt* and the world of "everyday language," i.e. to the realization of actually being in a world where thought and language are *activities*. Anyhow, the notion of a logos common to language and to the world, even if expressed solipsistically, already goes beyond idealism : "Solipsism, when its implications are followed out strictly, coincides with pure realism. The self of solipsism shrinks to a point without extension, and there remains the reality co-ordinated with it "(5.64). This amounts to the denial of a philosophical — although not of a psychological — self. "The philosophical self is not the human being, not the human body, or the human soul with which psychology deals, but rather the metaphysical subject, the limit of the world — not a part of it" (5.641). And as for the psychological self, this is nothing but the history of the individual's aches and pains, joys, sorrows, desires, etc. ultimately reducible to physical conditions. In other words, the province of psychology is ultimately that of physiology.

Realism signifies : (1) there is a world; (2) this world is logic. We acknowledge that there is a world in a particular experience which precedes logic. Thereafter logic precedes every experience that such and such is the case. The mystical experience is "the feeling of the world as a limited totality" (6.55) : the experience of the What. There is no logic unless there is a world to inspire it. Formal and material, possible and real, are strictly bound together. Something must be given, but so soon as it is given it is given a logical form. In such a way is it assumed into language and rendered incarnate in this world of ours "which exists independently of what happens" (2.024). The logical form of objects forms the logical space of the world. Reality divulges areas of possibility whence thought returns from the possible to the real. It is at this juncture that thought is subsequent to logic instead of preceding it; and as to questions regarding which possibilities obtain and which do not, those are to be answered in terms of verification. "Each thing is found, so to speak, in a space of possible states of thing" (2.013). A spot on the visual field need not be red, but it must have a colour, a tone must have a pitch, a tactile object must have hardness etc. (2.0131). For Husserl, however, not only is logic formal ontology, but that formal ontology should be extended into a material ontology : "Does not every *a priori* form part of a universal *a priori*, precisely, that which prescribes to matter the *a priori* form for a possible universe of existence?" However, although formal ontology has logical priority it only governs material ontology in implicitly presupposing it. Epistemologically, no thought can dispense with examples, and this indicates the limitations of formalism. Logical systems cannot be totally self-justifying since they are both inspired by, and subject to, the world.

These latter considerations might have been advantageously borne in mind by Moritz Schlick when he wrote his article "Is There a Factual *A Priori*?" [4] This article, incidentally, is unique in constituting (however obliquely) some evidence that Wittgenstein was at least aware of the existence of Husserl's philosophy and had even arrived at some conclusions with regard to it. These, the two most influential philosophers of our era — both German-speaking, both associated with Vienna, both of Jewish descent — apparently ignored one another in their writings. However, Spiegelberg reports a conversation with Rush Rhees wherein the latter stated : "I know of only one reference which he made to Husserl. Schlick had asked Wittgenstein what he thought of the view that the statements of phenomenology are synthetic propositions *a priori*, and Wittgenstein gave a brief discussion of this." [5] Schlick, in the article mentioned above, acknowledges Wittgenstein as the source of the basic principles of his objection to what he takes to be the phenomenological doctrine of a "material *a priori*." For Husserl, the rationalization *of* experience necessitates the constitution of the object *by* experience, and in the third of the *Cartesian Meditations* this takes the form of a *material a priori* as opposed to the Kantian restriction of a merely *formal a priori*.

It is precisely this contention of Husserl's that Schlick is out to attack. Schlick argues that anyone who is dissatisfied with Kant's position regarding the status of *a priori* synthetic judgments is under an obligation to provide an alternative solution of that problem (i.e. the problem how the *a priori* element in our judgments — that element which anticipates and is independent of experience, and which is absolutely true, universally applicable, avoiding as it does the vagaries of the "outside" world — should yet be synthetic (not simply analytic). It was a source of wonder to Kant that this element should not only be applicable to matters of fact but also render objective predictability. The propositions of the physical sciences are *a priori* synthetic in this sense, but how are such judgments possible? Kant's "solution" was to restrict the "*a priori*" element exclusively to the *formal* aspects of judgment. And Schlick

[4] In Feigl and Sellars, eds., *Readings in Philosophical Analysis* (New York : Appleton-Century Crofts, 1949).

[5] *The Phenomenological Movement*, 2nd ed. Supplement (The Hague : Nijhoff, 1965).

believes Kant was right to do so. All *a priori* judgments (or "propositions," as Schlick would prefer to call them) are analytic (or tautologous). Phenomenology has failed to come away with an alternative to the Kantian solution of the problem of *a priori* synthetic judgments or propositions — it simply evades this issue.

Furthermore, Schlick continues, the propositions of phenomenology are not material or factual propositions at all — as phenomenology fondly imagines — but merely trivial tautologies. As Wittgenstein has established, once we are prepared to grant normal and proper language the status it deserves, it becomes clear that philosophical problems arise from the distortion of language. And once we reflect upon the nature of the language as it is normally and properly used, it also becomes clear that language is abundant in implicit tautology, which it is the task of the modern empiricist to explicate. The propositions of phenomenology are just such trivial tautologies, and that phenomenology should fail to recognize them as such arises out of the failure to recognize that language has a formal structure of its own just as much as mathematics. "The first who to my knowledge has given the correct solution of the problem is Ludwig Wittgenstein" (285) and the solution is to be forthcoming from the recognition that the logic of language itself determines the irrefutable — but trivial and tautologous — truth of such judgments as "that every tone has an intensity and a pitch, that one and the same surface cannot be simultaneously red and green" (280) which are the only type of proposition Schlick will allow to clearly characterize phenomenology. Everybody knows that a colour cannot at once be red and green, but nobody ever troubles to point out such trivialities. To do so would be something of a joke. What could such a proposition be intended to deny? That a colour *is* at once red and green? But any proposition embodying such a judgment as that would be simply meaningless, nonsensical. Belief in the factual *a priori* entails that "not only the form of our cognitions but also their matter springs from the knowing consciousness... This would amount to a subjective Idealism of the Fichtean variety ..."(280)".

It is hardly surprising that Schlick should have little trouble in demolishing this disingenuous caricature of phenomenology, and since not a single phenomenological principle is considered by Schlick, far less discussed, and since phenomenological experience is dismissed out of hand as "confusion confounded," the phenomenological discipline escapes virtually unscathed from his fulminations. However naive Schlick's essay may appear, and however discredited (at least for the time being) the "logical-positivist" school in philosophy which Schlick represented may be, there is certainly no hint of the possibility of any affiliation whatever between what, in its most general signification, may be described as "linguistic" philosophy and phenomenology. And yet...

The fact is that this essay of Schlick's is a much more curious affair than it seems. Indeed, if we think about it a doubt may arise in our minds as to whether Schlick was really aware of what he was doing. Why, as a self-appointed disciple of Wittgenstein, should he be so ostentatiously up-in-arms against the notion of a "factual *a priori*"? Schlick's essay was published in 1931, and the works of Wittgenstein referred to are the *Tractatus* and the paper delivered to the Aristotelian Society in 1929. But is it not the case that even at this earlier stage in his thought Wittgenstein himself was concerned with establishing something in the nature of an "ontological logic" which in certain respects at least is sufficiently close to Husserl's ideal of a "material *a priori*"? Nor does it seem to me that the later Wittgenstein (and of course a man's latest publications are always earlier than his latest thoughts) repudiates the search for an "ontological logic" along with the search for a perfect language. All that happens in this regard in the *Investigations* is that the search has a different orientation, i.e. it is in the direction of "ordinary language."

Almost equally strange is the main criticism which is advanced by Schlick (and for which he acknowledges his debt to Wittgenstein). These "tautologies" ("that every tone has an intensity and a pitch, that one and the same surface cannot be simultaneously red and green"), which Schlick assumes to be characteristic of phenomenology, and for which he expresses such contempt ("Nobody ever troubles to point out such trivialities"), were certainly pointed out by Wittgenstein. What is the difference in status between these "phenomenological" propositions and Wittgenstein's propositions that "a spot on the visual field need not be red, but it must have colour, a tone must have a pitch, a tactile object must have hardness," etc? The curious thing, then, about Schlick's essay is why (as a disciple of Wittgenstein's) he should have selected the material *a priori* as a target and why, having done so, he should have attacked it in the manner in which he did.

If what Schlick took to be profound differences turn out, upon reflection, to be really resemblances, will this imply some sort of fundamental kinship between phenomenology and linguistic philosophy? Unfortunately, for the peace of the philosophic mind, *no*. Schlick is incapable of grasping the essential distinctions, for in order to do so it would be necessary for him to emerge from his verbal Valhalla, and this of course he is unwilling to do. Because what is primarily at issue here *is* the status of language itself. Everyday language? We should hardly expect Husserl, who spurns the natural world as a ground of certainty, to build upon the even shiftier sands of everyday language. The bare suggestion moves one to laughter! And at this juncture I should quote Merleau-Ponty :

> The Vienna Circle, as is well known, lays it down categorically that we can enter into relations only with meanings. For example, 'consciousness' is not for the Vienna Circle identifiable with what we are. It is a complex meaning which has developed late in time, which should be handled with care, and only after the many meanings which have contributed, throughout the word's semantic development, to the formation of its present one have been made explicit. Logical positivism of this kind is the antithesis of Husserl's thought. Whatever the subtle changes of meaning which have ultimately brought us, as a linguistic acquisition, the word and concept of consciousness, we enjoy direct access to what it designates. For we have the experience of ourselves, of that consciousness which we are, and it is on the basis of this experience that all linguistic connotations are assessed, and precisely through it that language comes to have any meaning at all for us.[6]

In the *Formal and Transcendental Logic* Husserl was more concerned with the powers than with the limits of reason. Wittgenstein shared Husserl's "scientific" ambitions, but drew different conclusions. Analytic formal logic is not for Husserl the last word. Room must be left for a transcendental logic if the transcendental question (how logic is possible, and how it is possible as truth, i.e. as ontology) is to be answered. Wittgenstein's *Tractatus*, on the other hand, gives to the analytic the last word. And although there are no references, either direct or indirect, to phenomenology, any metaphysics is explicitly rejected as unsayable. Indeed, from the viewpoint of the *Tractatus* there is no call to transcend logic in the interests of ontology, for logic expresses ontology already, or at least formal language shows the form of the world. To be able to express the *logical* form of the world it would be necessary to be outside of language, outside of the world, which is impossible :

> Propositions can represent the whole of reality, but they cannot represent what they must have in common with reality in order to be able to represent it — logical form. In order to be able to represent logical form, we should have to be able to station ourselves with propositions somewhere outside logic, that is to say outside the world (4.12).[7]

[6] *Phenomenology of Perception* (New York : Humanities Press, 1962), Preface.

[7] So too with dancing a dance, smiling a smile, singing a song. Propounding goes

Thus, for Wittgenstein as for Husserl, there is only true language, that which is explicated by logic. There is no meta-language. When we think we have found one it is only an infra-language. (Already the road is open before us that will lead us back to the *Lebenswelt* of Husserl and the "everyday language" of Wittgenstein.) All we succeed in doing when we seek for an ideal meta-language, according to the *later* Wittgenstein, is to make ordinary language say what it doesn't say. Rather, then, should our efforts be directed at clarifying that meta-language (which is really an infra-language) by the light of the true language, which is everyday language. For Wittgenstein even the affirmation of the logos condemns philosophy to silence.

Husserl in the second section of *Formal and Transcendental Logic* gives logic an ultimate justification, getting down to the source of logical formalizations and revealing their genesis. This amounts to a "transcendental critique of knowledge" with subjective orientations. This logic *of* logic is phenomenology itself, consisting of both regressive and progressive analysis. Regressive analysis concerns itself with the noema of logical thought to seek its foundations : it would appear that the adequate evidence of the rational is based upon the inadequate evidence of the sensible, i.e. on the primitive evidence of the presence of the individual object. Logic in dealing with everything in general nevertheless in the last analysis is always referred back to this individual object, for logic desires to retain its applicability to concrete elements. Logic is rooted in life — although this is sometimes far from obvious. This world is the substratum of all possible judgments. Husserl denounces the naturalists' presuppositions of a psychology which ignores the idea of intentionality and which would reduce the ego to a "collection of data." Logic cannot avoid coming to terms with the "kernels," or "cores," or "nuclei" — which are "the moments which subsist when one has stripped a proposition of all its properly predicative relations, and which return irreducibly to an ante-predicative intuition." Nor can it neglect their material homogeneity (a point echoed in his own terms by Wittgenstein) [8] which prohibits saying that a sound is extended or a number is a thing. One thereby verifies that logic, even when it turns away from the world, remains a logic of the world, regardless of whether this world is possible or real.

by the board and only the proposition remains. From Wittgenstein's viewpoint, that is, there can be no propositions about propounding; nothing can be said about it.

[8] See quotations from the *Tractatus* above, p. 55.

But this world is always a world for consciousness. Having discovered that logic is rooted in the world, Husserl proceeds to consider the rootedness or entrenchment of experience in transcendental subjectivity. First he introduces the ἐποχή. This notion, which is fundamental to Husserl's thought, is clearly set forth in the well-known passage in *Ideas* :

We put out of action the general thesis which belongs to the essence of the natural standpoint, we place in brackets whatever it includes respecting the nature of Being : this entire natural world therefore which is continually "here for us," "present to our hand," and will ever remain there, is a "fact-world" of which we continue to be conscious, even though it pleases us to put it in brackets.

If I do this, as I am fully free to do, I do not then deny this "world," as though I were a sophist, I do not doubt that it is there as though I were a sceptic; but I use the "phenomenological" ἐποχή which completely bars me from using any judgment that concerns spatio-temporal existence (*Dasein*).

Thus all sciences which relate to this natural world, though they stand never so firm to me, though they fill me with wondering admiration, though I am far from any thought of objecting to them in the least degree, I disconnect them all, I make absolutely no use of their standards, I do not appropriate a single one of the propositions that enter into their systems, even though their evidential value is perfect, I take none of them, no one of them serves me for a foundation — so long, that is, as it is understood, in the way these sciences themselves understand it, as a truth concerning the realities of this world. I may accept it only after I have placed it in the bracket. That means : only in the modified consciousness of the judgment as it appears in disconnexion. and not as it figures within the science as its proposition, a proposition which claims to be valid and whose validity I recognize and make use of.[9]

This prepares the way for the decisive if obscure idea of constitution. Consciousness is *constitutive, not creative* of being, clarifying it in the process of endorsing it : intentionality bestows meaning. Just as the identity of the perceived object is constituted in consciousness, so likewise the ideality of the logical object. The subjective *a priori* is the correlate of every given, and precedes every given. Logic, even as ontology, proceeds from consciousness. Wittgenstein in the *Tractatus* comes close to this, also positing an extra-mundane absolute as giver of meaning : "the meaning of the world is to be found outside the world" (6.41).[10] Where? In the language, or rather in the logic implicit in the language. The difference is that Wittgenstein embraces an objective

[9] *Ideas*, trans. W. Gibson (New York : Collier, 1962).

[10] Just as the meaning of language is to be found outside language, and hence it is impossible to say anything about it.

a priori, Husserl a subjective *a priori*. And yet in spite of embracing objectivity Wittgenstein has said : *my* language. And Wittgenstein, like Husserl, evokes a transcendental subject as correlate of the world : "the subject does not belong to the world but it constitutes a limit of the world" (5.632). Hence, finally, the temptation of solipsism : "I am my own world" (5.632).

In this connexion he is in the same difficulties as Husserl. Husserl escapes by applying the idea of constitution to that of intentionality. The facts of my transcendental sphere are also the transcendental realities which my consciousness endorses. However, this solution is not very satisfactory. Husserl's difficulty arises from the subordination of logic to subjectivity. The transcendental ego is itself subject to eidetic laws, e.g. the laws of association, which leaves him in the unhappy position of subscribing to the notion of an ego whose constituting powers are themselves constituted. In this respect it might be regarded as an object, since it is subject *to* these laws. But if it is an object how can it be a subject? This difficulty may be met in several ways. Logic may be accepted as absolute and the attempt to base it upon constitutive subjectivity abandoned. This is what Wittgenstein does in the *Tractatus* which only introduces the subject episodically, and for Wittgenstein the absolute is rather the objective and impersonal logos of the language, the logical form communing both with thought and the world. But this absolute is only bought at the price of alienating the subject, which becomes the instrument of the logos.

In the *Tractatus* Wittgenstein argued that we are inescapably in language, which is another way of saying we are in the world. The *Philosophical Investigations* attempt the description of this *Sprachewelt* which is Wittgenstein's counterpart of Husserl's *Lebenswelt*, since language is a kind of living for the man who is speaking. Henceforth Wittgenstein renounces the idea of a unique, perfect language. If such exists, it can only be dispersed throughout real language, which is empirically given. "Philosophy may in no way interfere with the actual use of language; it can in the end only describe it." *Description* — the key word to phenomenology is brought to bear upon the behaviour of man speaking. Wittgenstein observes speech-behavior in order to interrogate language; this is the significance of his emphasis upon use as opposed to meaning. Hence, for example, "what we deny is that the picture of the inner process gives us the correct idea of the word 'to remember.' We say that this picture with its ramifications stands in the way of our seeing the use of the word as it is." We should therefore give credit to language : it doesn't fool us; it is we who fool ourselves. Everyday language is true — but in its ambiguity, not in its clarity; practically, not theoretically. To examine "the application of words" is to search for what they wish to say, thereafter to describe what is, and to deny what is not. Wittgenstein asserts that language is "a form of life." "What we are supplying are really remarks on the natural history of human beings; we are not contributing curiosities, however, but observations which no one has doubted, but which have escaped remark only because they are always before our eyes" (415).

Wittgenstein does not abandon the central problem of the *Tractatus* — the truth of language, i.e. the relationship between logic and ontology. But instead of looking for the answer at the level of a perfect logic, he looks to everyday speech. Truth is truth experienced in the practice of life as a relationship between man speaking with man and with the world : such is the material truth in which all truth is rooted. And logic still remains — only now embedded in everyday language. Even the *Tractatus* holds that "all the propositions of our everyday language are effectively, as such, logically ordered" (5.5563). But the logic embedded in ordinary language is not logician's logic, not a logic which would explicate the logos, the perfect logic which "represents the *a priori* order of the world." We had supposed that this *a priori* was analytic, i.e. that the order of the world should be supremely simple and perfectly transparent : this was only an ideal. Wittgenstein is now interested in the logic immanent in ordinary language as practised by the man in the street. "The more narrowly we examine actual language, the sharper becomes the conflict between it and our requirement. (For the crystal-like purity of logic was, of course, not a *result of investigation* : it was a requirement)" (104). And so "back to the rough ground"! But is not this move a mistake, considering the diversity of language and language games? "No, because the games are apparent to one another." There is a logic immanent in language, but it is far more complicated and obscure than anything envisaged in the *Tractatus*, for it is deeply entrenched in behaviour. There are rules, as in any other game, but they are very vague, because they are subtle. "And is there not also the case where we play and — make up the rules as we go along? And there is even one where we alter them — as we go along" (83). This logic is not systematic, formal, *a priori*, but practical.

To see "how language works," then, it is necessary to examine man speaking. Like Husserl, Wittgenstein opposes psychologism. For psychologism erects a dualism, not between transcendental subject and the world but a dualism within the world : there are on the one hand people who perceive objects, on the other, spirits which perceive psychic objects or internal objects. Such a point of view thus assigns to thought a psychic being. Psychologism is right in affirming that experience is a private matter, but it forgets that if I can say it — what I suffer, understand, etc. — it is thanks to the language which is not purely private, and this prohibits me from looking within for an ostensive definition of words like pain, pleasure, red, etc. : "just try — in a real case — to doubt someone else's fear or pain" (303).

But thought does pledge itself to exteriority in aiming at an exterior object. Here Wittgenstein rediscovers intentionality :

> This queer thing, thought — but it does not strike us as queer when we are thinking. Thought does not strike us as mysterious while we are thinking, but only when we ask as it were retrospectively : 'How was that possible?' How was it possible for thought to deal with the very object itself? We feel as if by means of it we had caught reality in our net (428).

What distinguishes thought from sensation is not just that I think, but that I think something and say it. "Misleading parallel : the expression of pain is a cry — the expression of thought a proposition" (317). To understand or to know is to be able to reply to a question, obey an order, follow a rule. "To understand a sentence means to understand a language. To understand a language means to be master of a technique" (199). Rather than subscribe to a *consciousness* or *ego* he attributes to behaviour itself the structures and powers proper to the intentional life. But this behaviour is admittedly that of an individual. "To have an opinion is a state. — A state of what? Of the soul? Of the mind? Well, of what object does one say that it has an opinion? Of Mr. N. N. for example. And that is the correct answer" (573). Thus Wittgenstein does not deny consciousness but conscious processes are not "interior." They exhibit themselves.

The locutor is a *cogito*. The speaking man talks to say something and the meaning is in the words. No need to look behind the words, for the words are thought itself, bearing their own signification. Because the interest of the *Investigations* as compared with the *Tractatus* is anthropological rather than ontological, it is concerned less with the proposition than with the intelligent activity which constructs it, less with formal syntax than with syntactical operation. In the second part of the *Investigations* Wittgenstein is concerned to analyse the manner in which signification resides in the word, and he mingles that analysis with an analysis of perception. In the first part he wrote : "Understanding a sentence is much more akin to understanding a theme in music than one may think" (527). It is in that prehistory, in that primitive relation of man and the world (which is perpetually renewed through perception) that there is established the expressive power of language and hence the foundations of truth.

It would be presumptuous to claim that this reading of Wittgenstein is even thus far correct. The best one can hope for is an acceptable variant. He himself plays the sort of language game regarding which he asks : "Is it even always an advantage to replace an indistinct picture by a sharp one? Isn't the indistinct one often exactly what we need?" (71). This allows him the luxury of a certain factitious difficulty (like that of T. S. Eliot when he declares that in the modern age poetry must be difficult) [11] and also the right to disallow any strict exegesis of his work during his own lifetime. Perhaps, like the world, Wittgenstein's philosophy should be "left exactly as it is." However, at least this much is certain, that the approach of the *Investigations* differs from that of the *Tractatus* in some important respects, the most significant being the shift from logic and the abstract ideal of a perfect language as the central interest to anthropological interests and the acceptance of everyday language.

There is even a certain humanistic tendency — albeit somewhat anaemic — involved in this development. The emphasis upon everyday language carries with it a certain aura of epicene democracy. It has often been pointed out that the use of technical terms in the *Investigations* is kept at the minimum, so that the style of the work exemplifies the ideal which it expresses. Here the philosophy of commonsense becomes not only the philosophy *of* commonspeech but philosophy *in* commonspeech, as it were. The question as to what "everyday language" entails has been raised by Russell and others, but there can be no doubt that Wittgenstein meant the language of the man-in-the-street. One wonders what brought about this *volte face*, this descent from the ivory tower of *Principia Mathematica* into the marketplace, or at least into the "Quad."

And yet Wittgenstein's complex nature does exhibit certain evidences of the common touch. Malcolm has told of Wittgenstein's liking for the "flicks," his preference for pulp magazine stories to the sort of article that appears in *Mind* and his approval of powdered-egg. In certain respects Wittgenstein even appears something of a Tolstoyan

[11] I am not denying there may be a certain *aesthetic* truth embodied in this viewpoint : "Lovely the face that hid its secret..." (Monk Gibbon).

and we know that between the *Tractatus* and the *Logical Investigations* there intervened Wittgenstein's experience in the First World War and his encounter with the later writings of Tolstoy. It is not surprising that Wittgenstein should find Tolstoy congenial — Tolstoy, the aristocrat revolté who went to work in the fields with his own peasants; Tolstoy the anarcho-pacifist; Tolstoy the denouncer of Royalty and renouncer of royalties... All this would appeal to Wittgenstein who on his side made a gift of his patrimony and went to work as a hospital orderly during the war. Commonsense, commonspeech, the commonman — they are not unrelated. Malcolm tells us how pleased Wittgenstein was to hear that he had read Tolstoy's *Twenty-Three Tales*, stories which embody at their most intense the anarcho-communist ideals of Tolstoy's fundamentalist Christianity — including his fanatical anti-intellectualism.

Typical of these tales is "The Story of Ivan the Fool," where the Devil tells the Peasants that they should work with their heads instead of their hands. "They say the gentleman is beginning to work with his head." Ivan was surprised. "Really?" says he, and he turned his horse round and went to the tower. And by the time he reached the tower the old Devil was quite exhausted with hunger and staggering and knocking his head against the pillars. And just as Ivan arrived at the tower the Devil stumbled, fell, and came bump, bump, bump, straight down the stairs to the bottom, counting each step with a knock of his head! "Well!" says Ivan, "the fine gentleman told the truth when he said that sometimes one's head quite splits! This is worse than blisters; after such work there will be swellings on the head." That Wittgenstein should approve of this genre is also not without significance.

But there is also in Tolstoy a certain narrow puritanism which has nothing to do with the common man but is rather aristocratic and aloof. There is more than a touch of pride in his humility, and it might even be argued that the sheer artistic virtuosity of such tales as "The Three Hermits," "A Spark Neglected Burns the House," "How Much Land Does a Man Need?" etc. tends to belie the simplicity of heart and mind that these magnificent tales would commend. There is certainly more than one way of reacting to Tolstoy. Gogarty wrote a poem called "Ringsend" which bore the subtitle "After reading Tolstoy." Here, assuredly is a common man's reaction :

I will live in Ringsend
With a red-headed whore,
And the fan-light gone in
Where it lights the hall door...

Wittgenstein, however, will assimilate the aristocratic puritanism with at least as much relish as the more democratic elements in Tolstoy, and also like Tolstoy he will, in his own way, be most uncommonly common, i.e. most intellectually anti-intellectual, and he will have as much contempt for his fellow philosophers as Tolstoy for his fellow landowners — only, I suggest, with hardly comparable justification.

The burden of Wittgenstein's argument is that meaning is exhausted in the language. For Husserl, on the other hand, meaning is bestowed by the action of consciousness, and is to be described in terms of "meaning-intention" and "meaning-fulfilment." Meaningful expressions may be absurd; or may refer to entities that are fictitious or no longer in existence; or to matters that are only "in principle" verifiable; or there may be references which are both meaningful and genuinely referring; or there may be "ostensive" references; or syncategorematic expressions such as "is," "or," "and," which are meaningful but which do not refer; and lastly there are "expressions" which are not expressions but which are strictly meaningless. In the latter case there can be no meaning-intention. It is precisely the meaning-intention, according to Husserl, which characterises the genuine expression and the absence of meaning-intention which characterises the nonsensical. In other words the meaning-intending act constitutes the expression, and is essential to all meanings whatever. This is a constant.

But to this constant of the meaning-intending act there is allied the variable of meaning-fulfilment — variable, for one thing, because it may be either successful or frustrate, and for another, because of the varying types of fulfilment possible. Mohanty [12] cites the following examples (the first of which is not, of course, an expression at all) : (1) 'Abcuderaf,' (2) 'Roundsquare,' (3) 'Pegasus,' (4) 'The present king of France,' (5) 'The other side of the moon,' (6) 'man,' (7) 'This white wall before me,' (8) Syncategorematic expressions like 'is,' 'or,' 'and.' All these examples, except the first, are bearers of meaning-intention. Some are susceptible of meaning-fulfilment, others are not; and the kind of meaning-intention appropriate to each case is different. However, it is obvious that there has to be intention before we have a genuine expression at all, whereas there can be genuine expressions which resist fulfilment. But there cannot be knowledge without fulfilment, since

[12] *Edmund Husserl's Theory of Meaning*. This author sometimes writes as though the preference for linguistic over phenomenological methods, or vice-versa, were merely a matter of taste.

knowledge consists in the fulfilment of the intentional act. Mere thinking is not knowledge, although the symbols employed in the thought may be meaningful enough. What is grasped symbolically has to be the object of an intuitive apprehension before there can be knowledge.

Meaningless "expressions" for Wittgenstein would be such as lack any rules or linguistic conventions for their use. We just don't know what to do with them. If, on the other hand, an expression is genuine, this signifies that we *do* know what to do with it. To understand an expression is to know how to use it, and that is all — no question of troubling ourselves with psychical research after some sort of astral body of meaning. The meaning *is* the use.

But there we might object, how are we to understand an expression *prior* to its application if our understanding itself *consists* in the application? Surely understanding an expression can hardly be *identified* with knowing the rules or linguistic conventions for its application? Even if application according to rule is the criterion, it can hardly constitute the *nature*, of understanding. The only resort seems to be to substitute *applicability* for application, so that understanding an expression consists in the *possibility* of its application, or rather, renders *possible* the correct application of the expression. In short 'understanding' is a capacity word.

But this won't do either. This argument, as Mohanty points out, is analogous to the old reduction of material-object statements to hypothetical sense-datum statements. Although it *follows* from the statement that there is a wardrobe next door that if I get up, open the door, and look in the next room I shall see one, nevertheless the statement is not reducible to this, so it only *follows* from the statement "I understand the series," that I can "go on" with it : the statement itself is not reducible to this consequence.

Wittgenstein is not unaware of these difficulties. We say that a machine has certain possibilities of movement. "What does this mean?" he asks. Not the actual movement, nor the conditions of movement. The implication is that when we refer to the possibility of application of an expression we cannot be referring to either the actual-application nor to the conditions of application. The supposed possibility of movement seems to Wittgenstein like the foreshadowing of movement. Meaning, then, is a foreshadowing of actual use? But this is hardly satisfactory. There is little to be said for chasing shadows.

The unsatisfactory nature of any attempt by linguistic philosophy to describe understanding prior to use or application follows from the fact that to do so would necessarily involve circularity. This becomes particularly apparent when we consider the situation of a child learning the language.[13] No child has ever learned a language linguistically. At the elementary level the word exists in isolation — one must begin somewhere — and yet stands for a whole sentence, *intentionally*. The meaning of a word is the response it evokes; and to begin with, other noises do just as well. Nor is the word merely a whole sentence, it is the whole language. And to bear all this meaning the word must have a structure of its own, but it cannot be a linguistic structure. A word cannot *be* a whole language even if it *means* a whole language. The meaning cannot reside in the word. Only the concept of an intentional structure — in linguistic terms, a *private* language — can account for even the discussion of the matter. Otherwise, how can you understand me when I say that a word is a whole sentence? What whole sentence? If I tell you the sentence can you tell me the word? Or are you trying to tell me I've said it — which I shouldn't have done if I hadn't? Or that if the means of expression are not available, that which otherwise would be expressed does not exist? Or perhaps you would say that you do not understand what is meant when it is claimed that a word stands for a whole sentence? In which case...

As against this it might be argued that Wittgenstein could very well endorse the notion that the meaning of a word — for a child, at any rate — is the response the word evokes. For after all, isn't this a use? And doesn't Wittgenstein mean by "use" more than simple *usage* — he means communication, purpose, behaviour? But then, what I am arguing for is an *expressive* use, whereas the Wittgensteinians are very impressionable, i.e. "*impressed*" by the language in both senses of that word. Still, is it not the case that one must learn the word before one expresses even *that* much? Maybe so. But the original *use* is *expressive*. Human beings are noisy animals. Some noises work better than others. In the long run the ones that work best are words, and if there weren't a long run there wouldn't be any words either.

Wittgenstein's preoccupation is with the cognate-accusative.[14] He splits the cognate-accusative down the middle and then suppresses the subject term. And yet, after all, the cognate-accusative persists in ordinary language no matter how much Wittgenstein may dislike it. What,

[13] For more detailed consideration of this, see the present author's article, "Learning the Language," *Phil. and Phen. Res.*, 26 (1965-66), 561-77.

[14] E.g., "She sang a song," "He ran a race," etc.

then, can be the primitive source of this extraordinary preoccupation? In Wittgenstein there are involuntary undertones of some deeper and more original obsessions. There is a certain Wittgensteinian *mood* which stems, seemingly, from a genuine inner emptiness and desolation. He seems to suggest the poignancy and pathos of the incommunicable. This is one of the characteristics which gives Wittgenstein's writings a certain dignity, distinguishing him almost without exception from his many plagiarists. "How can we know the dancer from the dance?" [15]

Behind such questions there may loom a darker, more sinister obsession with the mutual exhaustion of expression and means of expression, in relation to which the preoccupation with the cognate figures as a mere logical analogue. Because I cannot see my seeing or hear my hearing, but can only see or hear, etc., Wittgenstein thinks I cannot say my saying or mean my meaning but only say or mean. Hence, his denial of any importance to meaning as a mental activity. Wittgenstein hears voices. There are no subjective realities in Wittgenstein's world. One imagines a sort of haunted ballroom — music in the air, the echo [16] of conversation between dances, and *no dancers.*

Consider his approval of behaviourism : "Here is the point of behaviourism. It isn't that they deny there are feelings. But they say our description of behaviour *is* our description of feelings." [17] The identification of expression with means of expression is more than a recurrent theme in Wittgenstein's writings; it is the cornerstone of his philosophy with respect to which even the enormous weight of linguistic preoccupations are, if not exactly secondary, at least derivatory. It is here that Wittgenstein most flagrantly exhibits that "desire for unity" of which he is so critical. Philosophically, however, this cornerstone doesn't hold up too well once we kick it around a little. The point, then, that Wittgenstein tries to make is that there can be no separating expression from means of expression, nor vice-versa. Expression and means of connection form an unbreakable unity, or are mutually exhaustive. In this expression he challenges his opponents with what might be called "the Quest for the Cheshire Cat" (i.e. the grin without the face.) Rush Rhees reports Wittgenstein as saying, "A man may sing a song with

[15] W. B. Yeats.

[16] The reference is to Rossetti's translation of Villon :
"Where is Echo, beheld of no man,
Only heard on river and mere...?"

[17] Wittgenstein, *Lectures on Aesthetics,* ed. C. Barett (Oxford : Blackwell, 1966), p. 33.

expression and without expression. Then why not leave out the song — could you have the expression then?" [18]

This distinction between singing with and without expression is rather odd. One wonders what Wittgenstein had in mind. Barbara Streisand compared with Astrud Gilberto perhaps? That sort of thing? But then, Astrud's "lack" of expression expresses a great deal. The trouble is — and it is not without significance in this context — that the noises emitted by a person who "sings" without any expression at all would not normally be reckoned song. Maybe I should count myself lucky, but although I have heard good singers, bad singers, and indifferent singers, I have never heard any expressionless singers. I *have* occasionally come across pianists who played their instrument as though it were a typewriter, but even although their performance was note-perfect it never occurred to me to confound their digital dexterity with music. However, *were* I to encounter an "expressionless" singer I imagine that I should still not regard the performance as devoid of "expression." It should at least express the fact that the "singer" couldn't sing. But what would this signify? A singer without a song? A song without a singer? Neither, so far as I am concerned, but characteristically Wittgenstein will settle for the latter alternative.

Of course what is not expressed is not expressed. There could hardly be any mistake about *that* tautology. And it would be rather ridiculous to suggest that because a song may be sung *con amore* that we cannot have *amore* without a song. What Wittgenstein seems particularly anxious to establish is that the song is not irrelevant to the expression, which is pretty obvious if the song is precisely what is being expressed. And this may sometimes be the case and sometimes not. Where it *is* the case, the word "interpret" might be more apt than "express." But in this case we have then to consider what the *song* expresses. There are cases, moreover, where the song *is* irrelevant to the expression. This occurs often in jazz, where some trite harmonic sequence with a poverty-stricken top-line unworthy of the name of melody is taken purely as a vehicle for improvisation and after a brief statement more or less ignored. But here again, what is expressed is not the song. The *performer* is expressing himself, just as in the first case the *composer* is expressing himself. In the first case the singer is the vehicle, in the second case the song. Abstract jazz is an attempt at total expression. Of course, as usual, music lags behind the times as compared with the

[18] *Ibid.*, p. 29.

visual arts. The sheer practical difficulties of music act as a restraint. However, abstract jazz does furnish us with an example of, as it were, "leaving out the song." Here it is a matter of pure musical expression. But then from Wittgenstein's viewpoint it may be argued that the "musical" aspect still remains, and that *this* is what is being expressed.

But what does such argument amount to except the assertion that what has been expressed has been expressed together with the dogma that there is no means of expression apart from the expression itself? That all art is art for art's sake? Temporal considerations alone are sufficient to absolve us from the penitential impositions of this bleak aestheticism. Certainly if an end is accomplished there is no call for further means, and if I have managed to express myself I have done so — and if not, not — but it does not follow from this that means and end are indistinguishable. Furthermore it is obvious that if I wish to express that I have "starved, feasted, despaired — been happy," I may do so via several different media, not just one. Here expression carries a similar relation to the arts as thought to various languages, and just as there is no language without thought, there is no art without expression. But then Wittgenstein — or his followers — may argue : "What we want of you is not the demonstration of the same expression through various media, but of expression itself — i.e. through no media at all." Very Socratic! The Cheshire Cat again!

In an essay that has become a modern classic, Gabriel Marcel writes as follows :

> The characteristic feature of our age seems to me to be what might be called the misplacement of the idea of function, taking function in its current sense which includes both the vital and the social functions. The individual tends to appear both to himself and to others as an agglomeration of functions. As a result of deep historical causes, which can as yet be understood only in part, he has been led to see himself more and more as a mere assemblage of functions, the hierarchical interpretation of which seems to him questionable or at least subject to conflicting interpretations... It is true that certain disorderly elements — sickness, accidents of every sort — will break in on the smooth working of the system. It is therefore natural that the individual should be overhauled at regular intervals like a watch (this is often done in America). The hospital plays the part of the inspection bench or the repair shop. And it is from this same standpoint of function that such essential problems as birth control will be examined. As for death, it becomes, objectively and functionally, the scrapping of what has ceased to be of use and must be written off as a total loss. I need hardly insist on the stifling impression of sadness produced by this functionalised world. It is sufficient to recall the dreary image of the

retired official, or those urban Sundays when the passers-by look like people who have retired from life.[19]

In terms of the foregoing, Wittgenstein emerges not as a "behaviourist" but as a *functionalist*. People are what they say. Ergo? Behaviourism, taken as a philosophy, becomes a "functionalism." It was above all the enormous success and even greater prestige of the physical sciences that led to the emergence of Watson's "behaviourism" just prior to the first World War, and it is easy enough to understand that Watson's "stimulus-response" reaction against introspective psychology, his "mechanism" and theories of "adaptive behaviour" should prove congenial to Wittgenstein. (Later behaviourism was in turn directly influenced by the logical-positivist school of philosophy.) With his engineering background Wittgenstein is naturally attracted towards mechanism, and in his later writings often has recourse to mechanical analogies. The "stimulus-response" idea becomes in Wittgenstein our response to the laws, customs, and institutions of our society. Language itself is a form of such adaptation.

But the adoption of the tenets of behaviourism by philosophy inevitably results in a "functionalism," in Marcel's sense. When linguistic function is apparently inadequate to exhaust the human-subject, other functions may be grudgingly admitted, and then again should difficulties arise in the description of *this* function it remains possible to fall back upon linguistic function once more (e.g. if we are discussing man as a worker and difficulties arise as regards economic motivation, social purpose, etc., we have recourse to the question as to how the word "worker" is used). Linguistic function is the function of speech (*not* strictly, as has sometimes been asserted, "man speaking"). It is the language speaking through man that is Wittgenstein's concern. Not that he will deny outright the existence of mind or consciousness or "meanings," as in some unguarded moments did John D. Watson, but simply be quite unconcerned about such matters and, if not deny their existence, at least imply their insignificance. As contrasted with the occasional bravura passages of Watson the pianissimo of later behaviourists has been echoed by Wittgenstein himself: "What, then, shall we say about consciousness? Is its existence denied? By no means. But to recognise the existence of a phenomenon is not the same thing as insisting upon its basic, i.e., logical,

[19] "On the Ontological Mystery," in *Philosophy of Existence* (London : Harvill Press, 1947).

priority." [20] But what, we may ask, does this concession amount to? Little more than the determination to avoid metaphysics — even a negative metaphysics — in the interests of preserving the methodological model of the physical sciences in all its doctrinal purity.

One of the commonest — although hardly the subtlest — kind of joke consists in the literalization of metaphor. This is a technique particularly favoured by American humorists. For example, someone declares that he has a frog in his throat and is invited to sit down and let the frog speak; a stove is offered for sale and the prospective buyer is warned in confidential tones that "It's hot"; a convict is asked "What brought you here?" and answers, "The Black Maria and a great big Irish cop." Much of Thurber's work is of this genre; a woman addresses a man seated on a dog-sleigh drawn by a springer-spaniel : "I said the hounds of Spring are on Winter's Traces — But let it Pass, Let it Pass!" In this connection behaviourists of the Watsonian school are astonishingly humorless. They simply cannot see the joke. To refer literally to a machine "working" or to the "mechanics" of human behaviour is just as funny as the notion of really drinking a shot or hearing a horse laugh. And although it may not be immediately obvious, the notion that words *mean* something is no less metaphorical than the notion that money *talks*, and when taken literally constitutes no less something in the nature of a joke. It is as though Polly were to put the kettle on at the behest of the parrot.

Wittgenstein's "behaviourism" or "functionalism" is at bottom a form of naturalism which would have aroused Husserl's hostility.[21] It is at this point that humanistic differences between the two philosophers become apparent. Husserl's philosophy may not be particularly individualistic (his successors, the existentialists, have made up for that) but it is humanistic in its refusal to allow the spirit of man to be subjugated to the dictatorship of the physical sciences. He will not accept the view that man is susceptible of purely natural, and ultimately physical, explanation. The psychical cannot be reduced to the status of mere epiphenomena. Husserl sees a certain contradiction in the naturalist rejection of all values of "oughts," since there is an "ought" implicit in the persuasive character of the naturalist's argumentations. Naturalists, positivists, and pragmatists are obsessed with "facts," but then for

[20] Clark L. Hull, "Mind, Mechanism, and Adapted Behaviour," *Psychological Review*, 44 (1937), 1-32.

[21] As regards this point and what follows in this section, see Husserl's *Philosophy as a Rigorous Science.*

Husserl this means that their argumentation is merely relativistic since ideas are the sole province of the absolute. For Husserl, as for Plato, the natural world is a world of flux, hence all naturalism is bound to be relativistic. No doubt the aims of the naturalists are respectable enough, but there is madness in their method. Naturalism endeavours to apply the methods of the physical sciences to problems which fall outside their province. (Kierkegaard shared this viewpoint, regarding "objectivity" and scientific method as legitimate only within what he regarded as their own proper domain.) Husserl argues that natural science is naive, is basically an extension of the "natural" attitude of everyday, and hence ungrounded and "unscientific" in Husserl's sense.

However, on one or two occasions his criticisms of psychology do remind us of the *earlier* Wittgenstein's search for an "ontological logic." There is a similar concern with the problem of transcendence : "How can the play of a consciousness whose logic is empirical make objectively valid statements, valid for things that are in and for themselves? Why are the playing rules, so to speak, of consciousness not irrelevant for things?" Psychology never poses this problem. In its naiveté it takes everything for granted — a weakness inherent in every naturalism whatever, and "if certain riddles are, generally speaking, inherent in principle to natural science, then it is self-evident that the solution of these riddles... transcends natural science." So far as the problem of transcendence is concerned a mere synthesis between reason and experience is not enough for Husserl. Experience is to be rationalized "so that logic, the science of reason, may be a logic of experience," and Husserl's "logic of experience" aims at discovering the "logos," i.e. the fundamental rationality of experience as such.

This too is reminiscent of Wittgenstein of the *Tractatus*, but for Husserl the rationalization of experience entails that experience "constitute" its own object. The call is "to things themselves," *not*, however, to "things *in* themselves." The world we are to enter is neither the phenomenal world of empiricism nor the noumenal world of idealism but the world subsequent upon the phenomenological disciplines of (1) ideation (whereby the essential core persisting through the object's various modes of givenness is revealed) (2) *ἐποχή* (the cathartic evacuation of the inessential positings of existence associated with the natural attitude) and (3) reduction (which is merely the more *positive* aspect of *ἐποχή* wherein we encounter the residual field of pure essences which is the phenomenologist's main concern).

"Appearances themselves ... do not constitute a being which itself appears by means of appearances lying behind it" (*P*, 106). In *Philosophy as a Rigorous Science* Husserl argues that this would amount to postulating appearances of appearances, epiphenomena of phenomena. For Husserl, then, phenomena are outside nature, and hence (in complete contrast to Wittgenstein) he will maintain that they are also outside the sphere of causality. (Like Kant, Husserl regards causality as obtaining exclusively in the natural or material world.) Phenomena are immaculate of natural characteristics and (like the good rationalist he is) Husserl maintains that it is as absurd to seek for causal properties in the phenomenal sphere as in the mathematical sphere. To seek for causal connections among phenomena is to indulge in "the absurdity of naturalising something whose essence excludes the kind of being that nature has" (*P*, 104). Phenomena, then cannot be subjected to the objective analyses proper to the physical sciences.

The principles Husserl has attemped to establish are specifically invoked by Merleau-Ponty in his criticisms of behaviourism. Thus in *The Structure of Behaviour* :

> Behaviourism, solipsism, and projective theories all accept that behaviour is given to me like something spread out in front of me... Does not the *cogito* teach us once and for all that we would have no knowledge of any *thing* if we did not first have a knowledge of our thinking and that even the escape into the world and the resolution to ignore interiority or to never leave things, which is the essential feature of behaviourism, cannot be formulated without being transformed into consciousness and without presupposing existence for-itself (*pour soi*)? Thus behaviour is constituted of relations; that is, it is conceptualised and not in-itself (*en soi*) ... (pp. 126-127).

And again :

> The possibility of constructing a causal explanation of behaviour is exactly proportional to the inadequacy of the structurations accomplished by the subject. The work of Freud constitutes not a tableau of human existence, but a tableau of anomalies... (p. 179).

Husserl's idea of 'intention' is similar to, but not to be identified with, 'intention' in the psychological sense. There is always involved in Husserl's notion of intention the notion of intentionality, i.e. taking an object. With regard to language, the symbol or physical sign is the object "taken up." The sign has a meaning only if meant, and Husserl's concern is with the experience of meaningfully using the sign. Signs or symbols are not originally given as expressions, and that which transforms them into expressions is an act of consciousness. Wittgenstein might agree, but according to him there is nothing describable in the situation apart from the use of the symbols involved. Wittgenstein's notion of intentionality is thoroughly psychological : "An intention is embedded in its situation in human customs and institutions" (*P.* 60). Without rules and regulations you couldn't even intend to play the game, let alone actually play it. If I can intend to say something in advance this is only because I can speak the language in question. All intention is subject to objective conditions.

But where does this lead us? Of course you couldn't speak if there were no language, any more than you could see if there were no light. So? Husserl, on the other hand, does not deny the conventional nature of language, but neither does he accept the notion that linguistic expression is exhausted in the sign. The corpus of traditional language as evolved through the centuries, for all its richness, subtlety, and cultural associations, would mean *nothing*, would not *be* a language without the co-operation of the meaning-intended act. It doesn't follow from this that the intentional correlate of every speech-act is *inspected* during the course of speaking. We are not objectively aware of the meanings of our meaning-intending acts. Such meanings are only available to reflection. But "meaning-intention" is required to account for our merely symbolic understanding, our seeing things "in a flash." Thus the meaning-intention is always determinate, even if it is a determination of the indeterminate, i.e. it would, for example, still be determinate as an intention, even supposing what was intended was indeterminate. The possible fulfilment of the intention is always as it were pre-determined by the intention, otherwise it could not be fulfilment of *this* intention. In other words, the relation between intention and fulfilment is internal, not external.

In language as in life Husserl is concerned with *meaning*. There is no implication here that he sees some mysterious halo surrounding linguistic expressions, but his concern is with what is entailed in *meaningfully* using expressions. A linguistic philosopher asks "What time is it?" When I reply "Three o'clock," he further enquires "What do you mean?" (This, incidentally, could prove a dangerous gambit in certain sections of the city.) He does this in order to impress upon me that the words "three o'clock" entirely exhaust the meaning, and that there is no meaning running parallel, as it were, with the words. But even at a naive psychological level it is obvious that at least *one* thing I meant was to reply to his question. (For Husserl's type of analysis there are always the actual physical awareness of the sign *plus* the intellectual awareness that interprets the sign as an expression.)

But admittedly Husserl himself is disturbed about the linguistic status of question and answer. In what consists the meaning of sentences expressing wishes, questions, commands? Are such sentences meaningful *as such*, or meaningful *implicitly* as containing a concealed statement? Husserl's difficulty arises because he wishes to sustain a *radical* differentiation between such sentences and sentences making statements. But how can sentences expressing wishes, questions, commands, etc. be meaning-intending when they are not objectifying acts, i.e. statements? And they obviously are not, since they can be neither true nor false.[22] Or are they reducible to statements such as, "I ask if S is P," "I command X to do Y"?

Such reductions are hardly satisfactory. It would be just as legitimate to reduce sentences expressing statements in this way, so that "S is P" would be reducible to "I judge S is P." But these two expressions are not equivalent, since "S is P" might be true when "I judge S is P" was false. Furthermore, expressions are not names — not even names of that which is expressed. Nevertheless, Husserl's solution *is* along these lines. He maintains that although the acts expressed in wishes, questions, commands, etc. are not objectifying (i.e. are not statements) they nevertheless function as meaning-intending. Such acts *can* so function, according to Husserl, only if they are made objective in some way. Otherwise they would be meaningless. They are objectified, then, by means of inner-perception, and it is this inner objectifying act which bestows meaning upon them. What then is expressed is not the acts of wishing, questioning, commanding, etc. but the inner-perception of these acts. This is hardly satisfactory, and arises from Husserl's dogmatic position that only objectifying acts are meaningful, together with a certain lapse in technique (i.e. his approach at this point, admittedly, is insufficiently radical — scarcely more phenomenological than linguistic). However, it should be borne in mind that these reflections upon language belong to the period of the *Logische Untersuchungen*, before the disciplines of the ἐποχή had become firmly established. Husserl's chief importance in this respect is in the area of the programmatic rather than in that of applied theory.

Having considered some of the "linguistic" elements in Husserl's philosophy, we might now turn to review whatever phenomenological elements are to be found in Wittgenstein. In my opinion there is seriously only one : ἐποχή, and even then only in the negative sense that, like

[22] A perennial point that is made perennially.

Husserl, Wittgenstein brackets existence. But this is done more or less "by the way." In the course of reducing all philosophical problems to linguistic status and justifying such reduction he almost incidentally, as it were, brackets existence. If his reduction were to be regarded as a *phenomenological* reduction it would have to be accounted a very limited one. There is certainly no evidence that I know of that Wittgenstein endorsed the phenomenological reduction as a method, nor can I see in his philosophy any genuine indications of the application of the method. Admittedly, the disregard for concrete existence and the concern for pure meaning in their earlier work shows a degree of correspondence between the two philosophers, but these characteristics are commonplace in philosophy. Indeed they are entirely commonplace in idealism, and both philosophers have an idealist bias to their thinking : Platonic in the case of Husserl, Kantian in the case of Wittgenstein. To put the matter in another way, whereas Husserl *begins* with the phenomenological reduction, Wittgenstein *arrives* at it. And, what is more, he arrives at it via an *objective* method, Phenomenology is nothing if not subjective. Nevertheless with Wittgenstein there is this limited ἐποχή — one might call it a *travesty* of ἐποχή.

And yet it is easy to see how to some minds Wittgenstein's linguistic reduction might seem the more appealing. It is much simpler, tidier, less complex, easier to grasp. Words have their mysterious side, of course, but they seem rather less intangible than phenomena. More people would claim to know what a word is than what a phenomenon is. And then words have *meanings* like a dog has fleas, which seems to take care of *that*. But phenomena? Who knows! And, anyhow, what can we possibly lose? Will anyone tell me that there is a difference between the phenomenon "red" and the word 'red'? Even if there is, it's cancelled out as soon as you say so. Such is the "linguistic" argument. And then Husserl's famous "phenomenological reduction" — don't we manage, in our own way, to retain that? Of course we can put the world in parentheses. Look : world. And there : "world." [23]

Several other basic Husserlian techniques seem to have lost their way and wandered into linguistic philosophy. Intentionality for example, that complicated concept in phenomenology — but how simple it becomes within the confines of *linguistic* reduction. 'Intentional'?

[23] The whole world, that is to say, and everything that's in it — every single thing — we put into parentheses. It's simply a matter of punctuation, and it leaves us with nothing but words.

That means aiming at an object, taking an object, and the words that do that are called verbs — transitive verbs. So much for the intentionality of consciousness! And so a sort of caricature of Husserl's method remains even with regard to intentionality. We no longer have to examine ourselves (a tiresome and occasionally embarrassing business,) we are not interested in how human consciousness works, only in how *verbs* work. And so the phenomenologist's intentionality becomes the linguisticist's transitivity. (O, Johnny, I hardly knew ye!) It begins to look as though Husserl were a linguistic philosopher *manqué* — or could it be the other way round? Certainly one has the feeling that *somewhere* down the line *something* has got lost. Could it be oneself? And of course, following this sort of decadent Husserlianism, the subject too is put in brackets, becomes a voice, a linguistic analogue — that impossibility.

It need hardly be said that it is neccessary to have a considerable superfluity of inner emptiness to project like this. However, as it was in the beginning so it is at the end. Wittgenstein having adopted a total objectivism as his point of view is bound to finish up *objectifying the subject.* And although he castigated the impulse towards unity, the fact that he went to such lengths in the attempt to prove that people had no insides indicates that he was as subject to that impulse as anyone else — and perhaps more so, if for him the impulse was more than normally frustrated. (Nor is it irrelevant that he personally felt himself incapable of loving or of being loved.) It should also be noticed, however, that Husserl, whose approach was that of a total subjectivism, so that he attempts to subjectify the object, is also in difficulties when the question arises regarding the subject. For, adopting as he does a constitutive theory of consciousness, he runs up against the difficulty that whatever else I constitute, it can hardly be credited that I constitute my own or other people's powers of constitution. (One is reminded here of the Sartrean notion of "the desire to be God.") But this in turn constituted a difficulty for Husserl to which he devoted a great deal of thought. In a word, within the confines of their respective philosophies, the problem for Husserl was how the subject was to be resurrected whereas the problem for Wittgenstein was how the subject was to be annihilated.

Husserl's reduction is for him an absolute *beginning* in philosophy. For Wittgenstein, however, the parentheses of Husserl being themselves reduced to the status of punctuation, the reduction is the *end* of philosophy. Philosophy itself is put in parentheses, and the problems with which philosophy traditionally deals are thus reduced to the level of linguistic errors. Scholastic dialogues regarding the nature of substance arise from the misuse of substantives, the arguments around the Cartesian *cogito* arise from the impossibility of using the first-person singular demonstratively — and so on.

There is no need to expatiate upon such obvious and well-known aspects of Wittgenstein's philosophy, nor upon the associated theme that philosophical problems are not so much to be solved as dissolved by appropriate linguistic "therapy." Wittgenstein really represents an anti-philosophy. In his introduction to Gellner's *Words and Things*, Russell opined that although he thought highly of the book he didn't think that it would have any great impact because "fashion dies hard." But the tenacity of Wittgenstein's philosophy is no mere fashion. Nor does it derive its impact from the fact that it is truer or more convincing than other philosophy. Its tenacity derives from the fact that it is an *anti*-philosophy. Malcolm at one point in his *Memoir* quotes Wittgenstein as saying : "When a person has only one thing in the world — merely a certain talent — what is he to do when he begins to lose that talent?" The words are evocative — one thinks of Scott Fitzgerald, Hemingway, Marilyn Monroe... Certainly Malcolm's reaction was the fear that Wittgenstein might commit suicide, as three of his brothers had done before him. This is not an argument *ad hominem*, but it suggests that Wittgenstein was peculiarly well equipped to fulfill the task he set himself.

Wittgenstein's philosophy is a travesty. But just as his earlier work might be described as "nonsense, but important nonsense," so his later work may be described as *a significant travesty*. It is a travesty that accords well with the spirit of the age. In this age of ours which demands the anti-hero, the anti-novel, the anti-play, anti-God theology, there is obviously a place for the anti-philosophy. But why, we may ask, all this nay-saying? No doubt the pressures — individual, political, national, and international — that bring about such states of affairs are very complex, but certainly the situation has all the characteristics of fear, betrays the immediate consciousness of being under threat. Humanity commonly seeks to avoid destruction by means of self-destruction : the Roman falls on his sword, the Japanese commits harakiri, the Hitler mob resort to cyanide... An entire generation may take on the suicidal characteristics of lemmings. And even if we hesitate to draw such immense conclusions as regards our culture (shirking the thought of "prognosis negative") it is hardly questionable that *our* subject, i.e. philosophy, is, and has been for a long time, under threat.

One has only to take the most cursory glance at the physical sciences — or even psychology — to realize *that*. Fortunately this is not the whole story, but it is understandable, and even in a sense appropriate, that in such circumstances there should arise an anti-philosophy, and that it should prove welcome. That is why I call Wittgenstein's philosophy "a significant travesty." One is reminded of Sartre's comment on Baudelaire :

> In order to enjoy the results of his suicide, it was obviously essential that he should survive it... And if he did not kill himself at a single blow, at any rate he behaved in such a way that each of his actions was the symbolical equivalent of a suicide that he couldn't commit.[24]

Yes ... no doubt about it, Wittgenstein's was a paradigm case.

[24] "Baudelaire," p. 182.

HUSSERL AND WITTGENSTEIN ON LANGUAGE

by

PAUL RICŒUR

The kind of confrontation that I propose here is not intended to generate a hybrid offshoot. Each philosophy is an organism which has its internal rules of development. What we may best do is to understand each better by means of the other and, perhaps, formulate new problems that proceed from its encounter.

Husserl and Wittgenstein allow a certain amount of comparison, thanks to the parallelism of their development — that is, from a position in which ordinary language is measured on a model of ideal language to a description of language as it functions, as everyday language or as language of the *Lebenswelt*. (These are provisory terms that have to be qualified by the analysis itself).

Therefore I propose to consider two cross sections : one at the level of the *Logical Investigations* on the one hand and of the *Tractatus* on the other; the second at the level of the last works of Husserl and of the *Investigations*.

I

At the first level the comparison may be focused on the function played by the theory of meaning and by the theory of picture respectively. Why this choice?

In the first *Logical Investigation* the theory of meaning is put in an intermediary position. Before that, in the *Prolegomena*, Husserl had elaborated a pure logical theory, conceived as the axiomatics of all possible theories, i.e., of all necessary closed systems of principles. This was a pure logic in the sense that a logical proposition is free from contamination by anything psychological; it is a "truth in itself." It is the task of a phenomenology of meaning to locate the logical contents within the wider circle of "signs" (*Zeichen*); among "signs" they belong to the class of "signifying signs." Logical contents are thus considered as the meanings of certain expressions (hence the title : *Ausdruck und Bedeutung*). As such they are only kinds of signifying expressions — but not mere cases. They display a specific function : they represent the *telos* of every language or level of language. And because logical structure is the *telos*, meaningful expressions cover a wider field than logical contents, and phenomenology must precede logic. Two examples may be useful : the description of *Erlebnisse* may be rigorous, without being exact in the logico-mathematical sense : we may speak rigorously of inexact essences. Furthermore, ordinary language is full of expressions that are equivocal not by chance but by nature; these "circumstantial" or "occasional" expressions — such as personal pronouns, demonstratives, adverbial locutions ("here" and "now") — achieve their meaning in relation to a situation and an audience with which speaker and listener are acquainted. As to the analysis of the meaningful act, I shall not repeat it here (meaning as an "aiming" that animates and permeates the signifying layer and provides it with the power of representing something, of having something as its object). It is the position of this analysis in the course of the *Logical Investigations* which interests me. I said that this analysis occupies an intermediate position. What is beyond and why have we to go further?

We were brought back from logic to phenomenology. We are now brought back from a phenomenology of "expressions" (of signifying signs) to a phenomenology of *Erlebnisse* in general. It is the task of the fifth logical investigation to elaborate a concept of "consciousness" — not only of consciousness as a whole, as monad, but of consciousness as the transcending process implied in each *Erlebnis*, of consciousness as *intentional*. Signifying expressions were still facts of language; intentionality covers the field of all transcending acts : perception, imagination, desire, will, perception of, desire of, will of.

After having founded logical contents on linguistic expressions, phenomenology founds the latter on the power of intentionality, which is more primitive than language and is linked to "consciousness" as such.

Language is therefore an intermediary between two levels. The first one, as we said, constitutes its *ideal* of logicity, its *telos* : all meanings must be able to be converted into the logos of rationality; the second one no longer constitutes an ideal, but a ground, a soil, an origin, an *Ursprung*. Language may be reached "from above," from its logical limit, or "from below," from its limit in mute and elemental experience. In itself it is a medium, a mediation, an exchange between *Telos* and *Ursprung*.

Can we now compare the picture theory of the *Tractatus* with this theory of meaning? No, if we consider the context; yes, if we consider the position and the function of this specific theory.

Like Husserl, Wittgenstein intends to build "a discourse in the kind of philosophy that uses logic as a basis." The central part of the *Tractatus*, concerning propositions (*Sätze*), propositional signs, logical form, truth functions, and truth operations, agrees with this requirement. The "proposition" is the pivot : "An expression has meaning only in a proposition" (3.314). But the *Tractatus* as a whole overflows this structure and does not use logic as a basis. Why? Because logic is concerned with "possibilities of truth" (4.3; 4.4; 4.41). But tautology and contradiction are the two extreme cases among the possible groups of truth conditions (4.46). The *Tractatus* must also take into account a non-tautological concept of truth, truth as concordance between propositions and facts. The picture theory comes in here : "the totality of true thoughts is a picture of the world" (3.01). But "tautologies and contradictions are not pictures of reality" (4.462). We have therefore to elaborate a picture theory distinct from that of truth conditions, as Husserl had to elaborate a theory of meaning distinct from that of logical propositions.

The context is different, but the position and the function are comparable.

The context is different. First, because Husserl intended to overcome the absoluteness of logical truth, while Wittgenstein has to overcome the senselessness of tautology; second, because the *Tractatus* has to start with propositions concerning the world (1; 1.1; 1.11, etc.) — facts, states of affairs, objects (things). Whatever the status of these propositions (and everybody knows how controversial it is), they precede the analysis of the "picture" and must precede it, since the picture is itself a fact — "a picture is a fact" (2.141) — therefore something in the world. But it is an odd fact, since it is a fact that represents other facts (*vertreten*).

This context seems to exclude any kind of comparison. For a phenomenologist the starting point of the *Tractatus* would appear to be the ultimate expression of the "naturalistic" attitude (unless we reinterpret these first propositions in the terms of the later Husserl, as a description of *Lebenswelt*, or in those of *Sein und Zeit*, as an analysis of being-in-the-world; but this would be rather hazardous).

In spite of this difference concerning the course and the development of both works, the picture theory, once introduced, displays a range of implications that exceed not only the logical framework of that philosophy but also the realistic requirements of the starting point; an implicit

— and perhaps abortive — phenomenology of the "meaning" grows out of the ontology of facts, states of affairs, and world.

The picture — like the meaning for Husserl — is the essence of all language; it covers the field of spoken and written languages and of all articulated signs : photographs, diagrams, plans, maps, musical scores, records — i.e., all kinds of representations through which the disposition of elements or of parts in the "fact" is expressed by a corresponding disposition in the picture.

The picture is a correspondence between structure and structure (2.12). But as soon as we have introduced this concept of correspondence we must find *within* the picture the principle of it. Wittgenstein calls it the "pictorial form" (2.15; 2.151), which is the condition of the "pictorial relationship" (2.1513; 2.1514). In the case of factual truth there is no trouble; we may speak of an *identity* between the picture and what it depicts (2.16; 2.161); the pictorial form may even be conceived as what a picture has in common with reality (2.17). But a less realistic interpretation of the pictorial form appears with the representation of possibility, of nonexistence,[1] and above all with false representations. Here the "sense" is no more something in common, but an inner feature : there may be representation (*Darstellung*) without depiction (*Abbildung*). This concept of *Darstellung* as distinct from that of *Abbildung* is the closest to phenomenology (2.22; 2.221-2.224); it culminates in this assertion : "What a picture represents [*darstellt*] is its sense" (2.221). As in Plato, the idea is an idea of something but not necessarily of something which *is*. Here phenomenology occurs.

But this phenomenology tends to abort : the absence of reflectivity in the picture precludes all explicit phenomenology : "A picture can depict any reality whose form it has" (2.171); "A picture cannot, however, depict its pictorial form : it displays it" (2.172). Why? We don't know. Henceforth the picture theory has to be absorbed into the theory of logical forms (2.18); a picture, the pictorial form of which is a logical form, will be called a logical picture. The *Tractatus* will be mainly a theory of the logical picture.

Husserl helped us to discover within the *Tractatus* tensions, paradoxes, and above all an aborted phenomenology of meaning, crushed between the initial realistic propositions of the *Tractatus* about world and facts and the logical kernel of the *Tractatus*.

[1] Wittgenstein seems to admit possibilities and negations in his concept of reality (2.06; 2.201).

But at the same time, we may perhaps understand why Wittgenstein had to elaborate a new frame-work for the meanings of ordinary language and to substitute his conception of language-games and of language as usage for the picture-theory. But we shall better understand this new stand after having considered the corresponding development in Husserl.

The predominant problem in the late philosophy of Husserl proceeds directly from the early one. As we said, language is an intermediary between logical structures that constitute its *telos* and the lived experience that gives it an origin. It is mainly this second side of the problem which the late philosophy takes into account, without losing sight of the other side, as the *Logic* of 1929 proves.

But this relation between language and prelinguistic experience is not a simple one. It implies in its turn a new polarity between two trends : the first one, symbolized by the "reduction," implies a suspension, which does not necessarily mean a retreat within an ego secluded from reality but the kind of break with natural surroundings which is implied in the birth of language as such; there is no symbolic function without the sort of mutation that affects my relation to reality by substituting a *signifying* relation for a natural involvement. Reduction, we might say, means the birth of a speaking subject. This reduction has its reflection in the structure of the sign itself; the sign is "empty" in the sense that it is not the thing, but indicates the thing, and is not itself, since it exists only to indicate.

Now this distanciation, this suspension, this reduction, which constitutes the sign as sign, opens a new and complementary possibility, that of *fulfilling* or *not fulfilling* the sign. There is a problem concerning fulfillment because of the emptiness of the sign as sign.

The problem of fulfillment is in a sense as old as phenomenology; we find it in the sixth logical investigation. But as long as the reduction had not been explicated, as it was in the *Ideas* and the *Cartesian Meditations,* it was not a problem but only a solution. It becomes a problem as soon as a first naïveté is broken, the naïveté of vision as a given — as though vision were a ray of light filling the cavity of the sign. This naïveté, too, must be lost. The return to the things themselves is the name of a problem before being an answer. We have to discover that the idea of complete or ultimate fulfillment is itself an ideal, the ideal of adequation; more than that, this ideal cannot be fulfilled in principle; the perception is by nature perspectival and inadequate; syntactic and categorical factors are always implied in the least judgment of perception; and the thing itself, as a unity of all its profiles or perspectives, is presumed, not given. Therefore, what we call "intuition" is itself the result of "synthesis," of passive syntheses that already have their syntax, that are articulated in a prereflective and prejudicative (or prepredicative) sense.

This is why Husserl was led to raise in new terms the problem of fulfillment. The prepredicative and prelinguistic structures are not given; we cannot start from them. We have rather to be *brought back* to them by the means of a process that Husserl calls *Rückfragen* ("back-questioning"). This *Rückfrage* definitely excludes any recourse to something like an "impression" in the Humean sense. It is from within the world of signs and on the basis of the *doxa* in the sense of the *Theaetetus* — i.e., of judgments of perception — that we "inquire" regressively towards a primordial lived experience; but this so-called lived experience, for men who were born among words, will never be the naked presence of an absolute, but will remain that toward which this regressive questioning points.

We have elaborated in this way a model of analysis which can be called a *genesis*, but not a genesis in the chronological sense; it is a genesis of the meaning, sense genesis, which consists in unfolding the layers of constitution deposited as sediments on a presupposed raw, mute experience.

The dynamics of genesis has thus been substituted for the status of fulfillment : this genesis allows us to introduce, in the framework of "transcendental logic," the notion of individuals, of world as horizon, beyond the something in general required by "formal logic." But individuals and world are the correlates of the *Rückfrage*.

As we have seen, the latest philosophy of Husserl has developed one of the directions implied in his first analysis of meaning; it has only been dramatized by the episode of reduction, which made of fulfillment a problem for itself. But the position of language as the intermediary between logic and experience, between *telos* and origin, has been reinforced by this new function of mediation between the absence constitutive of the sign and the articulated world that always precedes it.

When we jump from Husserl to the *Philosophical Investigations* of Wittgenstein, we have the impression that the author does not even consider the possibility of coming back from a logical language to ordinary language by way of a regressive inquiry. On the contrary, he confronts language directly and notices how it functions in ordinary, everyday situations. We are told not to think but to look. Language is immediately removed from the field of philosophical perplexities to that of its successful functioning. This field is that of *use*, in which language produces certain effects, reactions, adapted responses, in the realm of human and social action. We may compare this field of use to that of *doxa* in Husserl, with the difference that Wittgenstein examines its actual functioning, not its transcendental conditions.

The first advantage of Wittgenstein's approach is to relax the hold of a unitary theory of the functioning of language; we start without a model. What does one find? Innumerable uses, a few of which Wittgenstein supplies in paragraph 23.

In order to do justice to this countless multiplicity, Wittgenstein introduces his famous *games*; the point of the comparison lies in the fact that the diversity of these games is not subsumed under what might be regarded as essential to a language and that each is appropriate to a particular situation. Each game delimits a field in which certain procedures are valid as long as one plays that game and not another. Each is like a condensed model of behavioral patterns in which several players occupy different roles.

The second advantage of this reduction of language to a bundle of particular games concerns denomination (naming). According to Wittgenstein, a good part of our philosophy of meaning proceeds from an overestimation of the role of denomination, which has been regarded since Augustine as the paradigm case of the speech act; but naming is a special game played under certain circumstances (for example, when I am asked, What is that called? Or when I resort to "ostensive definitions" that remain dependent upon the game of learning and assigning names).

This critique of denomination is liberating, inasmuch as it gets rid of any atomistic theory of language for which the simple constituents of reality would correspond to logically simple names, to true proper names. The critique of the picture theory is itself implied in that critique of denomination, if it is true that the picture relation is a privileged form of the relation "name-thing".

In this way the critique of denomination (para. 50) opens the horizon to a resolutely pluralist conception of the uses of language; these uses form families, without there being an essence to the language games and therefore to language itself (paras. 65, 77).

But has Wittgenstein succeeded in avoiding a general theory of language? There is at least one idea that looks like a general idea concerning language, that of usage : "for a *large* class of cases — though not for all — in which we employ the word 'meaning' it can be defined thus : the meaning of a word is its use in the language" (para. 43). It is worth dwelling on this notion of use which can initiate a discussion with Husserl.

Indeed the notion of use is primarily a way of resuming the old battle against entities. It is this critique that is at stake in the discussion of denomination : entities are sublimated names; language becomes a contemplative activity, a vision of the meaning of words. The notion of use is thus directed against any theory that would make meaning something occult, either in the sense of a Platonic reality or in the sense of a mental entity. As a result of its public character use conceals no mystery. In the practice of language everything is exposed; it is even a matter of indifference whether this use is or is not accompanied by a mental process, by images or feelings. "What we do is to bring words back from their metaphysical to their everyday use" (para. 116).

It is at this very point that Husserl and Wittgenstein dissent.

The flexibility of language as mediating between several levels, as pointing toward logicity but also towards life, has been eliminated by this closed definition of language as *use*. What is lacking here is the dialectic between the reduction, which creates distance, and the return to reality, which creates presence. The concept of use is undialectical in this sense. Language games, according to Wittgenstein, are directly incorporated into successful human activities; they represent forms of life : "hence the term language-game is meant to bring into prominence the fact that the speaking of language is part of an activity, or a form of life" (para. 23). But do we coincide with life? In Husserl the life world is not viewed directly but posited indirectly, as that to which the logic of truth refers back. Wittgenstein on the contrary seems to situate himself immediately in this world of everyday experience, in which language is a form of activity like eating, drinking, and sleeping.

I propose that a theory of meaning requires two dimensions, not one. According to the first, meaning is not use nor is language a "part of an activity or a form of life"; the meaning is a term within a system of inner dependences, as Hjelmslev used to say. This constitution of the sign as sign presupposes the break with life, activity, and nature which Husserl has symbolized in the reduction and which is represented in each sign by its emptiness, or its negative relation to reality. This constitution of the sign as sign, at the level of a system of signs, distinct from natural things, is the presupposition of the other dimension of the sign, i.e., the use of meanings, by combination in sentences in a given situation. The first side is the semiotic side; the second is the semantic one, that of the speech act — what Wittgenstein calls in an appropriate way "the speaking of our language." With this distinction it is possible to retain Wittgenstein's notion of use and even to draw from it all the advantages of its application to life in an indefinite variety of uses, exceeding its logical functions. The concept of language as *use* concerns only the speech act; it is true that it is a form of life, but this is no longer true of language as a system of signs; the symbolic function, which constitutes the sign as such, originates in the distance between thought and life.

It is because it does not belong to life, because it is, according to the Stoics, an "incorporeal" entity, a "lecton," that it can transform all our human activities, all our forms of life, into meaningful activity. But if the first trend in language is a centrifugal movement in relation to life and the activities of living, the *use* of language becomes itself problematic. It is no longer enough to look; one has to think. We are forever separated from life by the very function of the sign; we no longer live life but simply designate it. We signify life and are thus indefinitely withdrawn from it, in the process of *interpreting* it in a multitude of ways.

And, above all, if language is only a mediation, an intermediary between several levels, between *Logos* and *Bios*, a critique of ordinary language is itself possible; the philosopher is playing a game that is no longer a form of life.

We are no longer engaged in a practical activity but in a theoretical inquiry. It is for this attitude of reflection and of speculation that the life world figures simply as an origination of sense, to which a regressive inquiry refers back endlessly. But philosophy itself is made possible by the act of reduction, which is also the birth of language.

THE DOUBLE AWARENESS IN HEIDEGGER AND WITTGENSTEIN

by

INGVAR HORGBY

I

Heidegger and Wittgenstein are naturally to a high degree philosophical contraries. The aim of this article is not to deny this. But in spite of the difference in intention and philosophical attitude there is a similar awareness (consciousness) in both. The purpose of the article is to show this.

This special awareness is based on a particular experience. (The term "awareness" is used as a translation of the Swedish "medvetenhet", and "consciousness" as a translation of "medvetande.") This experience can preliminarily be defined as an experience of the world's "that," not only of its "what" or "how." This awareness is here called "that" — consciousness or the double awareness ("— — Sein besagt : Anwesen des Anwesenden : Zwiefalt." ("Being means : Presence of the Present : Duality.") (*Vorträge und Aufsätze*, 252).

II

Heidegger's philosophy is primarily ontology.

For this reason he distinguishes between "*Being*" and "*What-is.*" The *ontological* awareness relates to "Sein", the *ontical* to what is "Seiendes."

What "Seiendes" is, is not hard to grasp. Everything that is, of whatever kind it be, the empirical given or ideas or imaginings, everything is "Seiendes," that of which I am ontically conscious.

In Wittgenstein (*Tractatus*) this "Seiendes" corresponds to : How the world is (6.432; 6.44), that about which one can talk.

But what then is "Sein" when everything is "Seiendes?" It is, according to Heidegger, "dass Seiendes *ist.*" ("that what-is *is*") (*Einführung in die*

Metaphysik, 24; *Holzwege*, 53, 54). There is something and nothing is not, says Heidegger. It is this mystical (in Wittgenstein's sense) "Sein" which the ontological analysis will clarify. The question of "Sein" is formulated by Heidegger thus : "Warum ist überhaupt Seiendes und nicht vielmehr Nichts?" ("Why is there any being at all, why not far rather Nothing?") (*Einführung in die Metaphysik*, I; *Was ist Metaphysik?*, 21, 23.)

The "that"-consciousness is not a consciousness of something *in* the world, but a consciousness *that* we are, that something exists, etc. Not a consciousness of the content of the world, but *that* there is content in this world. "Diesen in seinem Woher und Wohin verhüllten, aber an ihm selbst um so unverhüllter erschlossenen Seinscharakter des Daseins, dieses 'Dass es ist' nennen wir die *Geworfenheit* dieses Seienden in sein Da, so zwar, dass es als In-der-Welt-sein das Da ist. Der Ausdruck Geworfenheit soll die *Faktizität der Überantwortung* andeuten. Das in der Befindlichkeit des Daseins erschlossene 'Dass es ist und zu sein hat' ist nicht jenes 'Dass,' das ontologisch-kategorial die der Vorhandenheit zugehörige Tatsächlichkeit ausdrückt. — *Faktizität ist nicht die Tatsächlichkeit des factum brutum eines Vorhandenen, sondern ein in die Existenz aufgenommener, wenngleich zunächst abgedrängter Seinscharakter des Daseins.* Das Dass der Faktizität wird in einem Anschauen nie vorfindlich." ("This disclosed character of Being of the Being-there which is veiled in its wherefrom and whereto but in itself even more unveiled, this 'That it is' we call the thrownness of the Being-there into its there but so that it, as a Being-in-the-world, is the there. The term 'thrownness' is to signify the *'Faktizität' of the responsibility*. What is disclosed in the 'Befindlichkeit' of the Being-there, namely 'that it is and has to be' is not that particular 'That,' which ontologically-categorically expresses the Being-at-hand, which belongs to 'Tatsächlichkeit'. — *'Faktizität' is not the 'Tatsächlichkeit' of the factum brutum of a Being-at-hand but a character of Being of the Being-there which is absorbed into the existence although at first it seems put aside.* The 'that' of the 'Faktizität' is never at hand in an experience.") (*Sein und Zeit*, 135). Heidegger refers to this "Seinscharakter des Daseins ("character of Being of the Being-there") with the word "Faktizität." "Sein" is not something "Seiendes" but "dass Seiendes *ist*." ("that what-is *is*"). Experience can tell how something (or everything) "Seiendes" ist, but not *that* something is. For this a special awareness is required. Wittgenstein says : "— that something *is*; but that is no experience." (5.552). The awareness of "Sein," that something is, is not a consciousness of something.

This fundamental question of metaphysics is as important to Wittgenstein as to Heidegger. The philosophical "atmosphere" is similar in Wittgenstein and Heidegger, and the reason is that they are conscious not only of *how* the world is but also *that* it is. (6, 44). In order to be aware of this, a special experience of the world is necessary : an experience and consciousness of the nothingness of the world and an experience of man as thrown out in this nothingness (A kind of counterpart to the difference between experience and consciousness in Heidegger is found in a passage from "Holzwege" : "Wieder eine andere Weise, wie Wahrheit zum Leuchten kommt, ist die Nähe dessen, was schlechthin nicht ein Seiendes ist, sondern das Seiendste des Seienden. — Wieder eine andere Weise, wie Wahrheit wird, ist das Fragen des Denkens, das als Denken des Seins dieses in seiner Frag-würdigkeit nenne." (*Holzwege*, 50). ("Yet another way by which truth appears is the closeness of that which as a matter of fact is not a what-is but the Most-is of what-is. — Yet another way for truth to become manifest is the questioning of Thought which, as the Thought of Being, names this in its question-evaluation.").) Such an ontical-existential experience is the basis of Heidegger's ontological-existentialistic talk about "das ursprüngliche geworfene In-der-Welt-sein als Un-zuhause, das nackte 'Dass' im Nichts der Welt." ("the originally thrown Being-in-the-world as not-at-home, the pure 'That' in the Nothing of the world.") (*Sein und Zeit*, 276-7).

H. Jonas has interpreted the gnosticism as being based on such a fundamental experience of the world. (*Gnosis und spätantiker Geist*). The reason why he has been able to interpret the gnosticism according to Heidegger's philosophy with such an ease and success is that the gnostic conception of the world is very similar to that of Heidegger. *Sein und Zeit* is a "gnostic" work. (Heidegger could say that *Sein und Zeit* is the ontological comprehension of the ontical experience of the gnostics; *Sein und Zeit*, 201). But Wittgenstein's (*Tractatus*) theology is also gnostic : "God does not reveal himself *in* the world." (6.432). To Wittgenstein the idea that God could be the Creator of the world was completely unintelligible. The same attitude is expressed in Wittgenstein's rejection of pantheism. "To say that Wittgenstein was not a pantheist is to say something important." (von Wright, *The Philosophical Review* 1955, p. 543). Likewise gnostic cosmology and anthropology are manifest in von Wright's picture of Wittgenstein : "Wittgenstein had the conviction, he sometimes said, that he was doomed. His outlook was typically one of gloom. Modern times were to him a dark age. His idea of the helplessness of human beings was not unlike certain doctrines of predestination." (*The Philosophical Review*, p. 543). (Cf. Heidegger's definition of "Dasein" as guilt, *Sein und Zeit*, 284 ff.)

The experience of the *fundamental question of metaphysics and this "gnostic" conception of the world* are intimately bound together. The fundamental metaphysical question brings us before "Sein", but this can only be done in such a way that the "Seiende" shows its nothingness (the "gnostic" vision of reality). The metaphysical question — about "Sein" — arises only when we first have experienced the "Seiende" as nothingness. Interpreted *à la* Heidegger : the ontological understanding has an ontic condition. (See the conclusion of this article!)

"Warum ist überhaupt Seiendes und nicht vielmehr Nichts? — Jeder wird einmal, vielleicht sogar dann und wann, von der verborgenen Macht dieser Frage gestreift, ohne recht zu fassen, was ihm geschieht. In einer grossen Verzweiflung z. B., wo alles Gewicht aus den Dingen schwinden will und jeder Sinn sich verdunkelt, steht die Frage auf. — In einer Langeweile ist die Frage da, —, wo aber die hartnäckige Gewöhnlichkeit des Seienden eine Öde ausbreitet, in der es uns gleichgültig erscheint, ob das Seiende ist oder ob es nicht ist, — (*Einführung in die Metaphysik* I). ("Why is the what-is at all and not rather Nothing? — Everybody is once, perhaps even at times, faced with the secret power of this question without really understanding what is happening to him. For instance, in great misery, when all importance seems to disappear from things and every meaning is obscured, then the question arises. — For quite some time the question stands there, —, but the obstinate commonplace persistence of the What-is here spreads a desertlike emptiness in which we do not care whether the What-is is or is not. —"). But even in Wittgenstein this question lies behind all other questions. Heidegger's words can be adapted to Wittgenstein : "Unsere Frage ist die *Frage* aller wahrhaften, d.h. sich auf sich stellenden Fragen und sie wird, ob wissentlich oder nicht, in jeder Frage notwendig mitgefragt." (*Einführung in die Metaphysik* 55). ("Our question is the *question* of all true questions, i.e. that is questioning the questions themselves, and it will necessarily be asked in every question, whether deliberately or not.") One can interpret Wittgenstein's philosophy as an effort to make simple that which seems enigmatic, to solve the puzzles which the philosophers have raised, and so leave everything as it was : "It (the philosophy) leaves everything as it is." (*Phil. Invest.*, 124); yet not in order to abolish the enigmatic, but in order to put the enigmatic in the right place. In his book on Wittgenstein Malcolm quotes Wittgenstein's remark that he sometimes is struck by the wonder that something exists, that the world is. This amazement has been expressed both in Wittgenstein's earlier and in his later writings. One may say the activity of Wittgenstein as a philosopher is based on this metaphysical wonder. There is nothing enigmatic in the world. An enigmatic content does not exist. (4.003) But *that* the world exists, that is enigmatic. "We find certain things about seeing puzzling, because we do not find the whole business of seeing puzzling enough." (*Phil. Invest.* 212a). In order to purify the "that" — consciousness, Wittgenstein wants, through his philosophical work, to do away with the feeling of amazement — a kind of giddiness — when faced with philosophical and mathematical statements; the proper amazement has to be reserved for the world's "that". *This* amazement cannot be dissolved, but amazement concerning the content of the world can be dissolved through the philosophical critique of language.

"What *we* do is to bring words back from their metaphysical to their everyday usage," (*Phil. Invest.*, 116. Also 118, 119, 126, 133, 196 and other places). The aim of the *Tractatus* is to show what is important by making all that can be said, all facts in the world, unimportant.

Wittgenstein is closely tied to the fundamental metaphysical question. "I believe that a certain feeling of amazement that anything should exist at all was sometimes expressed by Wittgenstein, not only during the *Tractatus* period, but also when I knew him." (N. Malcolm : *Ludwig Wittgenstein, A Memoir*, p. 70.) But this question is connected even by Wittgenstein with the "gnostic" experience of the frightening mysteriousness of the world. Wittgenstein was not unfamiliar with the dread. His philosophical therapy did not make the dread disappear, but instead it can be said to have led to a fixing of the dread. The dread, according to Heidegger, is especially caused by the fact that : "Die Welt, worin ich existiere, ist zur Unbedeutsamkeit herabgesunken, —" (*Sein und Zeit*, 343). ("The world in which I exist has sunk into unimportance.") This Wittgenstein makes clear in the *Tractatus* : the world, what can be said, is worthless. "The sense of the world must lie outside the world." (6.41). The World is a desert without the oasis of values. Wittgenstein presents a world of nothingness, and thus a world of dread. If one interprets the Wittgenstein of *the Tractatus à la* the Wittgenstein of the *Phil. Invest.* : Wittgenstein's "form of life" with its "gnostic" experience of the nothingness of the world has determined his language and what he lets go for truth : the work *Tractatus*. Interpreted *à la* Heidegger : the question of "Sein", the fundamental question of metaphysics, was raised even to Wittgenstein through the revelation of the Nothing, "das

Nichts". Nothing is revealed in "Dasein" by the dread. Heidegger has taken over Kierkegaard's definition of dread : dread — for Nothing. The question of "Sein" is possible only when the possibility of Nothing has been established. (*Einführung in die Metaphysik*, 85; *Platons Lehre von der Wahrheit*, 114). Nothing is not for Heidegger an hypostasis of the negation. "Das Nichts ist ursprünglicher als das Nicht und die Verneinung" (*Was ist Metaphysik?* 28). ("The Nothing is more original than the Not and negation.") "Entgegenhandeln," "verabscheuen," "verbieten," "entbehren" ("to counteract," "to detest," "to forbid," "to be deprived of") are more important and more characteristic forms of "das Nichten des Nichts" ("the negativing function of the Nothing") than the negation of thoughts. (*Was ist Metaphysik?* 37). It is characterized by "Unheimlichkeit" ("Uncanniness"), which is hidden for us in our daily "In-der-Welt-Sein" (*Sein und Zeit*, 277) but which is revealed for us through the Nothing. "Sein" : "dass Seiendes ist" is revealed in "Dasein" in the dread "Dasein heisst : Hineingehaltenheit in das Nichts" ("Being-there means : being projected into the Nothing") (*Was ist Metaphysik?* 35; cf. even 12 and 32 and *Einführung in die Metaphysik*, 135). The amazement which makes Wittgenstein and Heidegger raise the fundamental metaphysical question is roused when "die Befremdlichkeit des Seienden uns bedrängt" ("the strangeness of the What-is forces itself upon us"), and this happens by the revelation of the Nothing through the dread. That is why the "Dasein" determined by dread is the only "Seiende," which in itself is ontological and not only ontical : it is related to "Sein" (Heidegger), to the world's "that", not only its "how." (Wittgenstein).

Man, who by his essence (as "Dasein") belongs to "Sein" is "das Unheimlichste" ("the highest uncanniness") (*Einführung in die Metaphysik*, 113 ff.). Man is the metaphysical being, is oriented towards "Sein," and the fact that he is so oriented is "das Unheimlichste." The original in Heidegger's ontology is that, in order to interpret the most general of all concepts, "Sein," he uses terms of a very special kind, taken from a "gnostic" conception of reality (dread, dead, decay, guilt, silence, conscience etc.).

III

To characterize the double awareness is a difficult task. Difficult in a qualified way : its object "Sein" is beyond all "Seiendes," is something similar to the One in Plato and the Neo-Platonists, is inaccessible.

We stand before the unconditional abyss. (*Vorträge und Aufsätze*, 179). No reason can be given for the phenomenon that language-games are played, for all distinctions are given *within* the language-game. (Wittgenstein, *Phil. Invest.*) *That* the world is, is the mystical. (Wittgenstein, *Tractatus.*) It cannot be expressed in sentences; it is the awareness of that which is higher, that about which nothing can be said. (Wittgenstein.) It is awareness of "Sein", not consciousness of anything (or all) "Seiendes," and can only be attained by the "Denken" ("thinking") which has affinity with "Dichten") ("poetry"), not by scientific thought or by habitual philosophizing. (Heidegger.) (*Platons Lehre von der Wahrheit*, 54; *Vorträge und Aufsätze*, 192; *Einführung in die Metaphysik*, 131; *Was ist Metaphysik?* 50-51). Its verb is "show," not "say." (Wittgenstein, *Tractatus*). Even Heidegger uses the verb "zeigen" in this connection.

1

Awareness is to be lifted from the low-land of the habitual conceptions to see that which is invisible for ordinary eyes : become alive to something long known. Then "I become alive to" what it means to be a human being. In the "that"-consciousness I see everything as *new*. Thinking on the level of the matter-of-fact consciousness makes everything old, puts everything back in the medium of the past (to talk with Kierkegaard). "Nothing is new under the sun."

2

Characteristic of the double awareness is its contemplation of the *whole* (*Einführung in die Metaphysik* 2), Heidegger refers to Plato's and Aristotle's distinction between whole and sum, between ὅλον and πᾶν (*Sein und Zeit*, 244, the note). This concerns not a quantitative but a, so to say, qualitative whole. "The contemplation of the world *sub specie aeterni* is its contemplation as a limited whole." (6.45) The Philosophy of the *Tractatus* gives this contemplation *sub specie aeterni*. The philosophy shall from within the unthinkable circumscribe this through the thinkable (4.114). By clearly stating what can be said, philosophy shall "mean" that which cannot be said. Such an activity is possible only *sub specie aeterni*, whereby the world appears as a limited whole. And thus the question is about a "qualitative" whole. Wittgenstein does not give a complete description of the world; that is given in the sun of all true elementary statements. (4.26). It is, even for Wittgenstein, a question not about the sun but about the whole, not about the "Seiende" but about "Sein," not about an ontical, but about an ontological whole. This contemplation of the whole is not possible for the matter-of-fact-consciousness, but only for the "that"-consciousness.

It is impossible for Wittgenstein to express in language this whole of the world.[1] What is an impossibility for Wittgenstein is for Heidegger a difficulty. Wittgenstein does not mean, however, that such a *conception* of the whole is impossible, but only that it cannot be expressed. According to Wittgenstein metaphysics is an impossibility as statements, as system, but not as awareness. On the contrary he presupposes the possibility of the metaphysical consciousnes. "There is indeed the inexpressible" (6.522). By denying the possibility of metaphysical statements Wittgenstein thus affirms the possibility of the metaphysical consciousness and also assigns to it the predicate The Higher. Thus he indicates its priority over the world of language. (In *Phil. Invest.* : "form of life" determines the "language-game").

3

Heidegger, who does not have Wittgenstein's (*Tractatus*) narrow ideal of language, says much about the characteristics of the real existence. Real existence, being "Sein zum *Tode*" ("the Being towards one's *death*") is conceived as a whole, although this conception of the whole is an impossible possibility, as death is an impossible possibility for life (*Sein und Zeit*, 236, 265-266). *Possibility*, because we could not at all know the distinction between real and non-real existence, if it were not a possibility. "Sein zum Tode" is possibility to authentic existence. *Impossible* possibility : it is impossible to conceive "Dasein" as a whole, because "Dasein" is by nature "sich vorweg." (*Sein und Zeit*, 20, 236). ("in-advance-of-itself").

It is an impossibility in a categorical respect (as "Vorhandenes") ("What-is-at-hand"), but possibility, in an existentialistic respect (as "Dasein"). As "Dasein" is always " 'mehr' als es tatsächlich ist", ("As 'Being-there' " always is " 'more' than it really is"), it is an impossi-

[1] Because of this Heidegger and Wittgenstein are quite different in the use of the concept "Sinn" : "Only the proposition has sense; —" (3.3), whereas Heidegger holds that "Sinn ist ein Existenzial des Daseins, nicht eine Eigenschaft, die am Seienden haftet, — *Nur Dasein kann daher sinnvoll oder sinnlos sein.* (*Sein und Zeit*, 151). ("Sense is an existentialistic function of Being-there, not a quality attached to the What-is, — Only Being-there can thus make sense or be senseless.").

bility, whereas it is a possibility, as it is "nie mehr, als es faktisch ist" ("never more than it actually is"). Hence, the command is a right one : "werde, was du bist!" (*Sein und Zeit*, 145). ("become what thou art!")

In Wittgenstein : "Death is not an event of life. Death is not lived through." (6.4311). It is man in his unreal existence who conceives death as an event, whereas death for the real existence is its utmost possibility : "Der Tod ist die Möglichkeit der schlechthinnigen Daseins-unmöglichkeit." (*Sein und Zeit*, 250). ("Death is the possibility of the outright impossibility of Being-there.") Both for Heidegger and Wittgenstein the question about death is a question of the double awareness. For the simple matter-of-fact-consciousness the problem of death is a feigned problem. The existentialistic analysis of death is *before* all biological, psychological or theological questions of death. (*Sein und Zeit*, 248). Death belongs, like, for example, the self, to the metaphysical, and limits the world from the other side, one might say. But philosophy, the philosophy of the double awareness, is within the sphere of the unthinkable. "It should limit the unthinkable from within through the thinkable." (4.114). "It will mean the unspeakable by clearly displaying the speakable" (4.115).

The task of philosophy is to stand within the unthinkable and by clearly depicting the thinkable, point to the unthinkable (Wittgenstein). Being an expression of the real existence, the task of philosophy is to clarify the unreal existence and thereby express the real existence as a possibility (Heidegger.) "Sein zum Tode" is the "Ganzseinkönnen" of man (" 'whole' potentiality of Being") (*Sein und Zeit*, 266, 326). Both Heidegger's and Wittgenstein's philosophy stand within the unthinkable, and both point out the metaphysical self and death as the two limits within the unthinkable, between which the world is. Because both Heidegger and Wittgenstein are aware of these boundaries, they can contemplate the world as a whole. Their contemplation of the whole (of the world as a limited whole) is existentialistic metaphysics (the philosophical ego, i.e. the thinker who carries on the philosophical activity, is the metaphysical ego). The philosophy of Heidegger and Wittgenstein is the philosophy of the double awareness.

4

In this "that"-consciousness, the *ego* is not an object (5.641).

It is in relation to the whole life of a human being that the different characters of those two levels of consciousness become apparent. The simple matter-of-fact-consciousness does not put me under an obligation, and has nothing to do with my moral life. The matter-of-fact-consciousness does not change anything in any personality. I may have this matter-of-fact-consciousness even with myself as object. Then I am an object among other objects and thereby exposed to the same laws as other objects. Hume, who denies the validity of the concept of substance, is right in doing the same thing with the ego — on the level of the matter-of-fact-consciousness. As a thing among other things the ego is not anything *sui generis. Only through the double awareness* is it elevated to its *unique position.*

"Die Person ist kein Ding, keine Substanz, kein Gegenstand." (*Sein und Zeit*, 47; see even *Sein und Zeit*, 332) ("The person is not a thing, not a substance, not an object.") This I, the metaphysical subject, is, according to Wittgenstein, the philosophical subject. And philosophy is to him an *activity*, something which is done by somebody. "(Words are also deeds)" (*Phil. Invest.*, 546). "Philosophy is not a theory but an activity." (4.112). This implies that what is not linguistic in the activity of language, the one who speaks, the I, does not belong to the sphere of language, to the world. The I is not at home in the world, although the world is always my world. The I is an a-cosmic quantity. According to Heidegger : "Person" is "Aktvollzieher" ("someone accomplishing acts") and "Akte sind etwas Unpsychisches" ("acts are something unpsychical"). "Psychisches Sein hat also mit Personsein nichts zu tun." ("Psychical being has thus nothing to do with being a person") (*Sein und Zeit*, 48) (See III 7!).

This distinction between "Tatsächlichkeit" und "Fakticität" can clarify what Wittgenstein means when he says that the subject does not belong to the world, but is a limit of the world (5.632). "There is therefore really a sense in which in philosophy we can talk of a non-psychological I.

The I occurs in philosophy through the fact that 'the world is my world.'

The philosophical I is not the man, not the human body or the human soul of which psychology treats, but the metaphysical subject, the limit — not a part of the world." (5.641). The philosophical I (which carries on the philosophical activity) is the metaphysical I; it stands within the unthinkable and does not exist in the "Tatsächlichkeit" of experience but only in relation to the double awareness, which is aware of the "Faktizität."

The philosophical I, which carries on the philosophical activity, is, according to Wittgenstein, the metaphysical subject and does not belong to the content of the world. "The subject does not belong to the world but it is a limit of the world." (5.632). (*Phil. Invest.*, 404, 405, 410). Heidegger says : "Der 'Geist' fällt nicht erst in die Zeit, —" (*Sein und Zeit*, 436). ("The 'Spirit' is not at first in time"). Wittgenstein does not forget that he exists, when he thinks. The subjective thinker himself is the meeting-place for the intellectual (the language, the world) and the mystical, the higher, the meaning of the world. The subject when considered as an empirical fact, as an I, is not a subject. The subject is not the objective, fixed point (in Descartes' way). It exists, not for the matter-of-fact-consciousness, but for the "that"-consciousness. The metaphysical I is the invisible-point which is the union between the thinkable and the unthinkable, between the world of language and the higher. It belongs itself to the unthinkable, and is not a part of the world as the eye is not a part of the field of vision. (5.632, 5.633, 5.6331). Here is the place of wonder, where the metaphysical amazement arises : *that* something exists. Wittgenstein clears away all false puzzles about the content of the world in order to make room for this "real" puzzle : The fundamental metaphysical question. In the same way Heidegger turns against all traditional metaphysics, because its question is not of "Sein" but of "Seiende"; the traditional metaphysics answers the question of "what," but not the question of "that." The higher relates to the world only at this point, in the metaphysical I, and not elsewhere. *This* solipsism is the philosophical attitude. That something *is*, is not an experience : does not belong to the content of the world. (*Tractatus*). The real object of wonder is what is given and presupposed, what ordains the language-game, what tells what is the truth, what determines the essence of things (*Phil. Invest.*). In the "object" of wonder is included the metaphysical subject itself, to whom this amazement is given. (*Vorträge und Aufsätze*, 71 ff., 234 ff., *Einführung in die Metaphysik*, 136, 155; *Platons Lehre von der Wahrheit*, 50, 65). The metaphysical wonder is possible only if the philosophical subject is drawn into the realm of the unthinkable and itself belongs to the mystical. Wittgenstein's metaphysics is existential : the thinker, who carries on the philosophical activity that implies the unveiling of the limits of the thinkable, stands himself beyond the limits of the thinkable. Interpreted in Heidegger's way : the fundamental metaphysical question, the question of "Sein", is given only in "Dasein". It is only when "das Nichts" reveals "Sein" in "Dasein" that one asks "Warum ist überhaupt Seiendes und nicht vielmehr Nichts?" ("Why is the What-is at all and not rather Nothing?")

(Heidegger). This is the question which places philosophy within the unthinkable and thereby starts the philosophical activity : to point out the limit of the thinkable (Wittgenstein, *Tractatus*). Philosophy is, as a language game, determined by and presupposes the given, "forms of life," which ordain what the language can say. That the language-game is played is the fundamental phenomenon (*Phil. Invest.*, 654) that arouses our "real" metaphysical wonder that something is given, that which is presupposed in all language (Wittgenstein, *Phil. Invest.*).

Wittgenstein is a mystic; he is silent about the higher. He lets metaphysics remain mystical, and his metaphysics has the minimal form of the mystic. His *method* is a *via negativa* but thereby he has not denied but affirmed "das Höhere," and he stands with his philosophy (*Tractatus*) within the unthinkable and the inexpressible. (4.114; 4.115). Heidegger, on the contrary, chooses an ideal of language according to which even statements about "das Höhere" of Wittgenstein are meaningful (and meaningful *par préférence*). Heidegger and Wittgenstein differ on the question of ideal of language, but what they wish to show is basically the same.

5

The "*existential*" *character* of the double consciousness is due to its being a consciousness of the qualitative whole. (The word 'existence' is here not taken in Heidegger's sense. Especially in his later philosophy Heidegger interprets the concept as an ontological concept (*Platons Lehre von der Wahrheit*, 66 ff.). The word is here instead taken in its merely existential sense, implying that Heidegger's philosophy is regarded as dependent upon Heidegger's existential experience). In accordance with our programme (see part IV) Heidegger's ontological interpretation is traced back to its ontic-existential point of departure. This is done because the conception of the whole found in the double awareness implies that the thinker himself is drawn into thinking in terms of the double awareness. "Die Frage nach dem Nichts (only "das Nichts" can in "Dasein" reveal "Sein", which is the "object" of the "that"-consciousness) stellt uns — die Fragenden — selbst in Frage. Sie ist eine metaphysische." (*Was ist Metaphysik?*, 41). ("The enquiry into Nothing puts us, the enquirers, ourselves in question. It is a metaphysical one."). In the same way Wittgenstein is conscious that he is buried in his own philosophy. This is shown by the fact that Wittgenstein in the *Tractatus* at the end denounces even his own Philosophy as developed in the *Tractatus* (because there can be no philosophical statements);

in *Phil. Invest.* he indicates the "Weltanschauung" that is the base of what he expounds in this work. His own philosophy depends on the form of life which he has chosen. "The concept of a perspicuous representation is of fundamental significance for us. It earmarks the form of account we give, the way we look at things. (Is this a 'Welt-anschauung'?)" (*Phil. Invest.*, 122).

In our double awareness we have responsibility. Ethics, which is transcendental, sets, according to Wittgenstein, the limits of our world. It cannot change anything *in* our world, but it can change its limits. About the meeting between the unthinkable and the thinkable Wittgenstein says : "the 'world is my world'." (5.641). Neither for Wittgenstein nor for Heidegger is the subject ever separated from the world : "*Im Ich-sagen spricht sich das Dasein als In-der-Welt-sein aus.*" (*Sein und Zeit*, 321); ("In saying-I the Being-there expresses itself as Being-in-the-world."); "*eigentliches Selbstsein*" ("authentic self-Being") is nothing but "*In-der-Welt-sein*" (*Sein und Zeit*, 298, 13). This is not anything that can be said (Wittgenstein), nothing that belongs to "das Vorhandene" (Heidegger). It can only be shown (Wittgenstein); it belongs to "das Dasein", to the existentialistic (Heidegger). This existential relationship between the world of language and the mystical cannot be expressed, says Wittgenstein (in that case it would be within the world of *language*). It does not belong to "die Tatsächlichkeit" but to "die Faktizität." There is no question about a "*factum brutum eines Vorhandenen*", ("*factum brutum* of a Being-at-hand"), but instead about "Dass es ist" ("that it is"); "Dasein" is what is concerned, Heidegger tells us. (*Sein und Zeit*, 135).

For Wittgenstein the limit of language and the limit of the world coincide (5.6; *Phil. Invest.* 371, 373). What this implies becomes apparent in a parallel passage in Heidegger; the existential implications of Wittgenstein's statement are expressed by Heidegger as follows : "*Erkennen ist eine Seinsart des In-der-Welt-seins*" (*Sein und Zeit*, 61). ("To know is a kind-of-Being of the Being-in-the-world.") The concepts are not created by the constructive thinker but force themselves on us. "A *concept* forces itself on one. (This is what you must not forget.)" (*Phil. Invest.*, 204e). This power of the concepts to force themselves on us is due to the fact that they are founded in life. It is our attachment to life that attaches us to concepts. "What people accept as a justification — is shown by how they think and live." (*Phil. Invest.*, 325). Which are the concepts that become ours therefore depends on our life, on our world as a whole. And it is this whole world which is put into question in

Wittgenstein's and Heidegger's philosophy, not as something but as "that". A sign of this is that the thinker is not unaffected by his philosophy. The thinker, the acting subject, (the metaphysical subject according to Wittgenstein) participates in Heidegger's and Wittgenstein's "mystical" philosophy (in Wittgenstein's philosophy, since the philosophy is within the realm of the inexpressible and the unthinkable, it can comprise the metaphysical subject).

6

A very important difference between Wittgenstein and the logical empiricists is, as will be known, connected with how *Wittgenstein's last sentence in Tractatus* is to be interpreted. Wittgenstein is aware of there being things of which one cannot talk. The logical empiricists mean that whereof one cannot speak, thereof one must be silent, but thereby one is not silent *about* anything (Neurath). "What we cannot say, we cannot say, and we cannot whistle it either" (Ramsey, *Revolutionen i Filosofien*, Stockholm 1957, p. 77). Wittgenstein's view is clarified in, for example, 6.522 : "There is indeed the inexpressible. This *shows* itself; it is the mystical."

There are corresponding passages in Heidegger. Even Heidegger is silent *about* something. The silence which is not silence *about* something is not silence. "Schweigen heisst aber nicht stumm sein. Der Stumme hat umgekehrt die Tendenz zum 'Sprechen'. Ein Stummer hat nicht nur nicht bewiesen, dass er schweigen kann, es fehlt ihm sogar jede Möglichkeit, dergleichen zu beweisen. Und so wenig wie der Stumme zeigt einer, der von Natur gewohnt ist, wenig zu sprechen, dass er schweigt und schweigen kann. Wer nie etwas sagt, vermag im gegebenen Augenblick auch nicht zu schweigen. — Der Mensch zeigt sich als Seiendes, das redet." (*Sein und Zeit*, 164-165) (*Platons Lehre von der Wahrheit*, 92; *Sein und Zeit*, 273). ("To be silent does not mean to be dumb, though. A dumb person has not only not proved that he can be silent, but he doesn't even have the possibility of proving any such thing. And a person who by nature is accustomed to speak little shows that he is silent and is able to be silent no more than does the dumb person. He who never says anything is thus not able to be silent at a given moment. — The human being shows himself as a what-is that speaks.")

According to this interpretation of Wittgenstein, it is fallacious and against Wittgenstein's intentions to seek, as Russell does (in the Introduction to the *Tractatus*), to evade Wittgenstein's qualitative distinction between "say" and "show" by appeal to a meta-theory of language (in which theory "meta" does not mean that a special kind of consciousness is established. The theory is still a theory on the level of the matter-of-fact-consciousness). Russell's "intellectual discomfort" (Introd. to the *Tractatus*, P. 22) with regard to Wittgenstein's distinction is not evidence of any discomfort at the intellectual level (although this, of course, was Russell's "unconscious" view of the matter). On the contrary the intellectual level here crosses another level (the "existential"). That Wittgenstein succeeds in saying quite a lot about the inexpressible, the mystical, Russell cannot understand, except by thinking that there must be a way out through a hierarchy of language (or something like that). This implies a way out on the level of the language, of the world, which is completely incompatible with Wittgenstein's view. Russell and Reichenbach ("*Elements of Symbolic Logic*", 1952, p. 381, note) treat of Wittgenstein's distinction as if it were a distinction between two functions on the same level, whereas for Wittgenstein it is a distinction between levels of consciousness, an intellectual and an "existential" one, between consciousness and awareness. The distinction can therefore not be done away with at the intellectual level.

Seeking to abolish this distinction is not to improve or beautify the philosophy of Wittgenstein (*Tractatus*). Instead, it is to tear down its fundamental element. The difference between Wittgenstein and Heidegger, on the contrary, may be conceived as two different ideals of language (which of course in itself is an important difference). But the fact that Heidegger says much about that whereof, according to Wittgenstein, one cannot talk, does not prevent them from doing philosophy on similar premisses.

That Wittgenstein does not conceive his philosophy at the intellectual level, becomes manifest in 6.54. "In, with, and under" (to use the prepositions of the Lutheran doctrine of the Sacraments) the intellectual exposition Wittgenstein has in the end not *said* anything (6.54; 7) but he has *shown* something, and this is that whereof one cannot talk. The difference between Russell-Reichenbach (the meta-theorists of language) on the one hand and Wittgenstein on the other hand is no technical difference between the philosophers of the matter-of-fact-consciousness and the philosophers of the double awareness; it is an existential difference. Wittgenstein is a real mystic; he is silent *about* something.

The criticism which here could be raised from Heidegger's and Wittgenstein's philosophy against philosophers of the Ramsey-Neurath-Russell-Reichenbach-type is not an intellectual but an "existential" criticism. They don't fail in *something* but they have not seen *that* something is; because they have chosen to be deaf towards the claims of this awareness.

The solutions of the philosophical questions have been found to depend on an interpretation of life. The philosophical discussion no longer is theoretical but becomes "existential." Not new thoughts are demanded but a new act of awareness.

Through a new act of awareness my matter-of-fact-consciousness is elevated to be binding. Hume's sceptical question of how something that is can be made to mean that something ought to be, is not solved by increased knowledge but by an intensifying of the consciousness. That is, the consciousness which man already has is not supplanted but is chosen. But man has chosen to forget, has chosen the simple, non-committing matter-of-fact-consciousness.

7

Common to Heidegger and Wittgenstein is the interpretation of *philosophy as therapy*. They are both "psychoanalysts" as philosophers. Philosophy is an activity — not a doctrine — which aims at unveiling hidden connections and thereby liberating. They are philosophers of "enlightenment" who practise medicine of a spiritual kind. The hidden is exposed and a spiritual illness is thereby cured. "The philosophers' treatment of a question is like the treatment of an illness." (*Phil. Invest.*, 255). Man is made free to adapt himself to reality, and this implies that he is made free to act. Heidegger's and Wittgenstein's philosophy is therapy, action, and makes man free to act, by displaying even thinking as action. Philosophy is not only something theoretical that merely concerns the theoretically contemplating man detached from life. It is, on the contrary, something which is important to the acting man. The analysis itself is action and the result of this action is that the "enligh-tened" are made free to act.

To Wittgenstein the use of a thought is the criterion of how it is meant. Wittgenstein understands his philosophy by applying it and he teaches others to regard the application as a criterion. The therapeutic in Wittgenstein's philosophy is that he, through his philosophy, makes others free to regard the application of a thought as criterion of how it is to be comprehended. He wants to make others understand : he wants them to act. In the action it is shown that the understanding is based on a way of living and thinking. This is the implication of what here has been called Wittgenstein's existentialism.

Wittgenstein means, like Heidegger, that the task of philosophy is to free man from the bewitchment of the language (even if he, with his strict, ascetic ideal of language, does not feel compelled to resort to a terminology so abstruse as Heidegger's). Like Heidegger, Wittgenstein means that man gains "health" through philosophical clarification. The philosophical "sickness", a paralysis of action, is healed by the philosophical activity.

Heidegger means that his analysis of "Dasein" unveils the unreal existence, and thereby reveals the real existence. In the unreal existence the understanding of "Sein" is "verschlossen", ("closed"), whereas it is "erschlossen" ("disclosed") in the real existence, through the ontological-existentialistic analysis. The existentialistic-ontological analysis makes *conscious* what was unconscious, "verschlossen," in the unreal existence.

8

For philosophy in general *language* is a neutral means of communication. Language is (ought to be) an organ, for the pure thought, free from all contents. Against this Wittgenstein's criticism is directed : it is a superstition to believe that the logically purified concepts are the correct concepts. "The more narrowly we examine actual language, the sharper becomes the conflict between it and our requirement. (For the crystalline purity of logic was, of course, not a *result of investigation :* it was a requirement.) The conflict becomes intolerable; the requirement is now in danger of becoming empty. — We have got on to slippery ice where there is no friction and so in a certain sense the conditions are ideal, but also, just because of that, we are unable to walk. We want to walk : so we need *friction.* Back to the rough ground!" (*Phil. Invest.*, 107). Another image which Wittgenstein uses is that often we want just the unclear photography (*Phil. Invest.*, 71). To make the concepts logically pure is to abolish the dependence of the language on its surroundings, its world, in which the language has significance; it is to abolish the situation of the language.

"What is happening now has significance — in these surroundings. The surroundings give it its importance." (*Phil. Invest.*, 583).

It was such an abolition of the situation of the language that Wittgenstein himself made in the *Tractatus* in a radical way, but he also accepted the consequences : nothing important can be said.

That people agree in the language they use is "not agreement in opinions but in form of life." (*Phil. Invest.*, 241). That the language is an expression of man's attitude towards life, that it is always "polluted" with existential suppositions, that it is never a sterile organ, is a consequence of the general picture, which the double awareness provides. Hence, the futility of the attempts of certain analytical philosophers to translate existentialists and similar philosophers into the sterile language used by these analytical philosophers. Such an objectifying, de-existentializing, neutralizing, is an impossibility. "Ein Ausdruck hat nur im Strome des Lebens Bedeutung." (N. Malcolm : *Ludwig Wittgenstein, A Memoir*, p. 93, citation from Wittgenstein). Heidegger's terrific conceptual apparatus, which exploits the tremendous capacity for astonishing and untranslatable connections and constructions of the German language — all this Turkish music in Heidegger's philosophical language is the *correct* expression of his fundamental thesis that, through the usual language, we hide for ourselves the real structure of the world, that the habitual language expresses "das Verfallensein" ("Being-in-decay") with its absence of mind, and prefers "Vorhandensein" ("Being-at-hand") to "Zuhandensein" ("Being-by-hand") and "Dasein", which is just the contrary of the real state of affairs. If Heidegger had written an ordinary language, he would have abandoned his philosophy. He would have remained within the everyday existence, with its concealment of reality. Heidegger means that the ontological analysis is very hard to express, because what is ontically most close to us, is ontologically the most remote — since our everyday existence conceals reality. The ontical phenomena which are closest to us are just those which it is hardest to analyse ontologically. "Das ontisch Nächste und Bekannte ist das ontologisch Fernste, Unerkannte —" (*Sein und Zeit*, 43; 15). ("What is ontically closest and familiar, is from the ontological point of view that which is farthest away, the unknown.") The difficulty of the ontological analysis manifests itself in his difficult terminology. Its striking peculiarity has a special philosophical function : to make the ontically hidden ontologically clear.

To these philosophers language is not only an organ for communication of truths about the world. To philosophers with double awareness the language itself is not only a neutral means of communication but is dependent upon the author's "that"-consciousness and its character. Wittgenstein says that the world of the happy and the world of the unhappy are different, and that different ethics do not involve a change *in* the world but *of* the world, that they do not change facts in the world but the limits of the world. For Wittgenstein it is not language which can give this picture of the world's "Faktizität". But language determines what goes for truth and what the essence of the things is. "*Essence* is expressed by grammar." (*Phil. Invest.*, 371; 373). The question of which language to use is therefore just the question of the world's "Faktizität," not its "Tatsächlichkeit" and it is answered when man's form of life becomes clear to me. In this both the earlier and the later Wittgenstein agree. "In brief, the world must thereby become quite another. It must so to speak wax or wane as a whole." (6.43). The difference between Heidegger and Wittgenstein here is that Heidegger uses the concept "truth" for this existential state, whereas Wittgenstein (*Tractatus*) means that truth is not a quality; for Wittgenstein only statements are true or false. Man's form of life determines what shall pass for truth, according to Wittgenstein, whereas Heidegger holds that the truth already lies in man's form of life. In Heidegger's words : the truth resides in the relationship "Sein" — "Dasein". (This relationship itself is given different interpretations by the earlier and the later Heidegger).

For Heidegger (*Sein und Zeit*, 194) the various phenomena of the will are derived from "Sorge" (cura), which he regards as a philosophical concept. It is implicit in the fundamental structure of Heidegger's philosophy that "Dasein" is always "sich vorweg". (*Sein und Zeit*, 236). Heidegger's philosophy is teleological philosophy. In Wittgenstein : my *choice* of form of life decides my *language*. This fact is not altered by the tendency in Heidegger's later philosophy to stress "Sein" and not "Dasein" (instead of dedicating himself to "Analytik des Daseins" ("Analysis of Being-there") he becomes a "Mysten des Seins". (Löwith : *Heidegger. Denker in dürftiger Zeit*, 21).) "Wissen" and "Wollen" cannot be separated. The truth is found in their unity. (*Holzwege*, 55). Only apparently is knowledge neutral. The active will is higher than knowledge and determines it. (Not the will as phenomena, not "der Wille" but "das Wollen" is at stake (6.423, 6.43). This is of course even more explicit in Heidegger). The will determines the wholeness of the knowledge, not its contents : "The world is independent of my will." (6.373). This is where the concept "das Höhere" in Wittgenstein (*Tractatus*) has its root. Therefore ethics, as belonging to "das Höhere," is transcendental; it cannot be expressed in sentences.

9

The unity of "Wissen" and "Wollen" (Heidegger),[2] that the language games are determined by forms of life (Wittgenstein) becomes manifest in Heidegger's and Wittgenstein's view on the *question of values.*

The questions of values belong to the sphere of silence (Heidegger), of the mystical (Wittgenstein), in which "das Höhere," e.g., the ethics belongs. The meaning of the world lies outside itself. There are no values in the world, only "outside all happening and being-so." There are no ethical sentences. Ethics become transcendental (6.41; 6.42; 6.421). The bad or the good will does not modify any facts in the world, it changes the world, not the contents of the world (6.43). In our terms : the world's "that", not its "what" is the aim of ethics. The question of *qualities* of value perishes, since qualities exist only *in* the world. But this does not imply that the value-nihilists are right. On the contrary, they have not seen the realm within which the values exist (6.522). They have only simple consciousness, i.e. they are, in our sense, unconscious. If the question of qualities of values is raised on the level of matter-of-fact-consciousness the problem of values cannot be solved.

As the question of value concerns the relationship between the matter-of-fact-consciousness and the "that"-consciousness (in order that the question may be meaningful) the answer cannot be given as if it concerned relations only on the plane of the matter-of-fact-consciousness.

10

G. H. von Wright says (in "Dagens Nyheter" 16.3.1957 : "Wittgenstein's 'Tractatus' ") that Wittgenstein's views on the questions of value are similar to those of *Hägerström.* According to what has been said above, their concepts of the philosophical status of values are qualitatively different. Their difference discloses itself also in their diverging views on *metaphysics* in general. The same superficial resemblance with the value-nihilists is found in Heidegger. He criticises the objectivism of values, which regards values as particular quantities having a special form of being. (*Platons Lehre von der Wahrheit*, 99 ff.). On the contrary, Heidegger incorporates the questions of values into his philosophy as a whole. They cannot be separated from it. It is the "wertbehafteten"

[2] It is certainly important to remember that Heidegger studied medieval philosophy, and especially the "voluntarist" Duns Scotus, carefully. Heidegger's work about the latter is helpful for the understanding of Heidegger's position, as Löwith has rightly pointed out in *Heidegger, Denker in dürftiger Zeit.*

things ("things, to which we attach value") that really show in which world we live. The "wertbehafteten" things are "das Zuhandene", ("being-by-hand"), and have priority in relation to "das Vorhandene" ("being-at-hand"). (*Sein und Zeit*, 63-64). Hägerström is the great enemy of metaphysics; he tries to destroy it. Metaphysical statements are meaningless. Wittgenstein can apparently say the same. But — he declares his own philosophy to be metaphysics. For him metaphysics is statement about the inexpressible. Such statements are, according to Wittgenstein himself, meaningless as statements (belonging to the world of language). But in spite of this, he utters them, and wants to utter them. Certainly, he is very ascetic in his metaphysics, saying as little as possible about that which cannot be said. But this does not change the fact that he is doing metaphysics, that he declares that "das Höhere" exists, the mystical, the inexpressible. There is an essential difference between Wittgenstein and usual metaphysicians. Wittgenstein does not, like other metaphysicians, try to rehabilitate his metaphysical statements on the level of the world of language. Wittgenstein is rigorous in setting boundaries between the world of language and the mystical. Thus his *double concept of truth :* he must consider his metaphysics, i.e., his statements about the mystical, as meaningless (in the sense of the intellectual say-truth). Nevertheless he declares his philosophy to be absolutely true (in the meaning of the "existential" show-truth). The double awareness leads to a double concept of truth. Wittgenstein does not mean as Hägerström that the values are meaningless hypotheses. They exist. What Wittgenstein says is that they don't exist in the world. Ethics cannot be expressed in sentences; but he nevertheless talks about ethics as "das Höhere". Everything is "joint in an endless natural connection, where nothing in itself is lower or higher." (Hägerström). But — "das Höhere" exists! (Wittgenstein).

Heidegger is different. He rejects the traditional occidental metaphysics from Plato to Nietzsche. This is not done out of an antimetaphysical tendency, but because the traditional metaphysics belongs to the level of "das Seiende". Thus it conceals "Sein", "Sein" which for Heidegger is, beyond all "Seiendes", the real being. (*Platons Lehre von der Wahrheit*, 53, 80; *Was heisst Denken?*, 35).

Without this double concept of truth there would have been an evident contradiction between what Wittgenstein says in 6.53, 6.54 and what he says in his preface : "On the other hand the truth of the thoughts communicated here seems to me unassailable and definitive". The perface must be concerned with the truth of what Wittgenstein *shows* in the exposition itself in *Tractatus*. He denies the truth of what he *says*. What Wittgenstein shows is true, but as he shows what he aims at by means of philosophical statements, he must reject what these statements show, because that which can be shown, cannot be said. "What *can* be shown *cannot* be said" (4.1212).

Wittgenstein is conscious not only of how the world is, but also of what he calls the mystical, what cannot be expressed; *that* it is. (6.44). It may be compared with Heidegger's : "Das im Verstehen als Existenzial Gekonnte is kein Was, sondern das Sein als Existieren." (*Sein und Zeit*, 143). All knowledge, "Anschauung," "Denken" and phenomenological "Wesensschau," "gründet im existenzialen Verstehen." (*Sein und Zeit*, 147). ("The existentialia which you are able to be in understanding is not a what, but the Being as existence. All knowledge, "experience," "thinking," and phenomenological "Wesensschau" is rooted in existentialistic understanding"). I find that the difference between Heidegger and Wittgenstein is not a difference of kind, but of degree; Wittgenstein is extremely ascetic in his metaphysics, in saying (showing) with words what cannot be said, the mystical. Heidegger cannot be charged with such a metaphysical asceticism; he does not attempt to reduce the number of metaphysical statements to a minimum.

11

Dread expresses our attitude towards the world's "Jemeinigkeit," ("nature of being ever mine"). Dread does not relate to any object, because objects exist only within this world. Its "Jemeinigkeit" is not a quality *in* the world. It is a nothing. It is the object of the dread : nothing. This is Heidegger's solipsism.

In "Dasein", "Sein" is for Heidegger always "Jemeinigkeit." (*Sein und Zeit*, 42). In dread this *existential solipsism* is revealed. What is at stake is not any kind of categorical solipsism; only in the "Dasein" as conceived ontologically do we live in the loneliness of dread. This is so because the world is not something in which I find myself, but something which is always strange to me. (*Sein und Zeit*, 188).

The world is always my world, according to Wittgenstein. And : "I am my world". (5.63). But the metaphysical I does not belong to the world. In Heidegger : the "Jemeinigkeit" of "Dasein" (and thus that of the world, because "Dasein" is characterized by being "In-der-Welt-sein") is not a quality of the world. Likewise, for Wittgenstein the fact that I am my world is not a quality of the world. The solipsism thus becomes the basic philosophical position, the position from which the philosophical activity is carried on. This is, however, something which cannot be said, it shows itself (5.62).

On the view of Heidegger and Wittgenstein, the question of the existence of the outer world becomes meaningless. Solipsism usually implies that *the external world* is denied. Not so with Heidegger's and Wittgenstein's solipsism. For Heidegger : "Dasein" is always "In-der-Welt-sein" (*Sein und Zeit*, 202). For Wittgenstein : The world is always my world. (5.62; 5.63). The meaninglessness of the question is due to the fact that the two levels of consciousness meet here : "das Vorhandene" and "das Dasein," (Heidegger), say and show (Wittgenstein). If the existence of the external world is denied, this implies that "das Dasein" should not be "In-der-Welt-sein", (*Sein und Zeit*, 206), but "Dasein" should be something isolated from the world. It would be to regard "Dasein" as "vorhanden". If the existence of the external world is asserted, this implies that I am unaware that the assertion of the external world cannot take place in the world, but only in "das Dasein." This should imply that "das Vorhandene" would be put on a level with "das Dasein" (Heidegger), the world equated with the metaphysical Ego (Wittgenstein). "Das Dasein" should be transformed into "das Vorhandene" (Heidegger). "Der Grund dafür liegt im Verfallen des Daseins und der darin motivierten Verlegung des primären Seinsverständnisses auf das Sein als Vorhandenheit." (*Sein und Zeit*, 206). ("The reason for this is to be found in the decay of the Being-there and the shifting of the primary understanding of Being into the Being as Being-at-hand, which is motivated by it.") The inexpressible should be something *in* the world, should belong to that which can be said (Wittgenstein).

13

This same circumstance makes *the absolute doubt* impossible (*Sein und Zeit*, 226-229). To believe in the possibility of the absolute doubt is not to have the double awareness. It is to let the matter-of-fact-consciousness answer a question which concerns the relationship between the matter-of-fact-consciousness and the "that"-consciousness. It is to be unaware of the existential presuppositions of the thought. What thinks, is always the metaphysical Ego (Wittgenstein). The thinker is always bound to his "Dasein" (Heidegger).

"Then what we do in our language-game always rests on a tacit presupposition." (*Phil. Invest.*, 179e). Even *all* doubt is based on such existential presuppositions. Hence, the absolute doubt is an impossibility. The doubt is possible only as a language-game, and all language-games are determined by forms of life. "What has to be accepted, the given, is — so one could say — *forms of life*." (*Phil. Invest.*, 226e). The doubt presupposes itself a language-game and is thus already existentially determined by a form of life. "Doubting has an end." (*Phil. Invest.*, 180e). There the doubt *must* end (N. Malcolm : "Wittgenstein's Philosophical Investigations." *The Philosophical Review* 1954, 547).

According to the *Tractatus* : one can only doubt *within* the limits of the thinkable and the expressible. Doubt beyond those limits is a meaninglessness; what is said can be doubted, but not that which is shown. "Scepticism is *not* irrefutable, but palpably senseless, if it would doubt where a question cannot be asked." (6.51).

According to Heidegger : Of all truth — even the truth of the doubt — it holds that it "... *ist ... relativ auf das Sein des Daseins.*" (*Sein und Zeit*, 227). (" '... is ... related to the Being as the Being-there' "). "Dasein" is always "in the truth" (*Sein und Zeit*, 226), since the truth is a determination of Sein. Therefore the absolute doubt is an impossibility. The *real* sceptic need not be refuted; he has already done it himself, because he has "in der Verzweiflung des Selbstmords das Dasein und damit die Wahrheit ausgelöscht." (*Sein und Zeit*, 229). ("In the despair of the suicide he has extinguished the Being-there and the truth with it.").

Heidegger's and Wittgenstein's philosophy is existential presupposition-thinking; the thinking proceeds from something existentially given, from the concrete "Dasein" of the thinker (Heidegger), from the form of life of the thinker (*Phil. Invest.*). The philosophizing Ego is the metaphysical subject, which stands within the realm of the unthinkable and the inexpressible and from there sets the boundaries of the thinkable and expressible. (*Tractatus*). To ask sceptically for the basis of this, is, even for Heidegger, to ask a meaningless question, to which no answer is possible. "Dies Unmögliche liegt nicht daran, dass unser menschliches Denken zu solchem Erklären und Begründen unfähig ist. Vielmehr beruht das Unerklärbare und Unbegründbare des Weltens von Welt darin, dass so etwas wie Ursachen und Gründe dem Welten von Welt ungemäss bleiben." (*Vorträge und Aufsätze*, 178). ("That this is impossible does not lie in the fact that our human thinking is unsuited to give such explanation and reasons. Rather, the inexplicable of the world and the fact that no reason can be given for the world, e.g. that it is, is caused by the fact that such things as causes and reasons remain inappropriate to the world : that it is.").

IV

The *ontological* analysis by Heidegger is necessarily built upon the *existentialistic*. This Heidegger founds in the relationship "Sein" — "Dasein". For "Dasein" is in itself as "Dasein" ontological, is already (although concealed) related to "Sein". (*Sein und Zeit*, 13). Our thinking necessarily takes place here in this relationship. "*Kein Weg* des Denkens, auch nicht der des metaphysischen, geht vom Menschenwesen aus und von da zum Sein über oder umgekehrt vom Sein aus und dann zum Menschen zurück. Vielmehr *geht* jeder Weg des Denkens immer schon *innerhalb* des ganzen Verhältnisses von Sein und Menschenwesen, sonst ist es kein Denken." (*Was heisst Denken?*, 74; 28, 45; *Holzwege*, 81; *Einführung in die Metaphysik*, 106 ff., 110, 134.) ("No way of thinking — not even the metaphysical one — originates from human essence and therefrom passes to Being or, *vice versa*, originates from Being and passes back to man. Rather, every way of thinking *goes* always already *inside* the entire relation between Being and human essence, otherwise there is no thinking.").

But this *existentialistic analysis* of "Dasein", which is the condition of the ontological analysis of "Sein" and is not separable from it, is in its turn founded in *existential experience*. In the existential situation lies already preformed, in embryo, the existentialistic insight (which man, true enough, always flees). Not only is this ontological "Sein" combined with the existential "Dasein". But this "Dasein" is always given as ontic existential experience and has already as such "Vorverständnis" of the existentialistic-ontological "Sein". According to Heidegger's own philosophy the ontological-existentialistic analysis is necessarily founded in an ontic-existential position. The existential position, based on an experience which awakes the existentialistic-ontological insight, is very rare. It is not rare as experience, but only seldom can it be resolved into existentialistic-ontological insight (Heidegger feels alone among his contemporaries on this point).

Only from this ontical-existential experience, one of many experiences, comes the ontological-existential analysis into being. From this special experience the general analysis of "Dasein" can proceed. With this special experience as material the whole essence of "Dasein" is revealed (and because "Dasein" is in itself "Seinsverständnis", the essence of being is revealed with the essence of "Dasein"). Heidegger is therefore conscious of the fact that *all* truth, all knowledge, is founded and rooted in a particular *existential position*. Even Heidegger's own existentialistic analysis is thus existentially founded. Knowledge and thinking are parts of our general attitude towards life; they depend upon and express an attitude of life.

What corresponds to this in Wittgenstein is what he calls "*forms of life*" (*Phil. Invest.*, 226e).

Man's form of life determines man's language-game. Man's way of living and thinking decides what he lets pass as truth. "One could hardly place too much stress on the importance of this latter notion (form of life) in Wittgenstein's thought. It is intimately related to the notion "language-game". His choice of the latter term is meant to bring into prominence the fact that the *speaking* of language is part of an activity, or of a form of life." (23; of. 19). (N. Malcolm : "Wittgenstein's Philosophical Investigations". *The Philosophical Review* 1954, p. 550). This may be called Wittgenstein's existentialism.

But the implication and meaning of the ontological-existentialistic interpretation is by no means given through the dependence of Heidegger's ontical-existential position. According to Heidegger, his ontological interpretation is generally valid and universally applicable. His claim is hence at least as big as, for example, Hegel's. He will not present his ontical-existential position but an ontological-existentialistic interpretation. He will not present a view of the world or of life but an interpretation that comes "before" all views of life and the world and makes them possible.

But Heidegger is not unconscious of the fact that his ontological-existentialistic interpretation (whose Heideggerian originality he is well aware of) is founded in his own particular ontical-existential position. This ontological-existentialistic interpretation is given from an ontical-existential point of view. He has seen that all interpretation, in order to get started, must be driven by something in the individual philosopher (Heidegger), who does the interpretation. An ontological interpretation does not make itself, but is done by somebody, who must have an existential occasion for doing it and making it a part of his own history.

Expressed in Heidegger's own way : the truth is "ontisch nur im 'Subjekt' möglich —" (*Sein und Zeit*, 227). ("the truth is ontically possible only in the 'Subject' ").

Heidegger himself recognizes that his ontical-existential position is the cause of his ontology. This is where this article ties on to Heidegger himself. He has himself seen the circumstances which we try to clarify here. But by exposing this standpoint and the experience on which it is founded, no total view of Heidegger's philosophy is given. On the contrary, an exposition of this kind presupposes that Heidegger's ontology is not contemplated separately. It is impossible to consider it an important task to see the experience behind Heidegger's philosophy, and at the same time to move philosophically within this ontology. If the ontology with its universal claim is accepted, the determination of Heidegger's ontical-existential position should be a task of no value. Heidegger himself mentions it only to point out that he will *not* expose it. The ontical-existential position-experience is for Heidegger himself only the catalysator which starts the philosophical process. It does not itself participate in the philosophical process. Heidegger is not an existentialist in the ordinary sense except by being aware of the catalytic character of the existential position. (His existentialism has nothing directly to do with what Heidegger calls existence. See e.g. *Platons Lehre von der Wahrheit*, 77 ff.)

The later Wittgenstein is, as we use the word here, an existentialist in a more unlimited way. To him the existential position (forms of life) are not only catalysts. By deciding which language-games are played, the existential positions determine in an unlimited way what shall be taken for truth.

Heidegger does not make the ontical-existential position a central object of investigation. He does not consider "Sein", but something "Seiendes". In his own words, this is a form of "Verfallensein" ("Being-in-decay"). He will not give a new interpretation of something (not even of all) "Seiendes" but of "Sein". He is not at all interested in the "Seiende" upon which his own ontology builds. But *this* ontical-existential position of Heidegger is what this article seeks to attain by means of Heidegger's work with its ontological-existentialistic intentions. Different characteristics and concepts in Heidegger's philosophy must be guides to the central ontical-existential position, which "underlies" the centre of Heidegger's ontology. (We believe that we have seen this centre as far as it is relevant to our task.) *Only* that part of Heidegger's philosophy which is necessary to show this has been utilized.

In order to make Heidegger's ontical-existential position a central problem, as is done in this article, the framework of the discussion must not be Heidegger's ontology. That is, in this article, we do not accept Heidegger's claim that his ontology is universally valid. *Why* it is not accepted needs no explanation, only *that* it is not accepted. Only then is the task possible. That Heidegger himself — as already pointed out — has seen the relationship between his ontical-existential position and his ontology, does not imply that he means that it is possible to let this relationship be a central problem *within* his ontology. On the contrary, to do this is, according to Heidegger, a phenomenon of "Verfallensein".

An exposition of Heidegger's philosophy, so organized that the relationship ontical-existential and ontological-existentialistic was studied as a whole, could perhaps have been a successful undertaking. Only Heidegger's ontical-existential position will be explained here, not the problem of its relationship to the ontology as a whole, though the explanation necessarily comes from the ontological-existentialistic interpretation Heidegger has given his ontical-existential experience.

A total view of Heidegger's philosophy is perhaps implicit in this undertaking (but this total view of Heidegger's philosophy cannot be similar to Heidegger's own). It is, however, not necessary to acknowledge as true this implicit total view on Heidegger in order to recognize as correct this exposition of Heidegger's ontical-existential position. Even an incorrect view of Heidegger's philosophy as a whole may perhaps give suggestions and hints about it.

Already the exposition of Heidegger's ontical-existential position goes counter to his ontology. Moreover, even the comparison between Heidegger and Wittgenstein is impossible within Heidegger's ontological frame. For Wittgenstein cannot be interpreted as presenting an ontology in Heidegger's sense. And only in that case would a comparison within Heidegger's framework be possible. Nor can one exploit Wittgenstein as Heidegger, within his ontological interpretation, has exploited philosophers whose ontology he regards as false; for example, Plato and Nietzsche (this is possible only for Heidegger, not for one who stands outside Heidegger). "That"-experience and -consciousness does not "underlie" Wittgenstein's philosophy, as it underlies that of Heidegger. It is not a part of Wittgenstein's philosophy, although it is expressed in his philosophical writings and is, in my opinion, the prime mover of his philosophy. The "that"-consciousness is not the centre of what he says but the expression of that which, according to Wittgenstein, cannot be expressed : the mystical, (*Tractatus*). But that which lies beyond the expressible is the important. Wittgenstein's "that"-consciousness is not a part of his philosophy in the same way as in Heidegger. The consequence of this is that it is not necessary to evaluate Wittgenstein's philosophy (in the case of Heidegger, one had to reject the universal claim of his philosophy in order to make possible the present task). Towards Heidegger's philosophy a (negative) position must be taken; within Wittgenstein's philosophy no evaluation is necessary here, be it positive or negative (because the "that"-consciousness is not a part of his philosophy, but remains beyond its limit).

A comparison between two philosophers should usually fulfil one requirement : that it starts from the centre of these philosophers, so that the comparison does not become a comparison between disparate utterances, a comparison which is of no importance. This natural claim must here be rejected as impossible. A Heidegger-Wittgenstein comparison is rewarding, but not from their philosophical centre. The standard of comparison in Heidegger is not important to Heidegger. On the contrary, such a comparison as this shows that there has been no attention to that which is central for Heidegger. (On the other hand, as mentioned, he does not deny that even for him the ontological-existentialistic analysis depends on the ontical-existential experience.) The standard of comparison by Wittgenstein is not philosophically central to Wittgenstein; this is a consequence of the character of Wittgenstein's philosophy both in its earlier and in its later form. For Wittgenstein's philosophy is not a doctrinal system but Wittgenstein's philosophical activity. Therefore it is misleading to talk about a centre of his philosophy. On the other hand it is meaningful to ask for the motive power in his philosophical activity, and this article has tried to give *one* answer to this. Heidegger elevates himself above his existential "that"-consciousness to the ontological plane of philosophy. Because of this, he does not pay attention to the relationship between ontical-existential and ontological-existentialistic which he has seen himself. Because Heidegger regards his ontological analysis as simply universal for all ontical-existential experience, his own ontical-existential position cannot be of any interest. Wittgenstein, on the contrary, descends from his existential "that"-consciousness to the plane of philosophy in order to free philosophy from all claims to state something factually important (and in this negative way express the important realm of the inexpressible). Therefore Wittgenstein in his philosophy is not able to express his "that"-consciousness.[3]

*

I am heavily indebted to magister D. Føllesdal and Diplomübersetzer Ebba-Maria Dudde, and a philosopher who wishes to remain anonymous, for translations. Some translations are taken from Martin Heidegger : Existence and Being (1956).

[3] No distinction is here made between the earlier and the later Heidegger and Wittgenstein. The distinction is not denied, but it does not concern our task, which is to study the double awareness in both philosophers and see its origin in a "that"-experience. We don't ask whether and why the "that"-consciousness is purer or stronger in the earlier or the later Heidegger, or in the earlier or the later Wittgenstein. Sometimes a thought in the *Tractatus* is shown to have a parallel in the *Phil. Invest.* and *vice versa.* (This is done in order to bring into prominence that Wittgenstein's philosophy in all its stages had an existential foundation.)

HEIDEGGER'S CRITICISM OF WITTGENSTEIN'S CONCEPTION OF TRUTH

by

J. MORRISON

In *Being and Time* Heidegger characterizes the traditional concept of truth, which comprises three theses :

(1) The 'place' of truth is the statement (the judgment).
(2) The essence of truth lies in the 'correspondence' of the judgment with its object.
(3) Aristotle held theses (1) and (2).[1]

In a later work, *On the Essence of Truth*, he gives the following account of the traditional concept of truth. "A statement is true if what it means and says corresponds with the thing about which it speaks. Also we say here : it agrees (*es stimmt*). But now, what agrees is not the thing but rather the proposition." [2]

Heidegger goes on to say that this agreeing has a twofold character : "... on the one hand the agreement of a thing with is meant in advance about it and on the other hand the correspondence of what is meant in the statement with the thing." [3] That is, since the agreement or correspondence is a relation between two "terms" — the statement and the thing — it presupposes that *both* terms can enter into the relation, i.e., agree with one another. The two-fold character of this agreement is determined by

[1] Martin Heidegger, *Sein und Zeit*, 10. Aufl., (Tübingen : Max Niemeyer, 1963) 214. Hereafter : SZ. All translations of Heidegger's texts are my own. Here I translate "*Aussage*" as "statement", "*Urteil*" as "judgment," and "*Übereinstimmung*" as "correspondence." I will adhere to these renderings throughout.

[2] Martin Heidegger, *Vom Wesen der Wahrheit*, 4. Aufl. (Frankfurt am Main : Vittorio Klostermann, 1961) 7. Hereafter : WW. I translate "*Satz*" by "proposition" and "*stimmen*" by "agree". Note that "*stimmen*" is the root word of "*Übereinstimmen*," "to correspond."

[3] WW 7.

these two "aspects" of the relation : the first is the "objective" aspect, where the thing corresponds to the statement or what is meant by the statement, the second is the "linguistic" aspect where the statement or what it means corresponds to the thing. The first is "objective truth," the second "propositional truth." [4]

In this essay I propose to discuss Heidegger's first two theses about the traditional concept of truth ((1) and (2) above) [5] in terms of Wittgenstein's own concept of truth as it is presented in his *Tractatus Logico-Philosophicus*. My main purpose in doing so is to see to what extent Heidegger's criticism of this concept is *relevant* to Wittgenstein and what this criticism really is. That is, I wish to generate a philosophical "dialogue" between these two thinkers who, on the face of it, are worlds apart in their philosophical methods, aims, interests, and conclusions. Many philosophers today, especially those in the English-speaking world, would seriously doubt the possibility of such a dialogue. Even if they admitted that Heidegger's views are meaningful and important they might suppose that what he says is not really relevant to the kinds of problems Wittgenstein, or any other philosopher sharing his philosophical tradition, is concerned with. Thus, my first task is to show what Heidegger says about the traditional concept of truth is *relevant* to Wittgenstein. Second, in order to show the *force* of his criticisms they must be presented in such a way that they can be seen to meet Wittgenstein on his own terms. To achieve this a mere confrontation of two opposing philosophical positions must be avoided, at least so far as this is possible. Such an arbitrary confrontation would simply beg the question and lead nowhere. Rather, it must be shown that Heidegger's criticisms point out the inadequacies of Wittgenstein's position *from within*, and that these inadequacies point to, and can only be overcome by, Heidegger's own position. Heidegger's criticism of the traditional ("correspondence") theory of truth is that it is ultimately inadequate, i.e., it is only *a partial* and *hence dependent* explication of the nature of truth, and thus requires a foundation in a radically different understanding of truth, which understanding Heidegger claims to provide. Thus, I must try to show the nature of, and reasons for, this partiality and dependence. In the end, I hope to have indicated why a radically new rethinking of the essence of truth is necessary, and that Heidegger himself has opened up the path for this rethinking. I have

[4] Cf. WW 7 *passim*.

[5] I omit any explicit discussion of thesis (3) which deals with Aristotle's relationship to the traditional theory, since this question is not directly relevant to my purpose.

tried to keep to a minimum any discussion of Heidegger's own positive views on the essence of truth, since this would lead beyond the scope of this paper. I will begin by discussing thesis (2) (above) — that the essence of truth is a correspondence between judgment and object — and will then turn to thesis (1) — that the "place" of truth is the judgment. However, I wish to emphasize that this division is adopted only for the purposes of exposition. It will be seen that they are both intimately related, and that this relationship is a necessary one.

A. The essence of truth

First, let us examine the second thesis which Heidegger claims characterizes the traditional concept of truth.

> The essence of truth lies in the 'correspondence' of the judgment with its object.[6]

Does this thesis apply to Wittgenstein's concept of truth? I think it does in all essential respects. To see this, let us first consider the passage from *On the Essence of Truth* quoted above. According to it, the traditional view has four basic constituents which I will indicate here by (a), (b), (c) and (d) : a statement (a), what the statement means and says (*meint und sagt*) (b), the "thing" the statement is about (c), and the "relation" of corresponding (d). Now, each of these constituents can be found in Wittgenstein. For Wittgenstein truth is the agreement (d) of the sense (*Sinn*) (b) of a logical picture or proposition (*Satz*) (a) with reality (*Wirklichkeit*) (c). Compare the following two remarks :

> What a picture represents is its sense. (2.221)[7]

> The correspondence or non-correspondence of its sense with reality constitutes its truth or falsity. (2.222)

Let us examine each of these in detail. In regard to (a) Wittgenstein talks about a picture (*Bild*) and Heidegger about statements (*Aussagen*). Heidegger also uses the term "*Satz*"-"proposition". For Wittgenstein, a picture, i.e., a *logical* picture, is a proposition, and what he means by

[6] SZ 214.

[7] Ludwig Wittgenstein, *Tractatus Logico-Philosophicus*, trans. by Pears and McGuinness (London : Routledge & Kegan Paul, 1961). All references are to this edition, though I will not always follow the translators' renderings. Also, in the case of direct quotations, instead of giving page numbers I will simply give the number of the passage.

proposition and picture is basically what Heidegger means by statement. In regard to (b), Heidegger talks about "what the statement means or says." Wittgenstein also distinguishes between the proposition or statement and what it means or says. For him, what a statement means or says is its *sense* (*Sinn*), for it is by means of its sense that a statement, proposition or picture can picture (*bilden*) reality or the world. The condition for the *possibility* of a proposition-picture is its logical form, which it has in common with reality (2.16 ff). Further, reality (*Wirklichkeit*) or the world (*Welt*) are ultimately reducible to facts, in particular, the existence or non-existence of states of affairs (*Sachverhalten*) (1-1.21). Thus, in regard to (c) — the "thing" the statement is about — what Wittgenstein means by world, reality, fact, state of affairs — is basically identical with what Heidegger means by things (*Sachen*). Finally, in regard to (d), — the relation of correspondence — both Heidegger and Wittgenstein use the term "*Übereinstimmigkeit*".

So far it looks fairly obvious that Wittgenstein does indeed hold the view which Heidegger terms the traditional concept of truth. But it may be objected that Wittgenstein makes subtle distinctions between world, fact, reality and state of affairs. This is no doubt true, but I do not think these distinctions are relevant here. Also, it may be objected that Wittgenstein uses the term "*Sachen*" to mean the same as "*Gegenstand*" (object) (2.01). And since for him objects are radically different from facts, the term "*Sachen*" cannot be applied to facts. But it must be remembered that Wittgenstein gives a quite technical meaning to "*Gegenstand*" and "*Sache*", and Heidegger is using the latter term in a loose and non-technical sense. Thus, I think it is correct to say that what Heidegger means by "*Sachen*" applies to what Wittgenstein means by facts, reality, world and states of affairs. Secondly, these same considerations should, I think, show that Wittgenstein's view also falls under what Heidegger in *Being and Time* calls the second thesis of the traditional idea of truth, namely, that the *essence* of truth is the correspondence of the judgement (*Urteil*) with the object (*Gegenstand*). Here Heidegger again uses "*Übereinstimmung*", but instead of "*Aussage*" he uses "*Urteil*", and instead of "*Sache*" "*Gegenstand*".But again, it is obvious from the context that he is construing these terms very broadly, and it would therefore be incorrect to make any sharp distinction between them. So much then, for a preliminary characterization of Wittgenstein's views in terms of Heidegger's formulation of the traditional view of truth. Let us now examine Heidegger's argument in more detail, first in regard to the notion of *correspondence*.

The correspondence of the statement with the thing is taken to be a *relation* (*Beziehung*) between the two. Heidegger then asks, what is the nature or basis of this relation? Now, every correspondence is a relation, but not every relation is one of correspondence. For example, a *sign* (*Zeichen*) relates to something else by pointing to or indicating it, but in doing so it does not correspond or "agree" with it.[8] Further, all instances of correspondence are not like the corresponding of a (true) statement with a thing or fact. Equality (*Gleichheit*), for example, is both a relation and a *way* of correspondence.[9] Thus, two 5-Mark pieces are equal to one another in the sense that their shapes correspond, e.g., they are coincident and "look alike".[10] But the statement and the thing are not equal in this sense, for they neither "look alike" nor physically coincide. Thus, their agreement or correspondence is *not* that of a relation of equality between two *things*, but between a statement and a thing.

> In what, however, are the thing and statement supposed to correspond, where the things referred to are obviously different in their appearances? How can the completely unequal, the statement, approximate (*Angleichen*) itself to the coin? [11]

Wittgenstein, I think, may have an answer to this problem. Having agreed with Heidegger that the correspondence of statement (picture) and thing (fact) cannot be grounded in a material likeness [12] he nevertheless holds that there must be some kind of likeness between them — they must have something in common.

> If a fact is to be a picture, it must have something in common (*gemeinsam*) with what it depicts. (2.16)

> There must be something identical (*identisch*) in a picture and what it depicts, to enable the one to be a picture of the other at all. (2.161)

For Wittgenstein, what picture and fact have in common is pictorial form (2.17) which in turn is grounded in logical form (2.181-2). These notions of logical and pictorial form are the core of Wittgenstein's conception of meaning. A proposition can have sense, i.e., can picture a possible state of affairs, only because it shares a common logical form

[8] SZ 215.

[9] SZ 214-5.

[10] WW 10.

[11] WW 10.

[12] An instance of a material likeness (in addition to the example of the two coins) is that between a portrait and the person portrayed. Both have roughly the same material properties, e.g., colour, size and shape.

with that state of affairs. Whether or not a proposition corresponds with a fact cannot be determined *a priori*, i.e., by determining that they have (and must have) an identical logical form. The logical form is only the condition for the possibility of correspondence. But if this correspondence is *actual*, then the proposition is *true*. Wittgenstein's theory of truth is thus grounded in his theory of meaning, the identity of logical and pictorial form between proposition and fact. Without this identity of form propositions could not "picture" facts, hence could have no sense, and hence could never be true.

By means of his notion of logical form Wittgenstein *seems* to have answered the question of the necessary condition for the *possibility* of correspondence. But this is so only at a superficial level, for certain fundamental problems remain. For example, has he really clarified the "relation" of correspondence *itself*? In *Being and Time* Heidegger maintains that what is true — what corresponds — is *not* the psychical process of judg*ing* but rather the "ideal content" (*idealen Gehalt*) of the judgment.[13] This ideal content is what Wittgenstein means by the pictorial form of the proposition. Truth, then, seems to be a "relation" between the ideal content of the proposition (judgment) and the fact (what is judged). But Heidegger goes on to ask a further question : Is this relation *itself* ideal or real?

Thus, it seems that the relation of correspondence is not identical with the ideal content (pictorial form) of the judgment which makes possible this correspondence. This suspicion can be substantiated by the following consideration. It is the ideal content of the judgment that is true, and it is true in virtue of its correspondence with what is judged. This correspondence relation is not *itself* "true" and hence is not identical with the ideal content of the judgment (pictorial form). Thus, we seem no closer to determing the *nature* of the correspondence relation. In *On the Essence of Truth*, Heidegger talks about the correspondence of statement and thing in terms of an approximation (*Angleichung*) of the former to the latter. But this notion throws no light on the problem of the relation of statement and thing, since this is already presupposed.

> The essence of approximation is determined rather out of the kind of relationship which holds between the statement and the thing. So long as this "relationship" remains undetermined and ungrounded in its essence, any argument about the possibility and impossibility, about the kind and degree of the approximation, remains empty.[14]

[13] SZ 216. Wittgenstein, of course, accepts this distinction and the implied separation of psychology from logic and theory of meaning.

[14] WW 10-11.

Heidegger suggests the following analysis in terms of the notion of representation (*Vorstellung*) :

> The statement about the coin relates 'itself' however to this thing while it represents (*vor-stellt*) it and says of what is re-presented how it is with it ... The representing statement says of the represented thing that it is *such as* it is. This 'such-as' (*so-wie*) concerns the re-presenting and its re-presented.[15]

Further, Heidegger defines re-presenting as a non-psychological "letting-stand-against (*Entgegenstehenlassen*) of the thing as object".[16] Compare this with the following remarks by Wittgenstein :

> What a picture represents (*darstellt*) is its sense. (2.221)
>
> A proposition shows (*zeigt*) its sense.
>
> A proposition *shows* how things stand *if* it is true. And it *says that* they do so stand. (4.022)

Although Wittgenstein uses "*darstellen*" rather than Heidegger's "*vorstellen*" the thought is basically the same. To say that a proposition is a *picture* of reality is just to say (in Heidegger's sense) that it *re*-presents it such-as it is by saying *how* it is. If the re-presented (the proposition-picture) "corresponds" with the presented (the fact) it is true, if not, it is false.

But *how* is this re-presenting possible, i.e., how can an object-fact be re-presented? Heidegger answers this by saying that the object must be *able* to "appear" (*Erscheinen*), that is, it must be able to become something that is open (*das Offenbare*). But to become something-that-is-open, to be *able* to appear, there is presupposed a region (*Bereich*) "in" which this can (or does) take place. In *On the Essence of Truth* Heidegger calls this region the Open (*das Offene*). In *Kant and the Problem of Metaphysics* and *Being and Time* such a "region" is called a horizon (*Horizont*). Thus, time is the "horizon" of the Being-process, the coming-to-presence of beings as such, i.e., their manifesting themselves as beings. Here Heidegger is following Kant, who speaks of time as a pure form of intuition, that which makes possible the appearing of any and all phenomena as objects of knowledge. For Kant, time is the horizon within which the object, *qua* object of knowledge and experience, becomes something-that-is-open (*das Offenbare*). And since Kant conceives *all* knowledge and experience as a re-presenting of what is "given", time as the Open is a necessary condition for the possibility of anything becoming an object-of-knowl-

[15] WW 11.
[16] WW 11.

edge, i.e., a re-presentation. In other words, knowledge and re-presentation *presuppose* a temporal horizon "within" which they can be manifested. So for Heidegger, the openness (*Offenheit*) of the Open is a necessary condition for something becoming-open, for its "appearing". To re-present something — to let it stand opposed to us as object — presupposes that the "something" is already open to us, i.e., is something which *can* be represented. Thus, representation does not first *create* the openness of what-is-open (*das Offenbare*).[17] Rather, it is the reverse.

Heidegger tends to conceive the Open as a "matrix of relationships" (*Verhältnisse*) or potentialities in *Being and Time*. This "matrix" is the world (*Welt*), as understood in the context of the being-in-the-world (*Sein-in-der-Welt*) of Dasein. It is *because* Dasein's mode of Being is that of being-in-the-world that it *can* relate itself or "behave" (*verhalten sich*) towards beings in various ways, e.g., by knowing them theoretically, handling them as tools, etc. But these ways of behaviour in turn presuppose that beings are open, i.e., are manifest *as beings*, since all behaving is related to beings of one kind or another.

Now, the asserting and uttering of propositions are *ways* of behaving. In particular, they are ways of behaving "towards" things, or what Wittgenstein calls states of affairs (*Sachverhalten*).[18] But we have already seen that for Heidegger behaving always presupposes a "context," a matrix of relations (*Verhältnisse*) which makes it possible. (In *On the Essence of Truth* this is the Open, and in *Being and Time* it is the world.) Further, truth as the correspondence of proposition and state of affairs is the "result" of such behaving when (and only when) it is "successful", i.e., when the proposition is "correctly" applied to the state-of-affairs. We then say, following Wittgenstein, that the proposition is true, it corresponds to the fact (thing), it is correct (*richtig*). In short, the proposition re-presents the state of affairs *as* and *how* it is. But, as Heidegger has shown, this necessarily takes place in the region of the Open. The Open is a region "... within which the being can place (*stellen*) itself uniquely as that which and how it is, and can become sayable (*sagbar*)." [19]

[17] WW 11.

[18] Note too that Heidegger's term for "behaviour" or "relating oneself" — "*verhalten*" — is the root word of Wittgenstein's term for states of affairs (facts) — "*Sachverhalten.*" The latter thus means literally : "relations-of-things". What Heidegger means by world (*Welt*) was expressed above as a "matrix of relationships." Wittgenstein defines "*Welt*" as the *totality* of *Sachverhalten* (cf. 1.1-2) This "etymological" coincidence brings them close together, but the basic differences remain.

[19] WW 11.

Then and only then, can the being be "pictured", re-presented, expressed in a true proposition.

Heidegger's argument against Wittgenstein is now becoming clearer. Truth as correspondence between proposition and fact is grounded in the possibility of a *prior* openness of beings. Beings must first manifest themselves as and how they are before one can *say* (truly) how they are, i.e., say "what is the case". Wittgenstein tries to explain how it is possible for a proposition and fact to correspond in terms of an "agreeing" of form of proposition and fact. But as Heidegger shows, this "agreeing" itself presupposes that the fact *as such* is already manifest. Truth as correspondence presupposes the possibility of an *ontological* making-manifest, a becoming open. A fact, *qua* fact, is re-presentable. But to be *re*-presentable presupposes that it be presented. And it is the latter problem which takes us beyond the realm of proposition and fact into ontology, i.e., forces us to question the very *possibility* of *how* a fact or any kind of being can, as such, be presented.

But this ontological question of how it is possible for a being or fact to be present as such is a question that Wittgenstein did not, and indeed *could* not raise. And this failure is itself a necessary consequence of his own view of truth. "Truth" (*Wahrheit*) is reducible to the multiplicity of true propositions (*Wahre*), which in turn are defined in terms of states of affairs (facts). What cannot be pictured as a fact cannot be "a truth" or true. But the question of how it is possible for a fact to be present as such is not itself a question *about* facts, since all questions about facts presuppose that there *are* facts, the very problem at issue. Hence, no "truth" can be stated about any ontological question at all; indeed, ontological questions cannot even be *raised.*

This failure to raise the ontological question about the possibility of there being facts, and the failure to make a fundamental distinction between the essence of truth (*Wahrheit*) and particular truths (*Wahre*), e.g., true propositions, are closely related. This relationship, as well as the necessity of distinguishing "the true" from truth and the ultimate dependence of the former on the latter, is brought out by Heidegger in a discussion of Leibniz in *On the Essence of the Ground.*[20] In this work Heidegger quotes a passage from Leibniz's *Primae Veritates*, in which Leibniz tries to show that the *principium rationis — nihil esse sine ratione, seu nullum effectum esse absque causa* [21] — is *derived* from the nature of

[20] Martin Heidegger, *Vom Wesen des Grundes*, 5. Aufl. (Frankfurt am Main : Vittorio Klostermann, 1965). Hereafter : WG.

[21] "Nothing is without a reason, or nothing is effected without a cause."

truth, which in turn is analyzed into the *identity* of predicate and subject. That is, all first truths (*ersten Wahrheiten*), like the principle of reason, presuppose truth (*Wahrheit*) in general, the essence of which is identity (*Identität*). The latter is the "birth" of the *principium rationis*. Further, since this identity is that of the subject and its predicates the essence of truth is the *connexio* of the latter. Thus, to say that something has no reason is to say that there is a "truth" which cannot be analyzed into identities of the subject-predicate form. But for Leibniz this is impossible, since such a "truth" transgresses against the "nature" of truth in general.[22]

Now, Leibniz has distinguished between (particular) truths and the essence of truth as such, and grounded the former in the latter. But, according to Heidegger, his distinction is not radical enough. This can be seen by noting that the essence of truth, like the particular truth (e.g., the *principium rationis*) it grounds, is *also* defined in terms of the *statement*. In Leibniz's case, the identity is that of the subject of the statement with its predicates. Thus, Leibniz's view implicitly rests on Aristotle's concept of truth as statement — propositional-truth (*Satz-Wahrheit*).[23] For Leibniz, the predicate "inheres" (*inesse*) in the subject. In particular, this inherence is inherence as "sameness" (*Idem esse*). Heidegger concludes that for Leibniz :

> Truth means according to this the agreement (*Einstimmigkeit*), which for its part is such only as correspondence (*Über-einstimmigkeit*), with that which declares itself in the identity as one. The 'truths' — true statements — take their nature with reference to something *on the ground of which* they are able to be agreements.[24]

According to Heidegger, his discussion of Leibniz has shown that the latter's determination of the essence of truth as a characteristic *of statements* is an "indispensable but derived" one.

> The correspondence of the nexus (of subject-predicate) *with* the being and its consequent agreement do not *as such* make the being primarily accessible.[25]

These beings, as that which the statement is *about*, must *already* be manifest (*offenbar*). This manifestation itself is obviously *not* of the subject-predicate character, and hence propositional truth (*Satzwahrheit*) is grounded in a more original truth which is a pre-predicative unhidden-

[22] WG 11.
[23] WG 11-12.
[24] WG 12.
[25] WG 12.

ness (*Unverborgenheit*) or openness of beings.[26] The essence of truth, therefore, must be radically distinguished from the totality of particular truths and sought in the openness and unhiddenness of beings themselves. It is the latter which points to the genuine *ontological* truth of being, i.e., their Being (*Sein*). Like Leibniz, Wittgenstein did not see this because he did not ask the ontological question of the possibility of there being facts at all, that is, the question of their *Being*. He merely "postulates" *that* there are facts and that the totality of these constitute the world, since this is the "ontology" to which his conception of language, meaning and truth commits him.

An "ontology", like Wittgenstein's, which "postulates" the reality of certain kinds of beings on the basis of a prior conception of language is not ontology in Heidegger's sense. The former view makes "ontology" *relative* to language. That is, *given* a certain "language" or conception of language it is then asked which ontological "commitments" (if any) one has, i.e., what kinds of beings are ontologically presupposed by that language. Aside from the fact that such "ontological presupposition" is itself problematic and unclear, this view never reaches what is for Heidegger the essential question of ontology, namely, how are such beings possible, what is their Being (*Sein*)? Genuine fundamental ontology has for its theme Being and the Being of beings (entities, things-that-are). It asks after the Being of beings (*das Sein der Seienden*) and thus cannot take for granted that there *are* such entities, that they are "presupposed" in the sense of "ontological commitments". To say, for example, that language presupposes the ontological reality of facts merely assumes that such beings have *Being*, i.e., are possible. Since Wittgenstein does not ask after the Being or possibility of facts he remains on the merely *ontic* level (in Heidegger's sense) and never approaches the ontological question of Being itself. At the same time his view *assumes* Being, since it assumes that facts are possible, that *there are facts*, which is just to say that facts *have Being*.

It may be replied here that Wittgenstein's view of objects (*Gegenstände*) as the *constituents* of states of affairs is his attempt to deal with this problem. But it must be remembered that objects, through their "hanging together" (*zusammenhangen*) form the mere *structure* of the fact, they do not form the horizon or region — the Open — within which facts are encounterable as such. Wittgenstein's objects are intended to serve quite another function, namely, that of grounding the theory of meaning by

[26] WG 12.

serving as the simple referents of logically proper names. Without such referring propositions would have no sense (*Sinn*), since they would have no "point of contact" with reality. In other words, simple objects are a prerequisite of meaningful discourse, and their nature, function and necessity can be understood only within the context of the problem of meaning. The problem Heidegger raises is a problem of ontology proper, not of "postulating" quasi-ontological entities as a necessary condition of meaningful language. Wittgenstein remains solidly in the realm of *metaphysics* in Heidegger's sense, i.e., the realm of beings. He sees that facts are a necessary presupposition for there being true propositions, but the question of the very possibility of such facts, the question of their Being (*Sein*), is not, and indeed cannot, be raised.

Let us look at Wittgenstein's "ontology" more closely. What is ontologically "real" for Wittgenstein — what exists — are facts.

> The world (*Welt*) is all that is the case. (1) The world is the totality of facts (*Tatsachen*), not of things (*Dinge*). (1.1)
>
> What is the case — a fact — is the existence of states of affairs (*Sachverhalten*) (2).
>
> A state of affairs is a combination of object (things) (2.01).[27]

Now, facts are what the sense of propositions depicts, and are what makes them true (or false). Thus, when Wittgenstein says the world, as the totality of facts, is "all that is the case" we may take him to mean that the world, considered "ontologically", simply *is* the referent of all true propositions. And since all significant (*sinnvoll*) language is that which states facts, the world *is* what we can (significantly) *say* it is. The world cannot, for example, consist of *objects* because these can only be named, and since to name something is not to represent, depict, describe or picture it, one could not *say* anything about such a "world". In other words, Wittgenstein's "ontology" of facts is a necessary presupposition of his theory of meaning and truth, which holds that all significant and true discourse is that of stating facts. *Given* the latter position, no other "ontology" is possible, since one could not *say* anything about it and hence it is unthinkable and nonsensical (*unsinnig*). The theory of objects and logically proper names is in turn a necessary presupposition for there being propositions and facts, since without names and the objects they denote (*bedeuten*) a proposition's sense would depend on the actual truth of another proposition, which in turn would imply that the first

[27] "*Der Sachverhalt ist eine Verbindung von Gegenständen* (*Sachen, Dingen*)."

proposition had no sense. To avoid an infinite regress the sense of a proposition must be determinable independent of its or any other proposition's truth (2.021 ff).

This points to another serious difficulty of Wittgenstein's position. We said earlier that the correspondence of proposition and fact consists of *both* an agreement of the former to the latter, and vice-versa. That is, *if* a proposition is to agree with or picture a fact it must have a form *in common* with it, that is, it must have the same logical form. What he has *not* shown, and indeed, what has not even presented itself to him as a *problem* is what is the ground of the possibility for logical form *itself.* Now, since logical form is the "common" element between proposition and fact it is presupposed *if* there is to be agreement and hence true propositions. And given the concept of logical form Wittgenstein seems to be able to answer the question not only of how a proposition can agree with a fact but also how the fact can agree with the proposition, i.e., enter into the "relation" of correspondence with it. Heidegger, however, is aware not only that both "directions" of agreement must be accounted for if anything like truth as correspondence is to be adequately articulated, but he also sees that the condition (ground) for *this* possibility is *itself* problematic. How is *it* possible? Or, in terms of Wittgenstein, what is the ground for the possibility of logical form? For Wittgenstein, the logical form "common" to both proposition and fact is ultimately a "postulate" since without it propositions could not "picture" facts and hence could not "correspond" to them, i.e., be true. Logical form implies a kind of "pre-established harmony" between proposition and fact, language and the world. The question now is, how is this "harmony" *itself* possible? Is there a ground for the agreement of the logical form "common" to both proposition and fact? Wittgenstein himself, of course, does not even *raise* this question, much less answer it. Indeed, given his own conception of meaning it could *not* be raised.[28] But, according to Heidegger, this problem *was* raised in medieval philosophy.

The traditional theory of truth was formulated in medieval philosophy as follows : *veritas est adaequatio rei et intellectus.* Now, as Heidegger points out, this formulation as it stands is ambiguous. "It can mean : the

[28] Of course, strictly speaking, the question of logical form itself (aside from that of its possibility) cannot be raised either, since it is not a question *about* facts but rather a question about the possibility of the picturing of facts by propositions and of the possibility of their truth. Wittgenstein was also quite aware of this, since he ultimately rejects his own "questions" and "answers" as nonsensical (*unsinnig*), as trying to "say" what cannot be said.

approximation (*Angleichung*) of the thing to knowledge. It can however also say : truth is the approximation of knowledge to the thing".[29] But the former *grounds* the possibility of the latter, i.e. the intellect (knowledge) *can* approximate to the thing only because the thing is already "adequate" to it. "Yet conceptual truth (*begriffene Wahrheit*), propositional truth (*Satzwahrheit*), is only possible on the ground of objective truth (*Sachwahrheit*), the *adaequatio rei ad intellectum*." [30] Now, for the medieval philosophers, the adequacy of thing to intellect was grounded in the doctrine of creation. That is, God, the divine intellect (*intellectus divinus*), created both the (human) intellect and the things (the world). Thus both, in their actuality, are "adequate" to a preconceived thought in God's infinite intellect. Every thing, as a thing created by God, "agrees with" the idea of it in God's intellect. The human intellect, which is itself created, approximates to the divine one to the extent that it "agrees with" the things, i.e., asserts true propositions. And the possibility of such asserting is in turn grounded in the "adequacy" of both things and finite intellect to their idea in God's intellect and their common origin in His creation.

> The possibility of the truth of human knowledge, if all beings (*Seiende*) are 'creatures,' is grounded in the fact that thing and proposition (*Sache und Satz*) are correct to the idea (*Ideerecht*) and therefore, out of the unity of the divine plan of creation, are adequate (*zugerichtet*) to one another.[31]

What this reference to medieval philosophy is intended to illustrate is simply that the adequacy of intellect and thing — for Wittgenstein, the common logical form of propositions and facts — is *itself* problematic, in that the question of *its* possibility, its Being, is not "self-evident" and must be raised. The implication is that, since Wittgenstein did not and could not raise it, his view is inadequate and without a foundation. Again, all ontic phenomena require an ontological grounding, i.e., the question of their Being must be raised and treated thematically.

B. The "place" of truth

As we have seen, according to Heidegger's treatment of the traditional idea of truth (as in *Being and Time*) the latter consists of two fundamental theses. The thesis that the essence (*Wesen*) of truth lies in the correspon-

[29] WW 7.
[30] WW 7.
[31] WW 8.

dence (*Übereinstimmen*) of judgment and object has already been discussed. The other thesis, that the "place" (*Ort*) of truth is the statement or judgment is essentially related to the first. Both views, according to Heidegger, originated in Greek philosophy, and in particular, with Plato. A close examination of their origin and development will reveal the essential bond between them. In short, for Heidegger, the view that truth is the correspondence of statement and thing leads to the view that the statement is the locus of truth, and vice-versa. It is not merely a question of which view arose first in time (historically), but of seeing that this common ground is the "forgetting" (*vergessen*) of the original *ontological* meaning of truth as un-hiddenness (*a-letheia, Unverborgenheit*).

In Heidegger, the forgetting of the original ontological meaning of truth and the arising of the traditional theory of truth are ultimately one and the same. They have a common philosophical origin and occur at the same time in the history of philosophy. Heidegger's claim in this regard is that Plato is the beginning of this process, and Aristotle, the "father of logic", establishes it securely for the subsequent philosophical tradition, down to Nietzsche and our own time. Heidegger sees the roots of the traditional theory at the core of Plato's allegory of the cave in the *Republic.* Heidegger claims that this allegory about the "education" of the soul also contains Plato's "doctrine" (*Lehre*) of truth, although this doctrine is left "unsaid" explicitly. Nevertheless, it can be uncovered through a careful study of and philosophical reflection upon what Plato does explicitly say. More particularly, on the basis of what Plato says in the allegory of the cave about the "education" or "tendence" (*paideia, Bildung*) of the soul we can discern "... a shift (*Wendung*) in the determination of the essence of truth." [32] Let us see how this "shift" takes place.

> '*Paideia*' means the turning-around of the whole man in the sense of a transplanting out of the region of what is proximally encountered into another realm in which beings themselves appear.[33]
>
> That which is always unhidden to man and the manner of the unhiddenness must be changed. Unhiddenness in Greek means *aletheia,* which word is translated as 'truth.' [34]

Further, the various "levels" or "abodes" of the cave represent the various "levels" or degrees of unhiddenness, or truth. What is most unhidden relative to the soul is not necessarily what is most unhidden in itself.

[32] Martin Heidegger, *Platons Lehre von der Wahrheit*, 2. Aufl. (Bern : Franke, 1954) 5. Hereafter : PLW.

[33] PLW 25-6.

[34] PLW 26.

Thus, education consists basically of leading the soul away from what is least unhidden in itself towards what is most unhidden in itself, so that the soul will not confuse what seems most unhidden to *it* with what is most unhidden in *itself.*

It is not until the *third* level that the idea (*eidos*), what is most unhidden (true) in itself, emerges as the ground or *essence* of the unhiddenness of what appears (*das Erscheinende*). That which appears in this sense is the phenomenon. But at the fourth (and last) level the *transition* in the essence of truth begins. This transition is reflected by Plato's conception of the relation between education, truth, and idea. "The 'idea' does not just let something else (behind it) 'appear', it itself is what appears, it itself is the basis for its own appearing. The *idea* is the apparent." [35] The idea "brings into sight and offers to be seen", the thing as unhidden. "And so the unhidden is conceived primarily and solely as what is perceived in the act of perceiving the idea, as what is known (*gignoskemenon*) in the act of knowing (*gignoskein*)." [36] The apparentness of the idea thus becomes *relative* to the see*ing*. The "supreme" idea, the idea of the Good (*to agathon*) is that which "holds together" the knowing and what is known, i.e., *nous* and *noein*, and the ideas. It is that which is the most shining, the most apparent (phenomenal) of all beings.[37]

The substance of Heidegger's argument is as follows : Plato's allegory shows how the idea became "master" of *aletheia*. "*Aletheia* comes under the yoke of the idea"; the idea becomes both the "master" of truth and the "dispenser" of unhiddenness. The essence of truth "... shifts its abode to the essence of the idea. The essence of truth relinquishes the basic feature of unhiddenness." Since truth is grounded in the idea — the "outward appearance" (*Aussehens*) — it must be *seen.* Hence, a "right glancing" (*rechte Blicken*) becomes necessary, and *paideia* becomes the process of *seeing* correctly. "The transition from one situation (in the cave) into another consists in the becoming-correct of the glancing. Everything depends on the *orthodotes*, the correctness of the glancing." [38] There must be "... a correspondence (*Übereinstimmung*) of the knowing with the thing itself. Truth turns into orthodotes, the correctness (*Richtigkeit*) of perceiving and stating." [39] Heidegger's basic point is expressed in these words :

[35] PLW 34-5.
[36] PLW 35.
[37] PLW 35-6.
[38] PLW 41.
[39] PLW 42.

> In the change of the essence of truth a shift of the place of truth comes about at the same time. As unhiddenness truth is still a basic feature of beings themselves. As correctness of 'glancing' however truth becomes the designation of human conduct (*Verhaltens*) towards beings.[40]

For Heidegger, Plato's conception of truth is radically ambiguous due to his wavering between truth as a characteristic of beings themselves (ultimately of the ideas) and of the human ability to see and 'glance correctly'.[41]

Let me summarize the core of Heidegger's general argument as follows. Truth was originally conceived in early Greek philosophy (by Heraclitus and Parmenides) as *a-letheia* — unhiddenness (*Unverborgenheit*). Moreover, it was beings themselves, or more exactly their Being (*Sein*, *ousia*, *physis*) which was the un-hidden, the Truth. With Plato, however, given the notion of Being as *idea* and of *paideia* (the education of the soul) as a turning of the soul away from the appearances or phenomenal "copies" to the ideas themselves, a subtle transition begins to take place. The "place" of truth is not only the idea itself (Being), but it is necessary to "glance correctly" or "glance to the right place" in order to "see" this truth. Thus, the "place" of truth "shifts" to the soul and its glan*cing*. With this shift in the place of truth there is simultaneously a shift in the *essence* of truth. The essence of truth tends to become identified with the "correct glancing" itself, i.e., truth becomes "correctness", and ultimately agreement and correspondence.

In the *Introduction to Metaphysics* Heidegger connects these changes in the essence and "place" of truth with a parallel change in the essence of *logos*.

> Initially the logos as gathering (*Sammlung*) *is* the happening (*Geschehen*) of unhiddenness... Now the logos as statement becomes on the contrary the place of truth in the sense of correctness. This turns into the principle of *Aristotle*, according to which the logos as statement is that which can be true or false. Truth, originally unhiddenness, a happening of the dominate beings themselves and governed through the gathering, becomes now a property (*Eigenschaft*) of the logos.[42]

Thus, the two doctrines, that the *essence* of truth is correctness (correspondence, agreement, etc.) and that the *place* of truth is the statement

[40] PLW 42.

[41] Heidegger goes on to trace this same ambiguity in Aristotle, who locates truth in the understanding (*dianoia*, *Verstand*) and makes *aletheia* the opposite of *pseudos*, the false (*falsch*) which in turn is thought of as the *in*correct (Cf. PLW 44 *ff*).

[42] Martin Heidegger, *Einführung in die Metaphysik*, 2. Aufl. (Tübingen : Max Niemeyer, 1966) 142. Hereafter : EM.

(proposition, etc.) both *arose* together *and stand or fall together*. That is, if the *essence* of truth is conceived of as correctness of statement and thing (the soul's glancing and what is glanced) then the *place* of truth must become the statement, the intellect, understanding, the soul's glancing. The *essence* of truth must be changed and redefined in terms of its "place". We have already discussed in some detail Heidegger's criticism of the notion that the essence of truth lies in correctness or correspondence. Let us now complete this criticism by turning our attention to its other inseparable aspect, the view that the *place* of truth is the *statement*. It will be seen that his criticism of the latter is basically the same as the former; that the statement and the truth of statements are ultimately *derived* from and hence *dependent* upon *ontological* grounds.

I will not attempt to treat all of Heidegger's views on statement but will merely select those which are most pertinent to Wittgenstein's position and which best exemplify Heidegger's objections to that position. In *Being and Time* Heidegger gives three significations (*Bedeutungen*) of statement. (1) Its primary signification — pointing-out (*Aufzeichnung*) — which is identical with the Greek *apophansis*. As such it means : "to let a being be seen from itself." (2) Statement signifies predication (*Prädikation*), "a 'predicate' is 'stated' (*ausgesagt*) of a 'subject', the subject is given a specific determination by the predicate. (3) Statement signifies communication (*Mitteilung*).[43] Taking these together, Heidegger defines statement as : "a pointing-out which gives a determinate character and which communicates." [44] Further, every statement has a basic "structure", which Heidegger calls the "as-structure" (*Struktur des 'als'*), i.e., asserts "something-as-something." [45]

What Heidegger means by the "as-structure" of statements is, I think, essentially what Wittgenstein means when he says the sense (*Sinn*) of a proposition pictures a possible state of affairs, or "place in logical space" (2.19 ff). Or alternatively,

> A proposition shows how things stand *if* it is true. And it *says that they* do so stand. (4.022)

Further, since for Wittgenstein a state of affairs is a combination (*Verbindung*) of objects (2.01), and elementary propositions represent (picture) states of affairs, the elementary proposition is also a "combination" of *names* (4.0311). In particular, for Wittgenstein the as-structure of propo-

[43] SZ 154-5.
[44] SZ 156.
[45] SZ 154 ff.

sitions is reflected in the combinations of names which, by denoting the simple objects constitutive of a state of affairs (and doing so with the *same* order and multiplicity) "picture" that state of affairs. And this picturing of a (possible) state of affairs is the proposition's *sense*. Heidegger's criticism of this position is that the as-structure of statements (propositions), and hence their *sense*, is *derived* from a more primordial *ontological* as-structure. All statement is grounded in a *prior* understanding (*verstehen*) since it presupposes a prior grasp of sense. That is, to make a statement *about* something presupposes that the thing is already to some extent understood. Now understanding is essentially a pro-jecting (*entwerfen*) towards possibilities.[46] These possibilities and their sense — their as-structure — must be grasped *before* they can be asserted (pictured) in a proposition. The sense of a proposition is derived from, and grounded in the sense of the possibilities (e.g., states of affairs) themselves. Thus, sense or meaning is not restricted to the "content of judgment" (*Urteilsgehalt*) but rather is grounded in a prior understanding and interpretation of what is judged *about*.[47] For Heidegger, this prior understanding arises first out of what is encountered as ready-to-hand (*Zuhanden*) within the environment (*Umwelt*) of circumspective concern (*Besorgen*). When making statements we "abstract" ourselves from involvements and practical dealings with beings and treat them as merely present-at-hand (*Vorhanden*). In this context, what Heidegger means by a being *present*-at-hand would be Wittgenstein's facts or states of affairs. Thus, the "as" of statements is *derived* from the more primordial "as" of our circumspective dealings and concern with the ready-to-hand.

Heidegger points out that Aristotle was the first to realize that every judgment was a "binding (*verbinden*) and separating (*trennen*)" (*synthesis* and *diairesis*) of its elements.[48] We have seen that for Wittgenstein an elementary proposition is essentially a combination (*Verbindung*) of names. But Heidegger has shown that the as-structure — the "something-as-something" — of every statement is grounded in, and has as its necessary condition, an as-structure which is more primordial than any binding of the present-at-hand elements of statements. This as-structure is that of the totality of references and involvements — possible uses, functions, applications, etc. — of what is encountered as ready-to-hand equipment (*Zeug*) in the environment. Only on the basis of our under-

[46] SZ 148 *passim*.
[47] SZ 156.
[48] SZ 159.

standing and interpreting of the *sense* of the latter can we make *statements* about them, i.e., re-present (or picture) their sense in propositions. Thus, statement and the sense of statements are grounded in, and derived from a prior understanding and interpretation of the ontological structure and sense of beings encountered as ready-to-hand within the environment. It is not the sense of *statements* which is primordial, but the sense of the *beings* which statements are "about". Thus sense, like truth, does not have its original "place" in the statement (proposition).

> The statement is not the primary 'place' of truth, but *on the contrary*, the statement as a mode of appropriation of uncoveredness (*Entdecktheit*) and as a way of being-in-the-world is grounded in the uncovering... The most original 'truth' is the place of the statement and the ontological condition of the possibility that statements can be true or false (uncovering or hiding).[49]

The above is the real heart of Heidegger's disagreement with the traditional concept of truth. Truth is not primarily "in" the statement, nor is truth a "corresponding" of statement and fact. *Truth is ultimately an ontological-existential concept grounded in Dasein and Dasein's being-in-the-world.*[50] Truth is not a "property" of statements which "correspond" to something in the world. Truth is the uncoveredness of beings encountered within the world by the uncovering of Dasein.

Our statements are "about" real beings in the world, and it is the latter which "confirms" (*bewährt*) the statement. But the statement also *uncovers* (*entdeckt*) beings in the world by saying *as* and *how* they are.

> The statement is *true* means; it uncovers the being in itself. It speaks out, it points to, it lets be seen (*apophansis*) the being in its uncoveredness.
> The *being-true* (*Wahrsein*) (*truth*) of the statement must be understood as *being-uncovered*. Truth thus does not at all have the structure of a correspondence between knowing and object in the sense of an appropriation of a being (subject) to another (object).[51]

A true statement *can* be true, and *can* be confirmed to be true, only because the being can be uncovered in its *ontological truth* by the statement. This ontological truth — the uncoveredness and unhiddenness of beings — is in turn grounded in their Being and the uncovering of Dasein. Only because there is (ontological) truth can there be true propositions, since only then can the (true) statement express the already uncovered being

[49] SZ 226.

[50] "*Dasein*" is ultimately untranslatable into English. Literally it means : "to be there", and less literally : "to exist". A *rough* English equivalent might be : "human existence."

[51] SZ 218-9.

as and how it is. A statement *can* "correspond" to a being (fact) *because* that being has already been uncovered, at least as a possibility.

Truth as being-uncovered is in the oldest tradition of philosophy, and is the "soil" out of which the notions of statement, thing, fact and correspondence grew. The *logos* of Heraclitus is ultimately *aletheia*, that is, the *logos*, as true, takes beings out of their unhiddenness, i.e., un-covers them. Also, for Aristotle, the phenomena, the "things themselves" (*Sachen selbst*) show themselves in the "how of their uncoveredness.[52] This "showing" and uncovering can then be "appropriated" by a statement, and one can *say* how the beings are. Now this being-uncovered, the showing-itself of the phenomena, is always relative to *Dasein*, for it is Dasein that *makes possible* the uncoveredness and unhiddenness of beings. "Being-true as being-uncovering (*entdeckend-sein*) is a way of Being of Dasein." [53] It is Dasein that uncovers. Dasein as uncovering is "true" in the *primary* sense, beings in the world (e.g. facts), as what are uncover*ed*, are true in a *secondary* sense.[54] Here Heidegger is pointing to the distinction between *ontological* truth (Dasein and Being) and *ontic* truth (beings). But if the latter are only true in a secondary sense, i.e., their truth is *derived* from the ontological truth of Dasein and Being, then the truth of statements is less original still, since the statement as true presupposes the truth and uncoveredness of the beings they are "about". The uncoveredness of beings in the world (and hence of statements) is grounded in the *disclosedness* (*Erschlossenheit*) of the world and the disclosedness of Dasein's *there* (*Da*), i.e., Dasein's understanding (*Verstehen*), discourse (*Rede*) and attitude (*Befindlichkeit*). "Dasein is 'in the truth'." [55]

The view that the essence of truth is correspondence and the 'place' of truth is the statement both have their origins in Dasein's being-in-the-world. Dasein, as being-in-the-world encounters beings in the world and "speaks out" (*aussagt*), makes statements, about them. When the statement is thus expressed it becomes something ready-to-hand in that it can be used in certain ways, e.g., repeated. The being the statement is about (e.g., the fact) is in turn something ready-to-hand or present-at-hand. Finally, the *relation* between statement and Being tends to be conceived of as present-at-hand. Statement, Being, and relation are thus all ultimately conceived of as present-at-hand. In this way truth as uncoveredness

[52] SZ 219.
[53] SZ 220.
[54] SZ 220.
[55] SZ 220-1.

becomes truth as *correspondence*. This whole phenomenon, for Heidegger, is a result of Dasein's tendency to interpret Being and its own Being in terms of what is closest to it, i.e., what it encounters "proximally and for the most part" (*zunächst und zumeist*). This of course, is beings ready or present-at-hand within the environment.[56] Heidegger calls this tendency, this fascination, this being "taken-up" (*aufgenommen*) by beings *in* the world (rather than by Being as such), Dasein's fallenness (*Verfallenheit*). Thus, Heidegger claims to have shown not only that the truth of statements is a secondary, derived phenomenon — depending for its possibility on the original *ontological* truth of Dasein's disclosing of the Being of beings — but also to have shown *why and how* statement-truth can be *thought* to be *itself* original. For Heidegger, the traditional theory of truth is not an "accident of history" — it has its roots and causes in Dasein's way of being-in-the world and Dasein's disclosing or failure to disclose the truth of Being. Indeed, although it was the Greeks who first disclosed the ontological meaning of truth as *aletheia*, this disclosure itself contained the seed for the eventual hiding and covering-up of Being and truth, which covering-up we know today as the "traditional theory" of truth and ultimately, metaphysics. Hence, metaphysics and the traditional concept of truth have one and the same origin and are intrinsically wedded to one another. And since the latter is grounded in Being and Dasein's disclosing of Being, so is the former. Both demand a radical rethinking out of their forgottenness back into their common ground, the existential-ontological truth of Being.

[56] SZ 223 *ff.*

MEANING AND LANGUAGE

by

S. A. Erickson

One of the central topics of concern for contemporary philosophers, both analytical and phenomenological, has been the nature of meaning. Members of both groups have intimated on more than one occasion that the domain of meaning(s) is the exclusive preserve and only battleground of philosophy. Many of these same philosophers have also suggested that the only way in which one can reach this domain is through an examination of language. What I wish to do in this paper is not so much to question these doctrines as to try to make them clear in the way in which they are held by particular philosophers. More specifically, I wish to discuss some of Heidegger's views on meaning and language, and then, by some critical comparisons with both the "earlier" and the "later" Wittgenstein, to show the philosophical peculiarities of both men's positions — positions which, as I shall argue, are intriguingly similar. If successful, my essay can be construed, then, roughly speaking, as a building block in the service of *rapprochement*. But *rapprochement* is only valuable as an ideal if it is in turn put in the service of philosophy. I shall conclude, therefore, not on a note of comparison but with a question which I think needs posing and for which I cannot provide an answer. My essay divides quite naturally into three sections. In the first I shall discuss Heidegger's understanding of meaning. In the second I shall explicate Heidegger's view that language provides a means of access to meaning and compare this view with what I take to be Wittgenstein's position in the *Tractatus* and in thc *Investigations*. In the third and final section I shall pose my question and reflect briefly on the factors that make it so problematic for both Heidegger and Wittgenstein, and therefore, in a sense, for contemporary philosophy.

I

Heidegger's remarks about meaning are peculiar from the start, so peculiar, in fact, as to make one wonder whether the topic is worth pursuing through the tortuous labyrinth of his prose. It is surely odd that he should state the central question of his philosophy in the way he does. He asks after the meaning of *Being* [1] rather than the meaning of 'Being'. Here obviously there is a problem. It is generally agreed upon that words have meanings. It is not altogether as clear, however, that the items referred to by these words have meanings. To make such a claim may well be to succumb to an uncritical and illicit employment of what Carnap and others refer to as the material mode of speech.

Let us consider Heidegger's case. Interestingly enough, in ordinary language the term 'meaning' and its variants often do function in a way which supports Heidegger's phrasing of his question. Consider the following examples, examples which clearly represent the sorts of ordinary language contexts out of which 'meaning' arises as a *terminus technicus.*

She means everything to me.
For those with no background in industrial psychology, his decisions have very little meaning.
What do you take their presence to mean?
I found the Klee exhibition quite meaningful.
The sacraments mean nothing to some churchgoers.
Just having the opportunity means a great deal to him.
A red light means that you must stop.
Nature is more meaningful to some than to others.

On the surface at least, meaning is here ascribed to such disparate items as persons, acts, paintings, religious rites, objects produced by modern technology, nature, and abstract entities. A translation of any of these statements into a formal mode of speech presents all but insuperable difficulties. What these translations must produce are statements in which the term 'meaning' is no longer predicated of or ascribed by indirection

[1] I understand Being for Heidegger to be a happening — an *act* in the broad Aristotelian sense — in some way akin to a "living," "emerging," and "enduring," not itself an entity, but which happens only with respect to entities and happens with respect to every entity. Being serves (at least) a Kantian transcendental function for Heidegger. One experiences entities because one experiences the Being of these entities. The latter is a necessary condition for the former. If one puts Heidegger's doctrine in a formal mode of speech, Being would be the pure form of connection which holds together yet articulates the various structural ingredients that go into the makeup of statements in their formal constitution — thus akin to Wittgenstein's notion of *logical form* in the *Tractatus.* Since Heidegger's understanding of Being — surely an agonizing topic in its own right — is not central to my argument, I shall leave my exposition of it to these brief remarks.

to the various entities just mentioned. The term 'meaning' must in effect drop out of the straightforward statement made in the object language and reappear, if it is to appear at all, as a metalinguistic notion embodied in a metalinguistic statement which serves as a commentary on the (now modified) object language statement. Quite clearly this is a formula for visiting abuse upon ordinary language remarks.

I need not pursue this point, however, though I shall return to it later on. Heidegger's position here is not what one might expect — granting, even, the ordinary language genesis of 'meaning' as a technical term in his philosophy. Heidegger writes,

> When entities ... have come to be understood ... we say that they have *meaning* [*Sinn*] ... Meaning is ... not a property attaching to entities, lying "behind" them, or floating somewhere as an "intermediate domain." ... *only Dasein can be meaningful* [*sinnvoll*] *or meaningless* [*sinnlos*]. ... all entities whose kind of Being is of a character other than *Dasein's* must be conceived as *unmeaning* [*unsinniges*], essentially devoid of any meaning at all.[2]

If we are to take these statements seriously it follows that, strictly speaking, the term 'meaning' is not applicable to entities other than *Dasein* — understanding '*Dasein*' for the present as a term roughly synonymous with the term '*man*'. In short, only *Dasein* has meaning. Yet Heidegger also writes,

> And if we are inquiring about the meaning of Being, our investigation does not then become a "deep" one [*tiefsinnig*], nor does it puzzle out what stands behind Being. *It asks about Being itself insofar as Being enters into the intelligibility* [*Verständlichkeit* — an alternative translation might be "*understandability*"] *of Dasein.*[3]

and

> In *Being and Time* the question of the meaning of Being is raised and developed *as a question* for the first time ... It is also stated and explained in detail what is meant by meaning (namely the disclosure of Being...[4]

In these passages resides what amounts, I think, to the greatest single difficulty in Heidegger's philosophy, a difficulty which is the cause of

[2] Heidegger, *Sein und Zeit* (Tübingen, 1957), g 151, e 192-193. (The English edition I refer to is the Macquarrie and Robinson translation, from which, with a few minor revisions, I have taken the wording for the quotations for this article. See *Being and Time*, trans. by Macquarrie and Robinson (London : 1962). Hereafter I will footnote references to *Sein und Zeit* simply by the letters SZ and the appropriate page numbers in both the German and the English editions.

[3] SZ g 152, e 193.

[4] Heidegger, *An Introduction to Metaphysics* (Garden City : 1961), p. 70.

many of the other problems which his work faces. With allowances for terminology this difficulty might in fact be said to be *the* problem of phenomenology. That this pivotal inconsistency has not been dwelt upon in greater detail by Heidegger's various commentators is surely remarkable.

Consider first the statement,

[our investigation into the meaning of Being] asks about Being itself insofar as Being enters into the intelligibility of *Dasein.*

On this account what distinguishes the *meaning* of Being from Being simpliciter is just this : the *meaning* of Being is Being itself, but only to the extent that Being has been revealed or brought to light. In short, the meaning of Being is Being insofar as Being has been understood. Roughly speaking, the distinction between Being and its meaning as described here is parallel to the medieval distinction between the formal and the objective modes of an entity's Being — between, for instance, the moon as it is in itself and that same moon as known.[5]

But now consider the phrase

... what is meant by meaning (namely the disclosure of Being ...

'Disclosure' is a member of a particularly dangerous family of slippery words in philosophy. Let me call these words "ing/ed" words. Beyond providing a convenient piece of shorthand for purposes of discussion, this nomenclature also names in a way the difficulty. The *Oxford Universal Dictionary* gives two meanings for the term 'disclosure'. It can either mean

the action of disclosing, opening up to view, or revealing; discover, exposure. (*ing* sense)

or

that which is disclosed. (*ed* sense)

If 'disclosure' is understood in the *ed* sense, then to refer to the *meaning* of Being as the *disclosure* of Being is to refer to it as Being itself *as disclosed.* This interpretation squares with the first statement which we have brought under consideration. If, however, 'disclosure' is understood

[5] I refer of course to this distinction as it was understood by the medievals, hard-headed realists that they were, and not as it was subsequently appropriated by Descartes. Descartes modified the doctrine in the service of a representationalism which leads to the conceptual schizophrenia at the basis of much nineteenth and twentieth century idealism. Whatever other philosophical peculiarities belong to Heidegger, he is neither a representationalist nor in any ordinary sense an idealist.

in the *ing* sense, matters are entirely different. To refer to the *meaning* of Being as the *disclosure* of Being is now to refer to it as the disclosing of Being. And disclosing is precisely the sort of thing done by human beings. The meaning of Being now becomes a property of one kind of entity, *viz.*, man, and not an aspect of Being itself. This interpretation in turn squares with these statements.

(a) ... *only Dasein can be meaningful or meaningless.*

(b) all entities whose kind of Being is of a character other than *Dasein's* must be conceived as *unmeaning*, essentially devoid of any meaning at all.

How are these last remarks to be reconciled with the *ed* interpretation of 'disclosure' and the first of the statements we have just considered? One might be tempted to offer the following argument : Being, after all, is a happening.[6] Now in some writings — particularly the later ones, though seldom if ever in *Being and Time* — Heidegger speaks as if Being discloses itself. Take the happening which is Being as a disclosing and the *ing* and *ed* interpretations coincide. Being itself is disclos*ed*, but since Being is a disclosing, what is disclos*ed* is precisely this disclos*ing*. The meaning of Being is thus that disclosing which is Being's disclosing of itself, a disclosing which in turn is Being itself and, as a disclosing of itself as a disclosing, Being itself as disclosed. Given the axiom of reduction plus definitions of the terms involved, this argument may in fact be analytic on semantic grounds. Leaving this question aside however, there is another consideration which recommends this interpretation : it is compatible with statement (a) above, *viz.*,

... *only Dasein can be meaningful or meaningless,*

a statement which on the surface at least appears to nullify the present attempt at reconciliation.

Heidegger's prose style, even in the midst of the most contorted of arguments, has a poetic undertone to it. This is a source both of brilliant particular insights and dubious lines of reasoning. Nuance and metaphorical suggestion yield relief from conceptual tangles, but used in an extended argument they lose their moorings, depending at this turn on one suggested meaning, at that turn on another. I mention this because the compatibility of statement (a) with the present effort to bring the *ing* and *ed* interpretations together depends flatly on a metaphor. Consider the term 'disclose'. 'Disclose' is an achievement verb which I use straightforwardly and properly only when two conditions are met. First, some-

[6] See Note 1.

thing must in actual fact be disclosed. Second, that something must be disclosed *to* someone. In particular if, as a special case, x discloses x, there must be some y *to* which x disclosed itself. This y may of course be identical with x itself, as is the case with some forms of "self-knowledge." For x to have truly disclosed x to y requires that y on its side *receive* (as opposed to *fail to receive*) the disclosure. Now there is a form of speech, not altogether common today, which has among its expressions such phrases as these,

'filled with the knowledge of'
'filled with delight'
'filled with wonder'.

In this language, to *receive* knowledge can under certain circumstances be viewed as tantamount to being *filled* with knowledge. And this is not always an innocent way of construing the situation. The metaphorical notion of the reception of knowledge as having something poured into one and being partially filled with that something has haunted epistemology and philosophy of mind during a number of periods in the philosophican past.

Consider now the term 'meaningful' [*Sinnvoll*]. It is easy for Heidegger to construe this in a metaphorical way to mean "filled with meaning". To say that Dasein is meaningful, then, is to say — now unpacking the metaphor — that *Dasein* has *received* meaning. In accordance with this line of reasoning, to say that *Dasein* alone can be meaningful or meaningless is but to say the following : entities other than *Dasein* cannot, as a matter of conceptual fact, receive meaning. Because it is a conceptual truth that they cannot be filled with meaning, it makes no sense to say of them that they are empty of meaning. In short, the predicates 'meaningful' ('*sinnvoll*') and 'meaningless', ('*sinnlos*') do not apply to them. Heidegger writes,

if we adhere to ... [this interpretation of the concept of meaning] then all entities whose kind of Being is of a character other than *Dasein's* must be conceived as *unmeaning* [*unsinniges*], essentially devoid of any meaning at all. Here 'unmeaning' does not signify that we are saying anything about the value of such entities, but it gives expression to an ontological characteristic. *And only that which is unmeaning can be absurd* [*widersinnig*].[7]

Unfortunately there are two major weaknesses in this attempt at reconciliation. But before I exhibit them, I want to mention a slightly more positive side of the attempt. It is this : for good or for ill this means of

[7] SZ g 152, e 193.

overcoming the disparate tendencies in Heidegger's interpretation of the concept of meaning is clearly the course Heidegger himself takes in his later writings.[8] It provides a clue for understanding much of what is going on in these writings, and it is what makes them at once both intriguing and to no small degree irritating — perhaps even scandalous. I might add parenthetically that the interpretation of the concept of meaning in such a way that strictly speaking it applies only to Being has also been the source of much of the recent interest in Heidegger on the part of some theologians. But this is another matter and a very complicated one. Let us turn back to the difficulties.

Being is always the Being of an entity. But, to quote the passage again.

> all entities whose kind of Being is of a character other than *Dasein's* must be conceived as *unmeaning*, essentially devoid of any meaning at all.

If meaning is a property of Being, and yet entities which possess a kind of Being other than *Dasein's* have no meaning at all, then either they have no Being — which the quotation denies — or only *Dasein's* Being has meaning. If only *Dasein's* Being has meaning, then the question of the meaning of Being is equivalent to the question of the meaning of *Dasein's* Being. In *Being and Time*, however, Heidegger claims that the question of the meaning of Being, though best approached through a consideration of the meaning of *Dasein's* Being, is *not* identical with the question of the meaning of *Dasein's* Being. And yet this latter question is the only one Heidegger is able to deal with in *Being and Time*. He answers it to his satisfaction and the book then ends, abruptly and far short of its projected goal.

If Being is the Being of an entity, and meaning is a property of Being, it makes some sense to ascribe meaning to entities — albeit in a roundabout and indirect way. This depends rougly speaking, on taking "belonging to" as a transitive relation. If one goes on to deny to entities other than *Dasein* any meaning whatsoever, though does not deny them Being, it then becomes tempting to ascribe meaning only to *Dasein* itself and not to *Dasein's* Being. Being is something all entities possess. If meaning were a property of Being why do entities other than *Dasein* have no meaning?

Add to this the realization that of all entities only *Dasein* is capable of receiving Being's disclosure — that other entities are, in a manner of

[8] See, for instance, Heidegger's *Gelassenheit* (Pfullingen : 1959). There is an English edition also. See *Discourse on Thinking* (New York : 1966).

speaking, ontologically mute — and the ground is fully laid for understanding meaning to be a characteristic solely of *Dasein*. And this of course is the reason why entities other than *Dasein* are viewed to be essentially devoid of meaning. 'Meaning' takes on the metaphorical commitments of 'meaningful', *viz.*, filled with meaning *qua* having received meaning by means of a disclosure. Meaning now becomes the disclosing of Being in the sense of *Dasein's* disclosing of Being. On this model the only meaning to be found belongs to *Dasein* or at best to *Dasein's* Being, not to Being as such, and the attempt at finding the meaning of Being ends in failure. This, I think is the unexpressed shortcoming which curtailed the argument of *Being and Time* before its completion.

There is another difficulty : understanding Being to be the disclosing of Being and meaning to be the disclosing of Being it becomes impossible to distinguish between Being and the meaning of Being. The two become simply one and the same — referred to by means of one expression on one occasion and by the other expression at a different point. Yet in *Being and Time* Heidegger clearly distinguishes between the Being of *Dasein* and the meaning of *Dasein's* Being. If the reconciliatory efforts of the later Heidegger are truly to be successful such a distinction should not remain. But it does, and with it remains the philosophically ambiguous doctrine of meaning.

Let us content ourselves with tracing out the *ed* interpretation of meaning — viewing meaning as Being itself insofar as Being is disclosed. Since in his later writings Heidegger, if I interpret him correctly, holds to the *ed* interpretation, this strategy will perhaps best represent his thought. The *ed* interpretation has the added advantage, I think, of holding the most interest for other philosophers.

Strictly speaking, the meaning of Being is not Being itself insofar as it *has been disclosed*, but Being itself insofar as it *can be* disclosed. Heidegger writes,

> That which can be Articulated in interpretation ... is what we have called meaning. That which gets articulated as such ... we call the totality-of-significations [*Bedeutungsganze*]. This can be dissolved or broken up into significations. Significations, as what has been Articulated from that which can be Articulated, always carry meaning [... *sind* ... *sinnhaft*].[9]

Aside from the puzzling notions it suggests concerning language, this passage is perfectly straighforward. It parallels in a rough and ready way

[9] SZ g 161, e 204.

Hegel's distinction between certainty and truth which appears in the *Phenomenology*. For Hegel reason is certain of that which it has in its grasp and whose content it is able to articulate. What is within reason's domain in this manner is referred to as *certain* in itself. To articulate that which is certain in his way is to bring it to its *truth*. Knowledge is obtained in the full-fledged sense only when certainty and truth become one and the same — in short, only when they coincide, which is the goal of the long-puzzling, and puzzlingly dialectical *Phenomenology* itself. (In contemporary thought the doing of what is often termed conceptual cartography parallels in spirit this conception of philosophical knowledge — minus, of course, most of the dialectic.) Similarly, for Heidegger one has knowledge of Being only insofar as its meaning — what can be articulated or explicitly revealed to be constitutive of it — coincides with the totality of its significations — what has actually been so articulated. Given an understanding of meaning (certainty) whereby meaning is not only limited to begin with, but limited even in the face of dialectical machinations, and given further a reinterpretation of what constitutes a proper "dialectical move" in philosophy, and the essential differences between Hegel and Heidegger come to light. To say anything more about this topic however, I fear, will be to risk illuminating the obscure by the more obscure. Let it suffice to say that the distinction between certainty and truth is itself just another variant of the more classical distinction between intentions and their fulfillments. Thus, as might be expected, the problem of meaning and the problem of signification are both properly considered only within the context of an extended discussion of intentionality.

Meaning, then, is Being insofar as Being can be articulated with respect to its structural moments. To seek the meaning of Being as Heidegger does in *Being and Time* is fully to articulate — to make totally explicit — what can be articulated as the content of Being. Thus, given Heidegger's doctrine of Being, the meaning of Being is that most peculiar happening, in some way akin to a living, emerging and enduring, not itself an entity, which happens only with respect to entities and happens with respect to every entity, itself brought to light and revealed. To express this point in its relevance to the domain of language, what is here revealed is the pure form of connection which holds together yet articulates the various structural ingredients that go into the makeup of statements in their formal constitution. In accordance with this view,

> the *concept of meaning* embraces the ... framework of what necessarily belongs to that which an understanding interpretation Articulates.[10]

[10] SZ g 151, e 193.

It is safe to say that the philosopher whose doctrines most pervade Heidegger's thought in *Being and Time* is neither Aristotle, nor Hegel, nor even Husserl, but rather Kant. This is true no less with respect to Heidegger's account of meaning than with respect to his account of Being — though generally speaking in Heidegger's hands Kantian points of view undergo subtle transformations. In *Being and Time* Heidegger understands meaning to serve a transcendental function of much the same sort as that served by Being. In fact, the former function is but an extrapolation of the commitment expressed in the latter. Entities can be experienced to be the entities which they are only because one already has some comprehension of the meaning of the Being of these entities. One understands entities in terms of the meaning of their Being, a comprehension of which — putting the point in Kant's language — serves as a necessary condition for the possibility of experiencing those entities. In characteristic Heideggerese Heidegger writes,

> ... what makes the relation to ... [entities] (ontic knowledge) possible is the precursory comprehension of the constitution of the Being of ... [entities], namely, ontological knowledge.[11]

and

> meaning is the upon-which of a projection in terms of which something becomes intelligible as something,[12]

What can be articulated as the content of Being makes possible an experience of entities which have Being. It is no less true — and I shall let this stand as the final point — that this meaning is said by Heidegger to make Being itself possible. Such a remark is open to the unfortunate interpretation of meaning as something which is in some way *beyond* Being. But this interpretation is simply unnecessary and, in terms of other of Heidegger's remarks, very implausible. The meaning of Being is to Being as the parts of a watch and their functional connections are to that watch itself — not as uncooked meat is to indigestion. About this matter nothing more needs, I think, be said, other than to point out what amounts to an analytic truth : the meaning of Being *does* make the *understanding* or *comprehension* of Being possible. Heidegger sometimes has this sort of thing in mind when speaking of meaning in the way he does.

[11] Heidegger, *Kant und Das Problem Der Metaphysik* (Frankfurt a.M. : 1965), g 20, e 15. The English edition I refer to is the Churchill translation. See *Kant and the Problem of Metaphysics* (Bloomington : 1962).

[12] SZ g 151, e 193.

II

Let me turn now to a consideration of language in its relation to meaning. Meaning, as we have seen, presents peculiar problems. There are two disparate tendencies with respect to the interpretation of the notion in *Being and Time*. The first of these, which is developed by Heidegger himself in later writings, understands meaning to be Being itself insofar as it can be disclosed — Being insofar as Being can be articulated with respect to its structural moments. The second — the *ing* as opposed to the *ed* interpretation — understands Being to be the disclosing of Being. This disclosing in turn is understood to be the special prerogative of human beings, and thus meaning is construed as a property of man (*Dasein*).

In contrast to the more cautious, piecemeal tendencies of the analytic tradition — tendencies which have resulted in a certain incompleteness in conceptual cartography — Heidegger presses toward a general doctrine of meaning. No general doctrine of meaning can be propounded, however, prior to setting the ontological question concerning Being — regardless of which of the interpretations of meaning one adopts. On the one hand, meaning as Being disclosed cannot be comprehended apart from the Being of which it is a mode. On the other hand, meaning as the disclosing of Being, takes its character from Being insofar as Being is its "intentional" object. Thus the status of meaning is, to say the least, highly problematic in Heidegger's philosophy.

Keeping in mind this problematic character and, more particularly, the dependence of meaning upon Being, let us consider how Heidegger relates language to meaning — leaving open for the moment the question of which interpretation of meaning is involved.

> That which can be Articulated in interpretation, and thus even more primordially in discourse [intelligibility-articulation], is what we have called meaning. That which gets articulated as such in discursive Articulation, we call the totality-of-significations [*Bedeutungsganze*]. This can be dissolved or broken up into significations. Significations, as what has been Articulated from that which can be Articulated, always carry meaning [... *sind* ... *sinnhaft*] ... The totality-of-significations of intelligibility is *put into words*. To significations, words accrue. But word-things do not get supplies with significations.
>
> The way in which discourse [intelligibility-articulation] gets expressed is language. Language is a totality of words.[13]

Language is said to *express* meaning — though the precise manner in which it does this is left unspecified. Clearly part of what is implied is

[13] SZ g 161, e 204.

that through language meaning, quite literally, gets *spoken out*. (The German verb is '*aussprechen*'.) At the same time however, something much less innocent than this is implied. Heidegger suggests a fairly sharp distinction between what gets expressed and the expressing of it. The former is given a definite independence of the latter. Meaning in the form of a totality-of-significations has a status of its own apart from language as a totality of words.

It is a peculiar truth of contemporary philosophy that Heidegger's position here is neither as odd nor as unorthodox as it might first appear to be. The failure of the phenomenologists to express themselves clearly on the matter has obscured this fact. Yet this doctrine is so basic to Heidegger and so pivotal to the development of phenomenological philosophy as a whole that virtually no discussion of Heidegger or of phenomenology can avoid a thorough investigation of it. As a means of examining the doctrine I shall discuss some very influential views of Wittgenstein, comparing them at various points with Heidegger's position.

In the *Philosophical Investigations*, section 15, Wittgenstein writes concerning names and naming,

> The word 'to signify' is perhaps used in the most straightforward way when the object signified is marked with the sign ... It is in this and more or less similar ways that a name means and is given to a thing. — It will often prove useful in philosophy to say to ourselves : naming is like attaching a label to a thing.[14]

And again in section 26,

> to repeat — naming is something like attaching a label to a thing. One can say that this is preparatory to the use of a word.[15]

To be sure Wittgenstein understands naming to be but a preparation for the full-blown use of a word in language games. A word may be used in a number of other ways than in its specific naming or referring function.

> As if what we did next were given with the mere act of naming. As if there were only one thing called 'talking about a thing'.[16]

Yet naming *is* a language game in its own right.

[14] Wittgenstein, *Philosophical Investigations*, trans. by G. E. M. Anscombe (Oxford : 1958) 7e. (Hereafter PI.)

[15] PI 13e.

[16] PI 13e (section 27).

... the processes of naming the stones and of repeating words after someone might also be called language games [17]

For Wittgenstein the language game of naming involves things, utterances, and a certain process, *viz.*, labelling. Through labelling, utterances come to be associated with the things in such a way that the utterances become names, and the things are said to be labelled, attached with labels, or alternatively, marked with signs. Labelling appears to be a linguistic process by which utterances acquire meaning — though in a minimal sense — and things are marked in some manner. In this account of labelling Wittgenstein clearly gives priority to language games.

Heidegger's explanation of labelling would be radically different. His view requires the substitution of the *Being* of entities for things, *intelligibility-articulation* [18] for the process of labelling, and the *meaning* of the Being of entities for those same things as labelled or marked. Notice that the expressing of meaning in language could be not mentioned here at all. In Heidegger's view such expression presupposes that the labelling has already been accomplished. In this account of labelling priority would clearly be withheld from language. Thus, on the surface at least Heidegger and Wittgenstein are poles apart. But let us look a little more closely at Wittgenstein's account of naming. In particular, let us consider his views on ostensive teaching of words.

Wittgenstein holds that a child learns a language not by having it explained to him but by being trained in it :

The children are brought up to perform these actions, to use these words as they do so, and to react in this way to the words of others.[19]

The words to stress here are 'perform', 'use', and 'react'. They indicate that in the learning process language, which is experienced initially by the learner as a natural (non-intentional) phenomenon, is fused with activity. Through this fusion language takes on the characteristics of what Wittgenstein terms a language *game*. Such games are for Wittgenstein

[17] PI 5e (section 7).

[18] By 'intelligibility-articulation' (*Rede*, λογος), Heidegger means : the making manifest or bringing out into the open of what is to be discussed in such a way that everything that comes to be said about what is to be discussed is drawn from what is to be discussed itself. Intelligibility-articulation is not language, and is thus neither written nor spoken, but it is that which makes language possible. It is, rougly speaking, a *pre-linguistic* structuring of experience. For an extended discussion of the notion see my 'Martin Heidegger,' *Review of Metaphysics XIX* (1966), pp. 462-492.

[19] PI 4e (section 6).

intentional in nature and are the minimal cognitive or conceptual units in our experience. They are forms of behavior : he often refers to them as "forms of life" (*Lebensformen*). Much like other forms of behavior, a certain training is required if the disposition to engage in them properly is to be inculcated. In short, the ability to play a language game is a conceptual *skill*, and training is viewed as the proper method of establishing such as skill. Whether the words in a language game are *understood* — which is required if the learner is to play the language game — is determined by the subsequent activity of the learner — by whether he is able to use the words, *perform* certain activities in relation to them, and *react* to them appropriately.

> Don't you understand the call "Slab!" if you act upon it in such a way : — Doubtless the ostensive teaching helped to bring this about; but only together with a particular training. With different training the same ostensive teaching of these words would have effected a quite different understanding.[20]

Ostensive *teaching*, as distinguished from training, is the act of pointing to a particular object or aspect of an object and uttering the name of that object or aspect — assuming of course that we are still talking about the language game of naming and closely related games. Training, on the other hand, involves the total behavioral complex with which the ostensive teaching is connected. The teaching is but one aspect of the total behavioral complex. Training might include praise when the learner becomes able to respond correctly to the words and use them correctly and punishment when his performance with the words is inappropriate. For Wittgenstein, language games are learned primarily through this training. The emphasis is not on the ostensive teaching, for the ostensive teaching may be the same in two different situations, but the results may differ if the accompanying training differs.

Wittgenstein carefully distinguishes between ostensive teaching and ostensive definition. For an ostensive definition to do its job, the one for whom one defines the word must already be within the language game in which the word plays a role, and must already have certain skills in playing that language game. Since training is the method by which the initial inculcation of these skills is accomplished, training is the means by which one first comes to language games. In view of Wittgenstein's remark that

> what has to be accepted, the given, is — so one could say — *forms of life*,[21]

[20] PI 4e-5e.

[21] PI 226e.

one is left with the impression that it is through training — in particular, linguistically oriented training — that there comes to be something like a cognitive world of experience (something *given* in a cognitive sense). In short, training appears to serve what other philosophers would call a transcendental function for Wittgenstein. Through training the learner makes the transition from non-intentional to intentional modes of behavior in any given domain.

One of the differences between the earlier and the later Wittgenstein, it has been suggested, is the account of how man comes to language. If one takes seriously the view that the possession of language defines man, this account is at the same time the account of man's coming into being — though Wittgenstein himself would surely be horrified by such talk. For the *Tractarian* Wittgenstein presumably — and here we must speculate a bit — this transition from non-linguistic and thus non-conceptual modes of behavior to linguistic-conceptual modes of behavior is holistic and in some instantaneous. Here we are speaking of course of the so-called "hidden" language in the *Tractatus*, the mechanism of sense as it is sometimes called.[22] Wilfred Sellars presents the rationale for this position quite explicitly :

> I want to highlight from the very beginning what might be called the paradox of man's encounter with himself, the paradox consisting of the fact that man couldn't be man until he encountered himself. It is this paradox which supports the last stand of Special Creation. Its central theme is the idea that anything which can properly be called conceptual thinking can occur only within a framework of conceptual thinking in terms of which it can be criticized, supported, refuted, in short, evaluated. To be able to think is to be able to measure one's thoughts by standards of correctness, of relevance, of evidence. In this sense a diversified conceptual framework is a whole which, however sketchy, is prior to its parts, and cannot be construed as a coming together of parts which are already conceptual in character. The conclusion is difficult to avoid that the transition from pre-conceptual patterns of behaviour to conceptual thinking was a holistic one, a jump to a level of awareness which is irreducibly new, a jump which was the coming into being of man.[23]

For the *later* Wittgenstein the transition is clearly piecemeal and takes place over an extended period of time. Note his famous remark that

> Our language can be seen as an ancient city : a maze of little streets and squares, of old and new houses, and of houses with additions from various

[22] In this connection see Bernstein's 'Wittgenstein's Three Languages,' *Review of Metaphysics* XV (1961), 278-298.

[23] Sellars, *Science, Perception and Reality* (New York : 1963), p. 6.

periods; and this surrounded by a multitude of new boroughs with straight regular streets and uniform houses.[24]

I mention this presumed constrast between the two Wittgensteins as a means of suggesting Heidegger's view, for if we take the contrast seriously Heidegger turns out to be very much of a "Tractarian." The sense in which this is the case, however, is odd indeed and requires some explanation. For human beings to be aware of anything at all, even of themselves, Heidegger thinks, is for them to be aware and to understand Being. Naturally, to the degree to which Being is understood (disclosed), meaning is disclosed, for meaning is the *disclosure* of Being in that ambiguous, twofold sense we have already discussed. Thus an awareness and understanding of meaning, the meaning of Being, is the means by which there first comes to be a cognitive world of experience — something *given* in a cognitive sense. It is the minimal cognitive, or conceptual, unit in our experience and it is clearly holistic. (Heidegger's term is equiprimordial (*gleichursprünglich*), which he predicates of the structures of Being.) This is to say that this minimal cognitive unit is not built up in piecemeal fashion out of disparate parts.

Throughout *Being and Time* Heidegger insists that an awareness of the meaning of Being is presupposed in all awareness of the meaning of Being's modes and characteristics. This holistic awareness and understanding thus serves the prime transcendental function for Heidegger. Now man cannot bring this transcendental condition into existence himself. Insofar as he is defined in terms of a reflexivity which takes the form of self-awareness, he himself first comes into being only *after* there is an awareness and understanding of the meaning of Being. Reasoning in this way, Heidegger is prompted to make very peculiar and oracular remarks. He says, for instance, that Being is the happening that has man. His meaning is not as dark as it first appears. He is simply saying that Being happens to man in such a way as to bring man into being as *man* — the being with an understanding of Being and through this understanding an awareness of entities, included among which is man himself.

Let me add a parenthetical note here. Though the line of reasoning which leads Heidegger to these assertions is a natural one for him to follow, it has dangerous implications. To say or suggest that Being brings man into being is to border on anthropomorphizing and reifying Being. Being begins to look like an agent — which, on Heidegger's own linguistico-grammatical analysis, is a misguided notion. Yet as grammar,

[24] PI 8e (section 18).

metaphor, and metaphysic begin to split asunder and war with each other as they do in the later Heidegger, this line of reasoning appears to captivate him. The progressive tendency to ascribe meaning to Being alone rather than to *Dasein* reinforces the haunting suspicion of Being's agency. As it does, Heidegger's philosophy takes on mystical overtones.

So far Heidegger has not mentioned language (or for that matter training). The comparison with Wittgenstein's *Tractatus* thus appears to be tenuous. Note, however, the sense in which there is a holistic and instantaneous transition to *language* in the *Tractatus*. To do this we must reflect for a moment on the various languages mentioned, used, or suggested by this puzzling book.

It is not an unduly speculative or bizarre interpretation of Wittgenstein to suggest that a number of languages can be distinguished in the *Tractatus*.[25] There is, first of all, our everyday or ordinary language. Wittgenstein makes a number of remarks about it.

> everyday language is a part of the human organism and is no less complicated than it. ... The tacit conventions on which the understanding of everyday language depends are enormously complicated. (4.002)

Further

> ... all the propositions of our everyday language just as they stand, are in perfect logical order. (5.5563)

Yet

> it is not humanly possible to gather immediately from ... [everyday language] what the logic of language is. Language disguises thought. [Here presumably Wittgenstein is still talking about ordinary language.] So much so that from the outward form of the clothing it is impossible to infer the form of the thought beneath it, because the outward form of the clothing is not designed to reveal the form of the body, but for entirely different purposes. (4.002)

Quite clearly the transition to language in this sense — *everyday* language — is neither holistic nor instantaneous. Everyday language is nothing more than the complex of language games which is Wittgenstein's concern in the *Investigations*. Presumably, therefore, it is learned in a successive, piecemeal way. There is certainly no evidence to the contrary to be found in the *Tractatus*.

Beyond ordinary language there is what I shall term, following Sellars, the "perspicuous" language. This is an ideal language which is to be

[25] The edition of the *Tractatus* I use for my quotes is the Pears and McGuinness translation. See Wittgenstein, *Tractatus Logico-Philosophicus* (London : 1961), trans. by D. F. Pears and B. F. McGuinness.

constructed for the purpose of showing perspicuously something that is hidden : the mechanism of sense — in other words the logico-conceptual process, the atomic propositions, etc., by means of which language as it is actually used makes contact with the world as it is or can be presented. It is one of the main tasks of philosophy to construct such a language. The process of construction is, again, piecemeal and dependent for its development upon the discovery of truths in logic as well as in metaphysics — truth, for instance, concerning the status of properties, relations, and truth-functional connectives.

There is also the language *used* by Wittgenstein in the *Tractatus*, which is neither the everyday language nor the perspicuous language. Wittgenstein employs a metalanguage as a means of describing the perspicuous language, and most of the propositions of the *Tractatus* fall within its scope. But to have a meta-language it is necessary first to have an object language, and thus the transition to *language* is not to be dealt with in the context of the metaphilosophical remarks which constitute the main body of the *Tractatus*.

The doctrine of the holistic transition to language, if it is to apply anywhere at all, must apply to the so-called "hidden" language in the *Tractatus*, the mechanism of sense. The mechanism of sense, however, is neither written nor spoken. Thus it is actually a language only in a very extended and metaphorical sense. Yet — and here is the paradox — it is not for that reason less than basic to the linguistically oriented Wittgensteinian philosophy which sets the limits of the world at the limits of language. The mechanism of sense makes it possible for everyday language to make contact with the world, and it gets expressed in disguised form in this language. It is also to be expressed in that perspicuous language which it is the philosopher's task to construct. The mechanism of sense thus resembles Heidegger's notion of intelligibility-articulation (*Rede*).[26] The transition to intelligibility-articulation is holistic, gets expressed in "the most elemental words in which *Dasein* expresses itself," and is to be expressed through the construction of an appropriate ontological grammar.

If the Tractarian conception of ordinary language is compatible with the doctrine of language games, then so is Heidegger's conception of language. One might go so far as to say that for Heidegger language takes the form of language games — at least in its initial stages and insofar as it is a "living" language. His way of putting this point would be somewhat

[26] See note 18.

indirect however. A totality-of-significations (*Bedeutungsganze*), Heidegger claims, precedes the significations into which it is (subsequently) analyzable. This totality is not to be built up out of separate items. Since language rests upon this totality and derives its character from it, it cannot itself be construed to be a conjunction of separately functioning units which come together in external fashion to constitute actual speech. Rather, language must be understood to be a whole of parts — as a living language, *wholes* of parts — in which the whole has some normative and thus prior status with respect to the parts. There is one passage in particular in *Being and Time* which well illustrates the close connection between language and the Wittgensteinian notion of language games. After having stated that assertion is a derivative mode of interpretation, a *founded* mode of Being-in-the-world interpretatively, to use phenomenological phraseology, Heidegger says that

> we can point out the modification if we stick to certain limiting cases of assertion which function in logic as normal cases and as examples of the "simplest" assertion-phenomena. Prior to all analysis, logic has already understood "logically" what it takes as a theme under the heading of the categorical statement — for instance, "the hammer is heavy." The unexplained presupposition is that the "meaning" of this sentence is to be taken as : This thing — a hammer — has the property of heaviness. In concernful circumspection there are no such assertions "at first." But such circumspection has of course its specific ways of interpreting, and these, as compared with the "theoretical judgment" just mentioned, may take some such form as "The hammer is too heavy," or rather just "Too heavy!", "Hand me the other hammer!" Interpretation is carried out primordially not in a theoretical statement but in an action of circumspective concern — laying aside the unsuitable tool, or exchanging it, "without wasting words." From the fact that words are absent, it may not be concluded that interpretation is absent. On the other hand, the kind of interpretation which is circumspectively *expressed* is not necessarily already an assertion in the sense we have defined ... Between the kind of interpretation which is still wholly wrapped up in concernful understanding and the extreme opposite case of a theoretical assertion about something present-at-hand, there are many intermediate gradations : assertions about the happenings in the environment, accounts of the ready-to-hand, "reports on the situation," the recording and fixing of the "facts of the case," the description of a state of affairs, the narration of something that has befallen. We cannot trace back these "sentences" to theoretical statements without essentially perverting their meaning. Like the theoretical statement themselves, they have their "source" in circumspective interpretation.[27]

Let us return now to our discussion of the learning of language games in the *Philosophical Investigations*, for if there is a striking similarity between

[27] SZ g 157-158, e 200-201.

the *Tractarian* Wittgenstein and Heidegger with regard to the status of language, there is as striking a similarity between Heidegger and the later Wittgenstein.

As we have seen, Wittgenstein makes a sharp distinction between ostensive teaching of words and ostensive definition. Ostensive definition, if it is to be effective, presupposes that the one for whom one defines the word is already within the language game in which the word plays a role and already has certain skills in playing that language game.

> So one might say : the ostensive definition explains the use — the meaning — of the word when the over-all role of the word in language is clear. ... One has already to know (or be able to do) something in order to be capable of asking a thing's name.[28]

Training is necessary in order to inculcate an understanding of the roles played by various words in the language. Take for example the case of color words — 'red', 'blue', 'green', and so on. By pointing to various colors and in connection with a certain training it is possible to develop in the learner the skill of being able to use color words. Through training the learner comes to know his way about in the "logical space" which color words occupy. He can then be said to understand the role played by color words.

But this is not all. When training in the skill is accomplished the learner may himself ask about colors, the names for which he does not have. For Wittgenstein, the learner is now open to the world of color itself, whereas before the linguistic training he was not. Having had the limits of his language expanded, the learner's world is expanded too. It is intelligible to him in a new dimension. In short, its intelligibility has been articulated for him in ways which go beyond for a time at least, the scope of the words he possesses for expressing its articulated distinctions. A gap exists between the colors the learner is able to discriminate and the words he possesses for making the discriminations. Yet more and more as names of colors are learned, the articulated intelligibility of the world of color gets *expressed* for him in language.

Granting this account, Heidegger's appeal to "phenomena$_H$" [29] in the

[28] PI 14e-15e (section 30).

[29] In accordance with the nomenclature I have used before in dealing with Heidegger's phenomenological method, a phenomenon in the ordinary sense is anything that can be brought to show itself. (See my 'Martin Heidegger', *Review of Metaphysics* XIX (1966), 465 ff.) On the other hand, a phenomenon$_H$, the phenomenon in the true *phenomenological* sense, is that which already shows itself *prior to* the phenomenon as ordinarily understood and which accompanies the "ordinary" phenomenon in

form of prelinguistic structures appears very much similar even to the later views of Wittgenstein and much less bizarre than one is initially led to think. What would Heidegger say about the world of color?

For Heidegger the colors the learner had become able to discriminate would be phenomena in the ordinary sense of the term. That by means of which this discrimination became possible — for Wittgenstein the logical or conceptual space of color to which the learner is brought through training; for Heidegger, intelligibility-articulation — would be phenomena$_H$, structures of Being. The names of the colors and their grammar would be the language by means of which the phenomena and phenomena$_H$ get *expressed*, and through an analysis of which the phenomena and phenomena$_H$ get *revealed.* For both Heidegger and Wittgenstein meaning thus transcends, in some contexts at least, language as language is ordinarily understood; yet it comes to be expressed in language.

Among the many differences between Heidegger and Wittgenstein there are perhaps two major ones. I shall mention them by way of concluding this extended excursus into the realm of philosophical comparisons. Heidegger would claim that meaning — the meaning of Being, roughly equivalent, I think, to the sum of the various logical or conceptual spaces suggested by the *Philosophical Investigation* — has an univocal pan-transcendentality which ranges in non-generic fashion over all language games and the forms of life (worlds of experience) which they adumbrate. He conceives it his task to bring this transcendentality to expression through the forging of a language grammatically equipped to deal with the conceptual difficulties and peculiar cartographical problems the meaning of Being presents. Secondly, Heidegger thinks that human beings are brought into the realm of meaning not through training but rather by means of the presence of Being itself — in short, that the transition to peculiarly human modes of behavior must remain somewhat of a mystery. Note finally however that Wittgenstein no less than Heidegger fails to present a theory or doctrine concerning the nature of meaning and how meaning is experienced by human beings. Thus both leave the status of language in a highly problematic state; both accounts of the relation of language to meaning are difficult to construe. As I have tried to point out however — and this is my final point — there are definite similarities of a positive sort between the two philosophies and these should not be obscured by the more obvious differences.

---

every case. A phenomenon$_H$ is a condition which makes possible the "showing of itself" of any ordinary phenomenon, for Heidegger understands 'prior to' in the Kantian sense of 'necessary condition for.'

III

Consider again the ordinary language statements, embodying the concept of meaning, which I listed earlier.

She means everything to me.
For those with no background in industrial psychology, his decisions have very little meaning.
What do you take their presence to mean?
I found the Klee exhibition quite meaningful.
The sacraments mean nothing to some churchgoers.
Just having the opportunity means a great deal to him.
A red light means that you must stop.
Nature is much more meaningful to some than to others.

As I indicated before, on the surface at least, meaning is here ascribed to a number of disparate items : paintings, persons, acts, religious rites, objects produced by modern technology, abstract entities, and nature. If meaning is to be limited to the domain of language and is to be understood solely as a property of words and complexes of words, all of these statements must be translatable into a formal mode of speech. That is to say, synonymous statements must be produced in which the term 'meaning' is no longer ascribed by indirection to or predicated of the various entities to which the original statements refer. In effect, the term 'meaning' must drop out of the straightforward statement made in the object language and, if it is to reappear at all, reappear as a metalinguistic notion embodied in a metalinguistic statement. The metalinguistic statement would serve in this context as a commentary on the object language statement which has now been modified. But without doing violence to the import and commitments of ordinary language, these translations simply cannot be performed.

Heidegger, on the other hand, ascribes meaning either to man or to the Being of entities, but not, as the above statements commit us, to entities themselves — entities which are independent of human beings in at least some senses. How can it be that in these straightforward, ordinary-language remarks 'meaning', an intentional term, is predicated of the extra-human world? This is the question I wish to pose and which the programmatic commitments of Heidegger on the one hand and the Wittgensteinians on the other make it exceedingly difficult to answer. What the question points to is the need for a reexamination of intentional predicates — of thirdness, to use the language of Pierce. It points further to the need for a close reexamination of the term 'language' as it functions in the statements philosophers make about their methods of doing philosophy. Though these tasks, which must be pursued in piecemeal fashion, are beyond the scope of this paper, I hope I have suggested some reasons for their undertaking.

AUSTIN AND PHENOMENOLOGY

by

HAROLD A. DURFEE

This brief note is to suggest that the philosophy of the late J. L. Austin offered largely unrecognized foundations for a significant dialogue between linguistic analysis and phenomenology, which positions have been so deeply divided in contemporary thought. I shall concentrate on two aspects of this relationship which, to my knowledge, have been neglected in the literature. The case should not be overstated, and I do not intend to suggest that Austin consciously or intentionally attempted to affect a relationship between these movements. Nevertheless, implicit in his position there are unexpected openings for dialogue which have been too readily overlooked in the studies of Austin's philosophy. The presence of such relationships does not minimize the many differences, both in content and in spirit, between Austin's philosophy and phenomenology, nor do such differences minimize the contribution he makes to the advancement of the discussion.[1]

1. Analytic and Phenomenological Methodology

Austin's wizardry with words is common knowledge and his perceptivity in noting subtle linguistic distinctions is itself a unique methodo-

[1] Two commentators have perceptively noted relationships between Austin's position and phenomenology. W. Cerf "Critical Review of *How to Do Things With Words*" in K. T. Fann, Symposium on J. L. Austin (New York : Humanities, 1969). This review originally appeared in *Mind* (1966). Cerf appropriately sees in Austin's concern with the "total speech act" a significant relationship to phenomenology and existentialism. The relationship is also noted in an apparently little known article by H. Spiegelberg, "Linguistic Phenomenology, John L. Austin and Alexander Pfänder," *Memorias del XIII Congreso Internacional de Filosofía, Volumen IX* (Universidad Nacional Autónoma de México, 1964). The relationships suggested in the main body of the present essay are not incompatible with, but are distinct from the connections noted in these essays.

logical contribution. Although it is difficult to specify with precision the nature of his method, his critique of the sense data theory suggests that he was not simply a Humean empiricist.

In order to mark an interesting comparison of methodological proposals, let us note some suggestions regarding the phenomenological method made by Professor H. Spiegelberg. He notes that phenomenologists, whatever other differences they may have, are agreed that at least they have something of a common methodology. In attempting to offer a phenomenological description of at least part of this method he writes :

> Describing is based on a classification of the phenomena. A description, therefore presupposes a framework of class names, and all it can do is to determine the location of the phenomena with regard to an already developed system of classes. This may be adequate for the more familiar phenomena. But as soon as we want to describe new phenomena or new aspects of old phenomena, we can do little more than assign them places within the wider framework of classes with whose other members they show at least some similarity or structural resemblance, being unable to indicate their distinguishing features.[2]

In further elaboration of the phenomenological method he continues a bit later :

> Going beyond Husserl, I would like to suggest an additional way by which we can proceed from particular to general essences. It consists in lining up particular phenomena in a continuous series based on the order of their similarities ... The elements for each such collection actually come from perception and imagination. The next stage is the observation that in some of these series, especially the qualitative ones, certain groups of phenomena cluster around cores that stand out as nodal points or vertices in the sequence of phenomena.[3]

Let us now set beside this methodological proposal some suggestions from Austin as to how one is to proceed in philosophical analysis.

> When we examine what we should say when, what words we should use in what situations, we are looking again not *merely* at words (or 'meanings', whatever they may be) but also at the realities we use the words to talk about. We are using a sharpened awareness of words to sharpen our perception of, though not as the final arbiter of, the phenomena. For this reason I think it might be better to use, for this way of doing philosophy, some less misleading name than those given above — for instance, 'linguistic phenomenology', only that is rather a mouthful.[4]

[2] H. Spiegelberg, *The Phenomenological Movement*, Vol. II (The Hague : M. Nijhoff, 1960) p. 673.

[3] *Ibid.*, p. 678.

[4] J. L. Austin, *Philosophical Papers* (London : Oxford, 1961) p. 130. This is a section of Austin's famous essay on "Excuses."

A bit later he continues :

Two methods suggest themselves, both a little tedious, but repaying. One is to read the book through, listing all the words that seem relevant; this does not take as long as many suppose. The other is to start with a widish selection of obviously relevant terms, and to consult the dictionary under each : it will be found that, in the explanations of the various meanings of each, a surprising number of other terms occur, which are germane though of course not often synonymous. We then look up each of *these* bringing in more for our bag from the 'definitions' given in each case : and when we have continued for a little, it will generally be found that the family circle begins to close, until ultimately it is complete and we come only upon repetitions. This method has the advantage of grouping the terms into convenient clusters.[5]

Let us note but one instance of Austin's application of this method, and that to the problem of action. He writes :

How far, that is, are motives, intentions and conventions to be part of the description of action? And more especially here, what is *an* or *one* or *the* action? For we can generally split up what might be named as one action in several distinct ways, into different *stretches* or *phases* or stages. Stages have already been mentioned : we can dismantle the machinery of the act, and describe (and excuse) separately the intelligence, the appreciation, the planning, the decision, the execution and so forth. Phases are rather different : We can say that he painted a picture or fought a campaign, or else we can say that first he laid on this stroke of paint and then that, first he fought this action and then that. Stretches are different again.[6]

Phenomenologists have already made enough of Austin's use of the phrase "linguistic phenomenology" in order to claim his sympathy so that I shall not take further note of that, although it should not be neglected. What is even more interesting and relevant is the similarity of methodological proposal between the two authors. These few lines quoted do not capture all of Spiegelberg's analysis of phenomenological method, nor do they capture all of Austin's methodology, but in both instances they are central methodological considerations. It is of course true that each writes from a different general frame of reference, especially regarding the metaphysics of these epistemological suggestions. Austin is no devotee of Husserlian essences. If, however, one were to search for an application of phenomenological method outside of avowedly phenomenological circles, one would be hard pressed to find a clearer application of the method which Spiegelberg suggests than the labours of Austin. The process of classification, the establishment of "continuous series

[5] *Ibid.*, pp. 134-135.
[6] *Ibid.*, p. 149.

based on the order of their similarities", the combination of perception and imagination, and the concept of "clusters" all would seem to be excellent illustrations in Austin's work of the very phenomenological description which Spiegelberg recommends. Austin, of course, proceeds to do this "linguistically", but surely the linguistic aspect is not ruled out by Spiegelberg's "class names," and Austin readily admits that the linguistic concern is to arrive at "the realities we use the words to talk about." Such similarity of methodological proposal would seem to be ready evidence that Austin's philosophy introduces ample opportunities for dialogue regarding the methodologies of two philosophical schools so often considered as proceeding very differently. Whatever ontological differences may eventuate, it is surely not necessary to start with ontology, in order to proceed to a fruitful discussion of comparative methodologies. In this regard Austin's creative work in philosophy would suggest that the conversation has already been started.

2. The Philosophy of Action

The second opening for continued conversation enhanced by Austin's work concerns the ethics of language and the philosophy of action. Although it has not as yet been sufficiently explored, it is already well known that the philosophy of action is a common meeting ground of these two movements. The concern with Being, doing, and having and with the embodied self acting when the body acts has been significantly explored in phenomenological circles. The nature of action, the relationship of thought and action, and the philosophy of the emotions is familiar territory in analytic philosophy. Austin makes his own unique contributions to many of these discussions. More specifically, however, I would suggest that he initiates conversation with the phenomenologists on two important aspects of the philosophy of action. (*A*) *The Ethics of Language*, (*B*) *Excuses and Justifications.*

(*A*) *The Ethics of Language*

He writes :

It is fundamental in talking (as in other matters) that we are entitled to trust others, except in so far as there is some concrete reason to distrust them. Believing persons, accepting testimony, is the, or one main, point of talking. We don't play (competitive) games except in the faith that our opponent is trying to win. If he isn't, it isn't a game, but something different. So we don't talk with people (descriptively) except in the faith that they are trying to convey information.[7]

This quotation suggests that the speech act definitely has an ethical or moral setting, and that such an ethical setting is crucial to the very nature of what goes on, or is supposedly going on, in the linguistic interchange. To the best of my knowledge Austin never developed the ethical analysis of language which is suggested above. His analysis of promising may be a step in this direction, but it is far from an elaboration of an ethics of language. Nor, to my knowledge, have other linguistic analysts developed this hint which Austin offers, in spite of their concern with language and in spite of their concern with linguistic ethics. In fact, we seldom think of language itself, including descriptive language, as having an ethical context.

In spite of the lack of attention to this problem raised by Austin but neglected by his associates, the phenomenological tradition has offered one major analysis of this very problem. Emmanuel Levinas, in his very creative *Totality and Infinity* deals directly with the ethics of language.[8] Philosophy of language is central to his entire position and within this context he offers not only a theory as to the relationship of thought and action but also a rather thorough analysis of the ethics of the linguistic situation. This is not the place to offer a study of his analysis of this problem but it may be sufficient to note that he considers in considerable depth the relationship of language and war, language and goodness, language and desire, language and justice, language and love, language and shame, language and anarchy, language and community, language and murder, language and responsibility, language and giving, language and mystery. Let me emphasize that his is not an analysis of the language *of* war or justice or desire, etc., but how language itself and the speech act itself is related to these moral concepts, and functions in the setting of such ethical contexts, of how language itself functions ethically.

I do not urge that Austin would be satisfied with Levinas' analysis, and there is ample reason to think that he would not be content, for Levinas works deep within the context of the phenomenological movement. Nevertheless, from that context he speaks directly to the problem of the ethics of language which Austin raises, and which Austin's analytic contemporaries and successors have unfortunately neglected. Thus Austin's thought has offered a further and more refined arena within

[7] *Ibid.*, pp. 50-51.

[8] E. Levinas, *Totality and Infinity* (Pittsburgh : Duquesne, 1969).

the philosophy of action and the philosophy of language for philosophical dialogue with phenomenology.

(B) Excuses and Justifications

It is a favourite technique of Austin to work on certain "preliminary" or peripheral areas surrounding classical philosophical problems. Thus he concerns himself with performative utterances in order to approach the classical epistemological problem of "I Know", or the phenomenon of pretending in order to approach a philosophy of the emotions. In his concern with excuses he notes that they differ from justifications, and that the investigation of such borderline phenomena in ordinary language may be a fruitful approach to the classical ethical problem of moral justification.

Austin recognizes that justifications and excuses function differently, and may be distinguished with some clarity, even though they can be confused. It is appropriate to call attention to the way in which justification and excuses seem to overlap in the lived world, but this is a phenomenon to which Austin devotes little attention, although he does note that certain speech acts offer "partial justification and partial excuse". His analysis seems frequently to be quite compatible with the phenomenological concern with the "lived world" and especially the lived social world. Austin's elaboration of excuses and justifications offers an excellent illustration of the philosophical dialogue possible at this point. Let me note but a single type of illustration supplementing Austin's legal illustrations. In a governmental or industrial budgetary crisis, administrators will constantly be called upon to curtail expenditures and to authorize expenditures only when they are thoroughly justified. To justify their proposed expenditure they will offer countless reasons for doing this or that, but as we all know these reasons will be very strange conglomerations of justifications and excuses. Many reasons will be offered which do not justify, but only excuse, although presented as if to justify. Many reasons will be offered to justify which are not the real reasons for doing the act, but a pretence offered under certain circumstances. As Austin is aware, what will be accepted as justification while remaining highly ambiguous, nevertheless offers a crucial context in which the justification is offered. Many valid justifications while justifying would not be acceptable as a justification. In that case the supporter of the proposed act is forced to offer what amounts to excuses, offered as justifications, although he is well aware that they do not justify, but will be acceptable as a justification. This obviously raises the problem of ethical honesty and integrity on the occasion of justification thus introducing a further aspect of the ethics of the language of excusing.

Consider the complex mixture of excusing and justifying which occurs in the political arena, and how central the problem of honesty becomes in the justifying language of politics. I suggest that this complex phenomenon of mixed excusing and justifying, as well as many other areas which receive Austin's attention, are prime data for one investigating phenomenologically the ethics of the social and lived world. Concern with the lived world is central territory within phenomenology at least since the late Husserl. Currently the social dimensions of such analysis are receiving increasing attention.[9] In view of Austin's contribution to the analysis of the language of excuses and justifications, as well as many other linguistic acts of our social life, he thereby has introduced one further avenue for dialogue with the phenomenologists of the social world.

In the above two contexts, therefore, as well as in methodological considerations Austin initiates occasions for philosophical discussion between analytic and phenomenological philosophy. In spite of the many differences that remain, this dialogue is surely one of the next steps in the development of both of these positions.

[9] For a major presentation of this type of philosophical analysis see A. Schutz, *The Phenomenology of the Social World* (Evanston : Northwestern, 1967).

META-PHILOSOPHICAL REFLECTIONS

SOME PARALLELS BETWEEN ANALYSIS AND PHENOMENOLOGY

by

D. IHDE

If one traces the history of the analytic philosophies in fairly broad expressionistic strokes rather than in pointillistic dots it appears that in certain ways that family of philosophies has more closely approached phenomenological insights than is generally noticed. And if one traces the history of phenomenological philosophy in the same size strokes it appears that language has become more and more a problem for it. This historical convergence can be seen in relation to certain views of the relation of language and experience.[1] In this paper I intend to first indicate what I take to be the movement of convergence and, secondly, show a certain parallelism between W. V. O. Quine and Paul Ricœur in terms of their respective views of language and experience.

In the beginning a rather stark contrast appears between phenomenology and the analytic movement. This is particularly so if one compares the most extreme type of logical atomism with the phenomenological view. The key notions of logical atomism developed among the early analysts derive mainly from the work of Carnap, Russell, and the "early" Wittgenstein. Wittgenstein's *Tractatus*, which may be taken as representative, gives the clear impression that the world is composed of *atomic facts*, of discrete building blocks. These facts, given in sensory experience, are reflected in language. Discrete protocol sentences are the linguistic counterparts to the discrete atomic facts of which the world is built. Moreover, the more elementary, simple, and clear the sentence, the closer to the fact it could be. Knowledge (science) could thus be built from the bottom up by the addition of elementary sentences about facts if it is arranged in proper logical order.

[1] I use the term experience because it preserves a certain neutrality between phenomenologists and analysts. Let each interpret it according to their own philosophical filter.

If one suspends what may be called the *philosophical filter* of interpretation lurking behind this construction, i.e., that all atomic facts are basically sensory in nature and given according to a stimulus-response pattern, then it becomes possible to discern several important ideas contained in the early analytic view of language and experience. In the first place the assumption seems to be that the world is basically transparent and orderly in its construction. The ideal for philosophical language is one which seeks clear and distinct statements about the isolatable atoms of the world. If ambiguity or opacity is discovered it must either be excised or counted as false. Indeed, the tendency is to believe that any ambiguity or opacity is a problem of language itself rather than of the world. The major task of the philosopher is to remove this flaw by philosophic operation.

This conception of philosophy continues the rationalist ideal of clear and distinct ideas and also preserves the traditional sense that the philosopher is basically an ideal observer who is able, through his philosophical surgery, to arrive at "literal truth." Doing philosophy means dissolving problems through the clarification of language. This motivation remains strong even in the case to be discussed. W. V. O. Quine maintains his task is the "clearing of ontological slums." [2]

Thus in the instance of early analysis the relation of language to experience is through clearly stated protocol sentences which express single facts. All systematic knowledge is built up from these foundations. To put it simply, factual sentences are the connection with experience; logic provides the framework of relations; and all other sentences are superfluous or meaningless so far as knowledge is concerned.

If one turns, in contrast, to early phenomenology it is not at all certain that linguistic problems are even major problems for the philosopher. And certainly the points of emphasis are quite distinct. For example, it appears that frequently a larger problem for the phenomenologist is the relation between the *speaker* and language. Speech as a type of intentional activity is more central.[3] But as the phenomenologists began to investigate wider areas it became apparent that language does constitute a major problem.

Husserl's aphorism, "all subjectivity is intersubjectivity," has impor-

[2] W. V. O. Quine, *Word and Object* (Cambridge : The Technology Press, 1960), p. 275.

[3] See the excellent summary of the matter in Merleau-Ponty, *Signs*, trans. R. C. McCleary (Evanston : Northwestern University Press, 1964), pp. 84-85.

tant linguistic implications.[4] It is through language that subjectivity and the ways of intending objects attain intersubjective value.[5] In later phenomenology the problem of language gains ground in several different ways. Heidegger introduces the notion of a hermeneutic, an exercise of philosophical clarification built upon meditations upon language itself in the hope of recovering the "pre-ontological" experience of Being. Mikel Dufrenne in *Language and Philosophy* traces language and its primary relation to experience to the poetic expressions of a first look at the world, he reaffirms J. G. Hamann's notion that "poetry is the mother tongue of the language." [6] And Paul Ricœur's reflective hermeneutic takes up the problem of language from within the richness of language.

If a phenomenological consensus about language exists it may appear like this : In contrast to atomism one might say that here the whole precedes the parts. Any meaning in the elements of language is to be found in relation to the whole of a given language. Language is not built up from discrete parts, but finds its significance in terms of indefinite possibilities within the living language.[7] Moreover significance may dwell even within the silences, intersections, and intervals between the words. Again contrasting with logical atomism, the discrete statement is always bound to be incomplete and dependent upon a wider meaning in the language as a whole. It is also possible that so far as language reflects experience the ambiguous statement may also mirror something about the world and not be merely a confusion of language.

In summary : it is the totality of a living and constantly changing language with its many functions and many-layered structures which best reflects experience. Language may contain semi-autonomous bodies of theory but they always remain at best incomplete and are but partial perspectives upon the world.

To stop at this point, however, would leave the two recent families of philosophy quite distant and unrelated. On the one hand we would have the early analysts doing a "logic of the sciences" based upon a type of reductive empiricism. And on the other hand we would have the phenomenologists doing a description of the many-layered structure of

[4] Edmund Husserl, *Cartesian Meditations*, trans. Dorion Cairns (The Hague : Martius Nijhoff, 1960).

[5] Quoted from Husserl's *Formal and Transcendental Logic* in Merleau-Ponty, *Signs*, p. 85.

[6] J. G. Hamann, a contemporary of Immanuel Kant, is an often overlooked philosopher who asserted the primacy of language as a philosophical problem.

[7] Merleau-Ponty, *Signs*, p. 42.

the world from their quite pluralistic view. But the story does not stop here. We now recognize two quite different directions in analytic philosophy.

The one side known as ordinary language philosophy may, in part, be traced to the "late" Wittgenstein. Wittgenstein evidently became less and less happy about his earlier statement of the problem and turned away from the atomism of the *Tractatus* to an interest in ordinary language. Evidently one of the problems became the complexity of the "facts." More flexibility was called for since language could not be simply reduced to protocol statements (nor the world to atomic facts). Wittgenstein indicated, "My propositions are elucidatory in this way : he who understands me finally recognizes them as senseless, when he has climbed out through them, on them, over them." [8]

What Wittgenstein came to believe, without ever abandoning his notion that the key to dissolving philosophic problems lay within the study of language, was that even an ideal language is no guarantee that one has adequately grasped the actual facts. An ideal language is no guarantee that what is taken as fact is so. Philosophy must become more a linguistic activity than ever if it is to discover the world aright.[9] Wittgenstein seems in some cases to have come to the conclusion that language itself is only a part of an activity which is at base non-linguistic.[10] He seems to have come close to the phenomenological position regarding the need to describe this pretheoretical world when he indicates in the *Blue Book*, "I want to say here that it can never be our job to reduce anything to anything, or to explain anything. Philosophy really is 'purely descriptive'. (Think of such questions as 'Are there sense data?' and ask : What method is there of determining this? Introspection?)" [11] Wittgenstein's following is also informative of certain parallels. Within the scope of ordinary language philosophy Austin appears quite interesting. Austin, with most of the linguistic analysts, insists that language cannot be reduced to the three simple categories of statements (empirical, tautological, and meaningless) of the positivists. Rather there are many dimensions and functions within language — and presumably within experience. With Austin the philosophical task becomes one of pointing out the subtleties of language. Austin attacks many of the

[8] Wittgenstein quoted in W. Barrett and H. Aiken, *Philosophy in the Twentieth Century*, Vol. 2 (New York : Random House, 1962), p. 490.

[9] *Ibid.*, p. 490.

[10] *Ibid.*, p. 490.

[11] *Ibid.*, p. 725.

historic problems by first accusing traditional philosophers of being a bit too debate-minded. Had the traditional philosopher paid more attention to the richness and flexibility of ordinary language he might not have gotten himself into the dichotomous controversies (such as free-will versus determinism) which so often debilitate philosophical advance.

From the "late" Wittgenstein on one sees this movement away from rigidity and towards a more flexible view of language. In addition one sees the emergence of the notion that language reflects experience in a multitude of ways. This approach obviously has a greater affinity to the phenomenological sympathy for a recognition of multiple dimensions to the world and experience.

But my main concern is not with the ordinary language philosophers. It is rather with what I take to be a development from the positivist side of the family. In this country there appears to have been a wedding of certain positivist and pragmatic views which I think are resulting in still another parallel between analysis and phenomenology.[12]

It is with the work of W. V. O. Quine that one finds this direction stated in its boldest terms. Quine is perhaps best known for his "Two Dogmas of Empiricism" in which he attacks the distinction between synthetic and analytic statements held so dear by the early analytic thinkers. Quine's attack was waged on behalf of a different view of the relation of language and experience. Quine puts the matter clearly :

> It has been the fashion in recent philosophy, both that of some of the English analysts and that of the logical positivists, to think of the terms of science and ordinary language as having some sort of hidden or implicit definitions which carry each such term back finally to terms relating to immediate experience. Now this view is clearly unrealistic. A better description, though countenancing the notion of immediate experience still, is as follows. On the one hand we have language, as an infinite totality of said or appropriately sayable phrases and sentences. On the other hand we have our sense experience, which by a process of psychological association or conditioned responses, is keyed in with the linguistic material at numerous and varied places. The linguistic material is an interlocked system which is tied here and there to experience; it is not a society of separately established terms and statements, each with its separate empirical definition.[13]

Quine's statement of the problem indicates both his connection with the positivist version of analysis and his rather distinctive modification

[12] James Edie has indicated that in certain respects William James approximates phenomenology.

[13] W. V. O. Quine, "On Mental Entities," *Proceedings of the American Academy of Arts and Sciences*, Vol. 80, No. 3, March, 1953, p. 198.

of that tradition. On the one hand Quine retains the same philosophical filter as the positivists. Wherever language does "key in" with experience it is primarily in terms of sensory experience interpreted behavioristically. These connections between language and experience Quine terms "surface irritations" upon the body of the language. And in some ways "surface irritations" appear to be quite like atomic facts — but not quite. Quine does insist that "occasion sentences," sentences which "command assent or dissent only if queried after an appropriate prompting stimulation," [14] and "observation sentences" which are "occasion sentences whose stimulus meanings vary none under the influence of collateral information," [15] are the closest to immediate experience.

But on the other hand, Quine's view of language seems to imply a strong rejection of logical atomism. The indefinite totality of language has what might be called a life of its own. It contains numerous interlocked systems and "bodies of theory" in addition to the most primary occasion and observation sentences. Thus if one wants to understand a term or a statement within the language this may be done only in relation to the wider linguistic connections.

What emerges in Quine's theory of language is what may be called a multiple-layered view of language and experience. The linguistic system is interlocked and connected in various (and often nonlogical) ways. And it is also layered. In short, a language is somewhat like a vast linguistic onion composed of many layers. Following this metaphor, the outermost layer is the one which "keys in" here and there with experience in terms of surface irritations. Here it is that one makes the primary statements which Quine takes to be quite neutral or objective. He says, "Observation sentences peel nicely; their meanings, stimulus meanings, emerge absolute and free of residual verbal taint. Similarly for occasion sentences more generally, since the linguist can go native." [16] But the inner layers have less and less "experiential purity," i.e., the inner layers of the linguistic onion become more and more dependent upon larger bodies of theory. This is the case with all theoretical statements.

> Theoretical sentences such as 'neutrinos lack mass' or the law of entropy, or the constancy of the speed of light, are at the other extreme. It is of such sentences that Wittgenstein's dictum holds true : "Understanding a sentence

[14] Quine, *Word and Object*, p. 36.

[15] *Ibid.*, p. 42.

[16] *Ibid.*, pp. 76-7.

means understanding a language." Such sentences, and countless ones that lie intermediate between the two extremes, lack linguistically neutral meaning.[17]

Here the picture emerges more clearly. At the surface there are more or less simple statements upon which agreement may be had; at the other extreme are the theoretical statements including philosophical ones. In between there are various connections and layers which span the gap, a rather great amount of linguistic onion skin.

The acceptance of this theory of language and experience in relation to philosophy has several results so far as Quine is concerned. In the first place it both relates philosophy to other types of theorizing and at the same time removes philosophy from any absolute position. The philosopher lives in the same linguistic world as anyone else and he must work his way around from within. This means that the philosopher cannot assume the "high and serene" balcony from which to observe the whole. The philosopher is within the maze; he is different from his peers only in terms of detail. Quine indicates :

> The philosopher's task differs from other's then, in detail; but in no such drastic way as those suppose who imagine for the philosopher a vantage point outside the conceptual scheme that he takes in charge. There is no such cosmic exile... He can scrutinize and improve the system from within, appealing to coherence and simplicity : but this is the theoretician's method generally.[18]

In addition to this relativity the philosopher has one further difficulty. He stands, as it were, the farthest removed from immediate experience so far as the layers of language are concerned. This means, Quine says, "No experiment may be expected to settle an ontological issue; but this is because such issues are connected with surfacc irritations in such multifarious ways, through such a maze of intervening theory." [19]

What, then, is the philosopher to do and how? The only help the philosopher-inside-the-onion has, according to Quine, is the device of "semantic ascent," that is, the philosopher shifts from talk about objects to talk about "objects" (words).[20] Or, if I may risk a paraphrase of this analytic version of the *epoché*, one may seek to discover something by refusing to talk in terms of literal truth, of belief, of the material mode, in short, of the natural perspective, and talk instead about words and the conceptual schemes.

[17] *Ibid.*, pp. 275-6.
[18] *Ibid.*, p. 276.
[19] *Ibid.*, p. 276.
[20] *Ibid.*, p. 272.

The major task of the philosopher is to reflect upon language through language in the hopes of *clarifying* and *describing* areas of linguistic relationships which have heretofore been either muddled or misleading. But even this is done within the linguistic onion.

For Quine and, as I shall try to show, for Ricœur, the border between language and experience is not a neat and clear one. Even the distinction between linguistic and non-linguistic phenomena, between words and their referents must be made linguistically. This *is* the hermeneutic problem.

In one sense Ricœur (and much of recent phenomenology) begins where I have just left off with Quine. It is indeed the recognition of the hermeneutic problem which has led some phenomenologists more deeply into the problems of language. A favorite phenomenological distinction has been that between the pretheoretical world and the world as presented theoretically. There was Husserl's noematic-noetic correlation. There is the life-world and the reflections of thought upon that world. But at the same time all of these distinctions must be made *within* language. It may be true that linguistically we point to that which is non-linguistic but our pointing is in terms of a language.

Ricœur deals with this problem as he struggles with his interpretation of man. In *La symbolique du mal* Ricœur deals with man's understanding of himself and his situation in terms of the problems of evil. Ricœur holds that the primary symbols and primitive myths of man hold a certain suggestive richness of thought which may be explored philosophically. That is, primary symbols and myths are expressions of man's self-understanding; they are "words" which man pronounces upon himself. Philosophy, if it wishes to approach any kind of universality in relation to human experience, must reflect upon these issues and self-confessions (*l'aveu*).[21] It is in the light of this particular problem that Ricœur raises the hermeneutic issues : "In contrast to philosophies concerned with starting points we must begin] from within language and of meaning already there. [Philosophy's first problem] is not how to get started, but, from the midst of speech, to recollect itself." [22]

From the very outset one must be warned : Ricœur's philosophical interest and also his philosophical filter are quite different from Quine's interests and filter. But this is not the focus of interest here. What is of

[21] Paul Ricœur, "The Hermeneutics of Symbols and Philosophic Reflection," *International Philosophical Quarterly*, Vol. II, May, 1962, p. 200.

[22] *Ibid.*, p. 192.

interest is the great similarity, in structural terms, of the understanding of language and experience.

As Ricœur orients himself "within language" it becomes apparent that he, too, accepts an "onion shaped" view of language and experience. In this case the place where language keys in with immediate experience is with various *primary symbols*. These are Ricœur's counterparts to Quine's surface irritations. At the outset one must not ignore the quite different problem and filter. Where Quine is interested in logical theory, Ricœur is interested in philosophical anthropology. Where surface irritations are linguistically neutral and expresss behavioral occurrences primary symbols are opaquely suggestive and are filled with poetic richness.[23] So here the connection with experience is interpreted quite differently, i.e., the philosophical filter has a different mesh. But that is not the main point.

The main point is that for Ricœur as for Quine there are certain privileged sentences or statements which afford a more direct connection between language and experience. (And who is to say at this preliminary stage that these connections may be or may not be of more than one type?) Both Ricœur and Quine maintain a sense that at various points language does key in with experience.

But language does not key in with immediate experience at all points. With Ricœur as with Quine, philosophy stands at a rather distant point from the primary statements. For Ricœur philosophy is to be a *reflection* upon the symbols, its ultimate goal is to go beyond the symbol as such — though care must be taken not to distort the intentionality of the symbol.[24] Philosophy must remain informed by the primary statements, but its theorizing goes beyond them. As such philosophy stands the same risk that theory in general does for Quine. It remains within the system and it must recognize the need for correction.

Again, for Ricœur as for Quine, between philosophy proper and the primary statements stands a maze of intervening interpretation or levels of expression. There is both interconnection, in which the philosophical task is the phenomenological job of understanding "symbol by symbol, by the totality of symbols," [25] and there are levels of interpretation. In terms of Ricœur's special problem there are primary symbols which are the most immediate responses of man's understanding of evil; then there

[23] *Ibid.*, p. 194.
[24] *Ibid.*, p. 201.
[25] *Ibid.*, p. 201.

are myths which are "first order spontaneous" interpretations of symbols; then there are theological doctrines which are third level interpretations, and so on. In brief, between philosophical reflection and primary statements stands a vast amount of intervening interpretation, many layers of onion.

How does the philosopher work through the layers? and what is his task? Again Ricœur and Quine resemble one another. Ricœur's version of "semantic ascent" is what he calls the *second naiveté* of a philosophical hermeneutic.[26] When the philosopher *qua* philosopher looks at symbols and myths he shifts from a material mode to a formal mode of understanding. That is, the philosopher is not interested in the "literal truth" which the believer may take the myth to hold. Rather the philosopher is already ascendant to the level of *interpretation.* He asks what is the intentionality of the myth apart from its cosmological scheme, apart from its logos. What is the theme of the myth? Ricœur's own exposition of his hermeneutical theory is quite complex and need not detain us at this point. It is safe to say that when he examines given symbols and myths he does it more on the model of a sympathetic literary critic than that of the fundamentalist to the Bible. The point is simply this : in order to gain a philosophical perspective within language the philosopher must ascend from the "literal" or material mode to the formal mode of interpretation. With this Ricœur stands with Quine.

But, the philosopher in his ascent must remain with his feet on the ground. He works out his problems within the fray rather than from above. Even philosophy cannot claim to be the concrete universal, says Ricœur, since the philosopher cannot view the whole. The philosopher stands within a relativity of language and situation. His task is basically a descriptive and clarifying one. For Ricœur this makes of philosophy basically a hermeneutic task, a process of reflection of language upon language in such a way that from within one may see the way from experience to theory.

Thus for Ricœur from the phenomenological point of view, and Quine from the analytic, both recognize that language does key in with experience, but this connection is neither simple nor sure. One must always be wary in the sense that language may reflect as much upon language as it does upon experience. The philosophic problem is always, at least in one of its most important dimensions, hermeneutic or lin-

[26] *Ibid.*, p. 202.

guistic. In this I suspect that both Ricœur and Quine understand the significance of Neurath's aphorism :

> Wie Schiffer sind wir, die ihr Schiff auf offener See umbauen müssen, ohne jemals in einem Dock zerlegen und aus besten Bestandteilen neu errichten zu können.[27]

[27] Quoted from Otto Neurath frontpiece to Quine, *Word and Object*.

IS THERE A WORLD OF ORDINARY LANGUAGE?

by

J. WILD

Having recently spent seven months on the continent of Europe and having conversed with philosophers in five different countries there, I was surprised to find, under wide diversities and sharp disagreements, a well-marked current moving in a single direction. Apart from members of traditional schools, the living thinkers of Western Europe are basically concerned with the human life-world, or *Lebenswelt*, as Husserl called it in his last published work, *Die Krisis der Europäischen Wissenschaften.* I am not suggesting that most European thinkers are now committed to any of the special methods and doctrines which Husserl defended at different stages of his long and constantly self-critical career. This is not true. Nevertheless his concern to achieve an accurate description of the concrete phenomena of the *Lebenswelt*, as they are experienced and expressed in ordinary language, is a constant theme of all his writings. And in this broad sense the influence of phenomenology has spread far and wide. There are, no doubt, other sources for this contemporary interest in the *Lebenswelt*. But Husserl is perhaps the focal center of this new empiricism and his influence the most widely recognized.

By *world* Husserl meant not a thing, not any set of objects, but rather an ultimate horizon within which all such objects and the individual person himself are actually understood in the "natural attitude" of everyday life. This horizon of concrete experience is sharply contrasted with the objective horizons of science which attend exclusively to objects via perspectives that are partial and abstract. As over against these, the world horizon of human life is concrete, subjective, and relative to man. This analysis has now been very generally accepted, and most European philosophers would agree that the task of describing the phenomena of this life-world and of analyzing its structure is of primary importance for philosophy. The scientist, like the rest of us, lives and moves within this world, and in a sense it is presupposed in his investigations. But we cannot expect him to perform the task of analysis, since he is interested in special, abstract objects of his own. Furthermore we must recognize that, since the time of Plato, philosophers have disregarded the *Lebenswelt* as a subjective region of shadows, and have turned their attention rather to transcendent objects and problems.

On the Continent, there is now a widespread skepticism concerning such objects and problems, and a widespread recognition of the need for a more radical empiricism, now generally referred to as phenomenology. The aim of this discipline is to describe the phenomena of everyday life as they are lived in the horizon of the *Lebenswelt*, and the foreign visitor is struck at once by the many philosophical studies of such concrete phenomena as laughter and tears, imagination, sorrow, the feeling of guilt, personal encounter, and so forth. In these studies, abstract terms and technical language are avoided, for it is recognized that the many shades of meaning and the very ambiguities of ordinary language are themselves significant and much closer to the concrete. Each abstract horizon of science has its own special mode of abstract speech. But to deal with the inexhaustibly open and ever-changing phenomena of the *Lebenswelt*, a richer, more flexible, and more far-ranging mode of expression is required. What we call "ordinary language" develops and lives in the *Lebenswelt*. Hence this radical empiricism has brought forth a deep and widespread interest in the modes and structures of common speech. This is of course only a brief sketch but, I believe, a true characterization of what is going on now on the continent of Europe.

After returning to this country via England and Oxford, I was deeply impressed by certain apparent similarities between the living philosophy of the Continent and the linguistic analysis which is now proceeding so widely and so intensively in the Anglo-Saxon countries. Here, too, I noted a similar distrust of transcendent, unobservable objects, and of the artificial problems engendered by such assumptions. One also finds a similar urge toward empiricism, a respect for what is called *fact*, and finally a similar recognition of the depth and fertility of that ordinary language which is presupposed in all the artificial constructions and abstract modes of speech which grow out of it. These similarities led me to reflect on the mistrust and suspicion which is so openly expressed on both sides of the English Channel, and to wonder if this is not somehow based on avoidable misunderstandings and misconceptions. Is not the ordinary language of daily life correlated with the ordinary phenomena of the life-world? Is it not true that the careful study of the one must require the careful study of the other? Are not phenomenology (in the current broad sense) and linguistic analysis both approaching the same thing (concrete experience) from different angles? Are they, then, not so much severely opposed as mutually supplementary and fructifying?

I think that these questions need to be asked, and that an affirmative answer is possible. But before an affirmative answer can be given, certain difficulties must be cleared away. There are, of course, evident differences between these two movements of thought. Perhaps the most basic of these is a tendency on the part of analytic philosophers to identify the world of everyday experience with the objective universe, or with the facts revealed by different sciences, and thus to follow our tradition in slurring over the concrete and humanly relative phenomena of the *Lebenswelt* with which ordinary language is primarily concerned. In this chapter, I shall first of all give a concrete illustration of this failure to distinguish between what we may call abstract facts of science and concrete phenomena of the *Lebenswelt*; second, I shall try to clarify the meaning of this term *Lebenswelt*; third, defend the distinction between scientific facts and world facts; fourth, offer some criticism of two recent attempts to avoid it; and finally, fifth, raise a question for analytic philosophers concerning the need for a distinctive kind of empirical analysis which philosophers alone can perform.

A Reduction of Fact to Scientific Fact

The above tendency to merge all facts together under a scientific rubric is at present very widespread in England and America owing to the prestige of science, and might be illustrated from many different works. I shall choose a recent essay by G. J. Warnock entitled "Analysis and Imagination," in the volume *Revolution in Philosophy*.[1]

Warnock is considering the different tasks which he believes need to be performed by philosophical analysis. The first is to exercise a therapeutic function in revealing "the distorted character" of certain general philosophical questions (p. 114) and "breaking down the cramping rigidities which generate some philosophical difficulties" (*ibid.*). No radical empiricist could possibly disagree with this recommendation, especially as the author points out that the only remedy for such misguided questions "is to put our concepts back to work again in actual examples, to observe how in concrete cases they do actually function" (*ibid.*). Next Warnock turns to "the 'systematic' work of analytic philosophy," which

[1] (New York : St. Martin's Press, 1957), pp. 111-126.

is to "examine language in the spirit of pure research, describing and ordering its features..." (p. 115). The phenomenologist can only applaud this aim.

After this, the "explanatory task of analysis" is considered. It is possible for the analyst to ask, "Why do we use language in this way? (p. 117). Why, for example, do we use the concept of cause as we do? In order to answer such questions, Warnock again recommends a procedure that is thoroughly empirical and phenomenological. "To explain our concept of causation," he says, "we need to trace its connections not only with other concepts that we employ, but also with empirical facts about the course of events in the world, and the ways in which we concern ourselves with these events" (p. 118). In this passage he seems to be speaking not merely about the objective facts of an abstract scientific horizon, but about concrete facts in the life-world with which we ourselves are concerned.

Finally Warnock turns to the "inventive" function of analysis : How can the analytic philosopher be original? We think at once of the array of divergent systems, and as soon as metaphysics enters into the picture, everything changes. The idea that philosophy has any empirical function to exercise fades away. The world of fact is the same for all of us. There are no philosophic problems here. A past metaphysician, like Berkeley, "saw the same world that the rest of us see, but saw it from a rather different angle" (p. 122). He may have invented a new "conceptual apparatus," but in claiming that he was "discovering something real" (*ibid.*) he was wholly mistaken. Real facts are the province of science. In this respect the logical positivists were quite correct. "It was precisely by making these claims, by presenting themselves as super-scientists, discoverers par excellence, that metaphysicians drew on their own heads the formidable bludgeon of Logical Positivism" (*ibid.*). In claiming any access to facts of any sort not thoroughly covered by some science, philosophy sets itself "on quite the wrong ground, ground from which it is liable to be destructively expelled" (p. 123).

After some reflection on these passages, the reader is led to ask, does philosophy exercise any factual function or does it not? Warnock seems to give a divided answer, and this ambiguity, I believe, is significant. In dealing with the therapeutic and systematic functions of philosophy, he recognizes that the analyst is not concerned with concepts alone but also with certain facts, recalling our attention to "the concrete and the familiar" (p. 115). Now science may begin with the concrete and the familiar but it does not end there. Indeed, to be in this condition is precisely the sign of imperfection and immaturity. Each science tries to move away from this, as soon as possible, to the abstract and the unfamiliar. To dwell on these familiar facts of concrete experience in the attempt to analyze them accurately and interpret them is not the function of science. If it is to be performed at all, it is the function of philosophy. If there are such *philosophic facts*, or world facts, as we may call them, not "covered" by any special science, then it is false to assert that philosophy is exclusively concerned with language alone, or with our "conceptual apparatus."

But then a few pages further on, after suggesting something of this kind, Warnock ridicules the whole idea that philosophers (now called metaphysicians) might be "discoverers" (p. 122), and asserts that any claim to factual evidence will bring them onto ground from which they are "liable to be destructively expelled," especially by Logical Positivists.

This, I believe, is a confusion, to which I desire to call the reader's attention. It is in essence the failure to recognize an important ambiguity in the English word "fact," which refers not only to scientific facts, such as that the boiling point of water at normal atmospheric pressure is 100° C., but also to *world facts*, as I shall call them, such as that the pencil I write with is on the table at my right. I shall maintain that these two senses of the same word "fact" are quite distinct, and that our constant tendency to reduce the second to the first leads to basic confusions concerning the nature of philosophy. Before turning to this distinction, however, I must first say a few words about the human world which has now emerged as one of the best confirmed discoveries of phenomenology. This is a term in ordinary usage which we have already used without special explanation. Now let us analyze it a little more carefully.

The Human World

The American philosopher William James played a vital role in this important discovery. In his *Principles of Psychology* (pp. 258, 281-82, and 471-72) he points out that the objects of experience are not insular impressions sharply separated from one another, as the British empiricists had supposed. This is a logical ideal of how we should experience them. In our actual perception, however, they are always surrounded by a field of meanings which refer them to other objects. These references are easily taken for granted, or forgotten, as we concentrate on the central object of our attention. But they play a vital role in all perception. James called them *fringes*, and the sections noted above were carefully read and annotated by Husserl.[2] They led Husserl to his notion of the *Lebenswelt*, the last horizon of meanings in what he called the natural attitude of our everyday existence.[3] After Husserl's investigations, this world horizon has been studied by many thinkers, including Sartre and Merleau-Ponty in France. One of the most thoroughgoing and disciplined analyses is that of Heidegger in his important work, *Sein und Zeit*. The chief results of these studies may be briefly summarized as follows.

The life-world is a horizon of meaning which, in some particular version, is always found with men. It includes all the persons, events, and things which we do or can encounter. When we wish to express the most far-ranging doubt concerning the location of anything in any region, we say, where in the world will you find it? This world includes not only spaces and places but things, persons, and modes of action. Hence when we seek to express the most far-reaching doubt concerning any of these categories, we use similar expressions, saying, What in the world is this thing? who in the world will do this for you? and how in the world will he do it? This horizon of meaning encompasses all that we can know by feeling, thought, imagination, and any natural power. Hence, to speak of another world, or of what lies beyond this world, is a reference to what transcends our experience in the widest sense of this word. Any person, event, or thing in the world presupposes this background of meaning, for something not in this world would not be intelligible and would no longer be a thing. Indeed, it would be doubtful whether we could meaningfully refer to it as a being, for what a thing really is, refers to its place in a final world horizon.

The world has a spatial aspect; though, as we have seen, the primordial space of the life-world is very different from any geometric space. These are later abstractions from it. Hence, when I think of myself or some other person as being in the world, I mean something more than mere spatial inclusion, as a cup is in the cupboard, or a shoe is in the box. I am in the world rather as in a field of care, as we speak of a woman as being in nursing, or a young man as in love. This world is divided into the different regions of my care, like the kitchen for cooking, the bedroom for sleeping, and the library for reading and study. The different utensils

[2] Cf. Aron Gurwitsch, "Les 'fringes,' selon James" in *Théorie du champs de la conscience* (Paris : Desclée De Brouwer, 1957). pp. 246 ff. for an account of Husserl's relation to James on this, as well as other matters.

[3] Cf. *Krisis der Europäischen Wissenschaften und die transzendentale Phänomenologie* (The Hague : Martinus Nijhoff, 1954), pp. 127ff.

in these regions are for some use, and are either in or out of their proper places. This referential for-structure is usually taken for granted and hidden under the "obvious." But when something is lacking or out of place, it may suddenly loom into view. The tools of a given region have a bearing on one another; the chair bears on the desk, and the desk on the paper for writing. Whole regions bear on one another, as the procuring of raw materials bears on manufacturing, which is for distribution. All these different regions are finally for the use of man who orders them in different ways, depending on the ultimate objects of his devotion. Hence the world order, or cultural pattern, of one people will differ from that of another; and in those where personal freedom is respected, the world of one individual may differ radically from that of another.

When we first become aware of these differences in world horizons of meaning, which enter into everything that we do and say, we are apt to think of them as isolated islands, each enclosed within itself. But this is a mistake which leads to the influential view now known as *relativism.* It arises from a failure to understand the perspectival character of human awareness. Thus I can never see or grasp, for example, the whole of the table before me, except in a partial perspective from the left or the right, from above or below. But this does not mean that I cannot see the whole table in this way. As I look at the table from above and in front, I can see the bottom of a rear leg, and also the table top that keeps me from seeing the rest. In this and other ways, each perspective leads beyond itself to other parts that it sees itself not to see. Hence, unless it becomes pathologically fixed and frozen, a single perspective remains open to other perspectives revealing other parts of the object without interference. Thus in and through a partial perspective or, even better, through a number of these, I can grasp the style and pattern of the whole.

The same can happen to our versions of the human world of meaning, though there is here an even greater danger of partial fixation and dogmatism. If I become, even to a slight degree, critical of my world of meaning, I can recognize gaps and areas beyond my horizon, involving vast regions that I know I do not know. This enables me, as well as those around me, to distinguish between our versions of the world and the world into which all these versions open. It is a main task of philosophy to keep these versions flexible, so that individuals and groups living in entirely different versions of the world may be able to communicate and to keep on growing. In order to do this, we must recognize, however, that there is no world in itself apart from our human versions, which are all real as far as they go, and must be taken account of in any interpretation of the world which is not hopelessly abstract and partial. There is no world apart from our human versions, and these different versions, unless they become rigid and congealed, open into *the world* which has a place for them and yet transcends them all.

Our lived existence is made up of encounters with powers and persons absolutely independent of us. Meaning is the human answer to these encounters. Man is the responsible being who can respond in this way, gather things together into a world that makes sense of everything, and, therefore, really is. The meaning of the Battle of Waterloo must take account of the plans and the actions of the men who fought and died there, to the last detail. It is inseparable from the concrete events, precisely as they happened. And yet meaning is relational or referential in character, and always points beyond to something further. Thus the meaning of the battle involves the public policies of France, England, and Prussia, the future course of history, and the projects of those of us who are now alive and trying to interpret it. The world is the ultimate horizon of meaning which tries to do justice to all events of which we are aware, and to all other perspectives alien to our own, by ordering them around our ultimate hopes and aspirations. To find a place for something in such a version of the world, which we have reason to believe fairly closely approximates the world, is to find out what it really is.

We do not know what these alien agencies are before we meet them and struggle with them. We call them beings a priori, in the hope that we may find a meaning in them and thereby find out what they really are. But these independent agencies do not give themselves up without a struggle. They resist not only our acts but our noetic powers as well.[4] Meaning has to be snatched from their hidden depths and brought up into the light of truth bit by bit. But further depths always remain. Being is an ambiguous word, which stands both for this resistance on the part of real beings, as well as for the hope that we shall find their real being or meaning in the world. At first, we grasp only a minimal meaning in these independent beings, their approximate location in space and in time, and whether they seem alien or friendly. These scattered findings we call *facts*. They may be trustworthy and hold up in time, but they are only a beginning. We do not find out what they really mean until we are able to fit them together in ways that make sense in a total horizon of meaning.

[4] For a fuller account of this noetic resistance, cf. my article "Contemporary Phenomenology and the Problem of Existence," *Phil. and Phen. Research*, Vol. XX, No. 2 (December 1959).

This discovering of the sense of things involves two distinct aspects that are usually opposed. On the one hand, full justice must be done to the scattered facts, down to the last detail. Any failure here will jeopardize the most coherent system. But on the other hand, the isolated facts must be fitted together in an overarching world of meaning. Only then can we catch a glimpse of what these alien beings and we ourselves really are. Each way of knowing has its own horizon, some being wider and some less wide. But in each of these we find a division of labor between those who are chiefly concerned with the detailed facts and those who are concentrating on the broader systems of meaning, though these diverse functions are inter-dependent and often overlap. Thus in science, for example, we find a division of labor between the experimental and the theoretical physicist, and in the life-world there is a similar division of labor between the historian, on the one hand, and the philosophically oriented student on the other.

But are there two horizons of this kind — science and the life-world? If so, these two ways of knowing must be concerned not only with different kinds of meaning but with different kinds of fact. We have noted how Warnock denies such a distinction. For him, there is only one kind of fact — the facts of science. There are no historical or, as we may say, no historical world facts. I believe that this reduction of fact to scientific fact is found not only in the thought of analysts, but also in that of many other philosophers at the present time. It has even begun to exert a marked influence on our ordinary language and our common sense. I have chosen Warnock's essay simply as a clear and fairly typical example of a tendency that is now widespread in English and American philosophy. Indeed, this tendency is firmly grounded in a traditional distrust of the supposedly confused and transitory data of immediate experience, which goes back to the origins of rational thought in the West. But I am not concerned here with this historical background. I am interested only in showing that there is an order of world fact which is bound up with ordinary language, and which is quite distinct from the different ranges and levels of scientific fact.

Two Kinds of Fact

Let us begin, in the first place, with the difference between the one as concrete, the other as abstract. Science certainly begins with individual world facts. But as we have pointed out, it moves as rapidly as possible to various abstract levels where it can formulate certain hypothetical laws of the type, "if A then B." As is well known, these laws do not attempt to describe the actual course of concrete events. They state rather what will happen in general under certain specified conditions. Thus, disregarding atmospheric resistance, a body will fall at such and such a rate, or at a certain pressure water will boil at such and such a temperature. These abstract generalizations are the facts of science. When a science has arrived at maturity, concrete occurrences come into the picture only insofar as they exemplify or conflict with such generalizations. The movement is away from the concrete toward the abstract. Let us now turn to a world fact such as : this yellow pencil is now on the table at my right. The pencil is now here before me as I face the world. Such facts as these are at least as certainly known and as well confirmed by critical observation and intersubjective testing as any scientific facts. But two differences need to be noted.

General terms, of course, like "pencil," "yellow," and "table," have to be used. Otherwise the fact would remain ineffable. But the fact is individual and concrete, as is indicated by the demonstrative words *this* and *my*. The universal terms are used not to express a universal connection, but to illumine an individual situation here and now which must constantly be recognized and held in mind, if this fact is to be properly analyzed and understood. Here the movement is not only from the concrete to the abstract and universal, but also from the abstract and universal back again to the concrete, which is always the center of attention. Such an entity, in its full concreteness, like this pencil or me, myself, is always envisaged in the world horizon, though this is often left unexpressed. Thus I do not normally think of myself as being in the solar system, or even in the Milky Way, though these statements are technically true and acceptable in certain artificial contexts. But the whole of my concrete being, to which I refer by the first person pronoun, is too rich and variegated to be included within such abstract horizons. So I say rather of myself in a concrete context that I am in the world.

In the second place, while a world fact may be illumined by universal terms and by hypothetical judgments involving special movements and conditions (if I looked at it from below, it would still look yellow), it does not necessarily involve such special conditions or abstractions. It is simply a concrete fact that has now emerged in world history. Of course one can analyze out certain conditions, like normal light, that do in fact hold. But these conditions hold after the fact and in it, not before. The fact is not dependent on adopting a certain abstraction or making certain arrangements. It simply happens in the world. Hence it is to be described in a categorical, not in a hypothetical or universal mode. These two differences, then, must be noted. The facts of science are abstract and partially dependent on special modes of observation. World facts are concrete and independent of any special mode of approach.

A third basic difference, clearly noted by Husserl, is that the various fields and regions of science are purely objective, and consciously removed from what is called *the subjective*, as something incidental and capricious. To observe something scientifically means to gain an attitude of impartial detachment, and to regard it as an object that is simply there before the mind. Whatever cannot be regarded in this way is dismissed as capricious and subjective. Non-living things cannot be examined in any other way, and probably not too much is lost in analyzing them. Every phase of human existence also can be regarded from the outside, even human thinking and action once it is finished, in its deposits and results. But something is missed by such an objective procedure. This is the act as it is proceeding, as lived and experienced from within. Thus it has now been shown that it is one thing to analyze the finished results of language from the standpoint of an external observer, and quite another to analyze it as it actually proceeds from the point of view of the living speaker.[5]

These inner factors of lived experience may be ignored as subjective by the detached attitude which is normal for science, but they are nevertheless important to living men and play an essential role in the world horizon, which, as Husserl said, is relative to man and subjective. This is certainly true in spite of the vast range of this world horizon. Thus it is clear that the organs of the human body map out a world pattern, and that the human infant, from the time of birth and before, is open to a world that answers positively or negatively to its needs. It is no wonder, then, that we speak of the human world in contrast to the life-fields of other animals with different organs and needs. We go even further than this and speak of my world, and of the world of a given individual, *x* or *y*, whose pattern is quite different. Such subjective factors have no place in the objective perspectives of science. Hence we do not speak of my galaxy nor of the Hindu solar system. It is perfectly natural, however, to speak of the Hindu world, for this horizon of concrete facts involves not only objects but also subjective factors which are normally omitted by science.

That this is no mere accident of speech, we can show by a brief analysis

[5] Cf. F. de Saussure, *Cours de linguistique générale* (Lausanne : Charles Bally et Albert Sechehaye, 1916).

of the world fact we have chosen : this yellow pencil now on the table at my right. Physical space does not lie around a vital center, and is not oriented with respect to vital directions. Hence, while the physicist may have to employ the notions of right and left in manipulating the instruments of his experiment, they have no place in the finished products of his analysis. But the space of the world is an oriented space, and we would at once lose our bearings if we could not distinguish in it the directions of right and left. Not only is this true, but the notion of the pencil being *on* the table refers to a subjective orientation that is wholly absent from physical space. It involves a category of above and below, which is derived from the relation of my body to external objects, which cannot be conveyed by any purely geometric or physical analysis. No matter how detailed such an analysis might be, unless it surreptitiously introduced "anthropomorphic" factors, I could not tell from it alone which of the extended objects was above or below, or whether they were merely side by side.[6]

The objectivist will no doubt wish to say that this is merely the introduction of a distorted and biased version of physical space. But this is also to express a bias. Without begging many questions it will perhaps be fairer to say, in the light of what is now known, that world space contains many human factors which are absent from any pure geometric or physical space. This should not be understood as implying that world space, or the world, is merely *subjective* in the usual sense of this confusing word. If we turn to ordinary language for guidance, we find it hard to imagine any situation in which it would be reasonable to say that space is in me, or that the extended things outside of me are in me, or that the world is in my head. The relativity of which we have been speaking makes no demand on us to accept any such absurdities. Neither does it necessarily imply that our experience is a distorted version of things as they are in themselves.

It does require that the things we know are in relation to us. But there is no reason for doubting that these relations are quite real; that we can know them, at least in part, as they are; and that by abstracting from these relations, science can give us some knowledge of what things are apart from them. The beings around us are quite independent. But we understand them and order them in a world horizon which is relative to us. This is a digression, however. The point we are concerned to make

[6] M. Merleau-Ponty, *Phénoménologie de la perception* (Paris : Gallimard, 1945), pp. 117-118.

is that this relative world horizon is different from the more abstract perspectives of science, and that world facts, therefore, include relative factors which are absent from what we may call normal scientific facts. What are these relative factors?

I shall not attempt to draw up an exhaustive list, but now, as a fourth point, will make a few comments on one of the most important of these, namely, value.

These phenomena can, of course, be regarded from a detached point of view as value facts. In this way they can be embraced within a scientific or objective framework. We can observe that such and such a person *A* has a desire for *B*, and that such and such a culture *Y* has a dislike for Z. But objective facts of this sort are quite different from values as they are directly experienced in the *Lebenswelt* and expressed in ordinary language. Hence the statement that science is neutral to value conveys a certain truth which needs to be spelled out. We shall take the time now briefly to note three differences.

First, we have inherited from our tradition a strong tendency to think of things as substances which are prior to their relations including value relations — a certain kind of accident. A thing must first be what it is before it can have a value. Thus for the objective analyst, the pencil is first of all an extended substance with a certain shape and point, a certain color, and so forth, which may be used for writing. Value predicates are later additions that things come to have in relation to human desire. In the *Lebenswelt*, however, values are original, and lie at the very core of things. Thus in ordinary conversation, we would never refer to the object at my right as a thing with certain properties adapting it to writing. We refer to it straight off as a pencil, which is not a neutral noun but a value term. This is not only true of artificial objects but of natural objects as well, like sunshine, storm, and fire. In the life-world, these objects are originally loaded with value meanings. To lose sight of these meanings is to fall into complete disorientation. In the *Lebenswelt*, value is not a later addition. It is constitutive of the thing.

Second, the realistic tradition has led us to make a similar analysis of the human agent or the human group. Good or evil desires and acts are later accidents which the agent may or may not "have." But the living agent is not separated from his acts in this way. He *is* a set of desires and aspirations. A human culture is not a neutral structure with approvals and disapprovals added on. It *is* a structure of approvals and disapprovals. To be committed to a value is very different from observing this from outside. When I actually hold to a value, it becomes essential to me, and affects my whole existence from the ground up. Thus in ordinary, moral discourse, as distinct from detached argumentation, we do not say that a friend of ours had courage on such an occasion. We say he was courageous. We do not speak of a person as developing attributes of slyness and greed. We say he is rapacious.

Third, we have already touched on a point which needs to be developed further. This is a tendency commonly found in objective analysis to regard value as a special kind of property, or genus, or region separate from other regions. One example of this would be the traditional way of distinguishing between value and fact. More specific illustrations would be Hartmann's realm of value, and even G. E. Moore's conception of value as a very peculiar, simple, and unanalyzable property. It is difficult, however, to find concrete illustrations of this restrictive character when one turns to the life-world. Here what we refer to by the term "value" refuses to let itself be confined within any special compartment or region but seems rather to run through various regions, even getting itself involved in whatever it is that enables us to distinguish between different regions, each of which is for some end. Thus the whole area of agriculture farms, fields, storage plants, and slaughterhouses, is for food; that of medicine, sewers, food inspection, research laboratories, medical schools, and hospitals, is for health; and so on.

In the light of these facts, it would seem to be hard to maintain that value is confined only to a single, special region of its own. It would seem rather to pervade the whole life-world. This pervasive character is reflected, as we should expect, in ordinary language, where value is not expressed by any special words or forms but by all words and all forms, including the tone of voice.

I believe that this is sufficient to show that there is an ultimate world horizon correlated with ordinary language, which has certain features distinguishing it sharply from the objective horizons of traditional realistic thought and modern science. This world horizon is (1) concrete and (2) categorical. It also contains (3) certain "subjective" and relative factors, among the more important of which is (4) a pervasive "value" factor which cannot be understood (as it is) from the outside, but only as it is lived, so to speak, from the inside. As over against this, the horizons of realist philosophy and science are abstract and hypothetical. They also have no place for the lived experience of value and other experiences of this kind, whose pervasive character they try to restrict, and which they neglect and dismiss as private and subjective. Hence I believe that the distinction between world facts and scientific facts is justified. World facts are in the former horizon, scientific facts in the latter.

We have pointed out that the world horizon is characterized by a certain ultimacy, and that, for ordinary language at least, what lies beyond the world possesses an unqualified transcendence which certainly does not seem to belong to any facts of science. We have also suggested not that every scientific fact, but that every type of scientific fact, can be found as an abstract aspect of some world fact. In the context of ordinary discourse, we should certainly find the statement that science is out of this world as odd. These observations might seem to suggest that the various perspectives of science, or *the* perspective, if there is such a thing, should be regarded as an abstract horizon within the *Lebenswelt*. Such a view is, I think, defensible and certainly does not imply any traditional form of idealism. But it raises many basic issues which I have not touched upon. So I am not considering it here. I am simply asserting that world facts belong to an independent world horizon quite distinct from the scientific universe, that this is the factual horizon of ordinary language, and that it deserves disciplined attention and study by philosophers. This is my thesis.

Two Ways of Reducing World Facts

As we have pointed out, the central tradition of Western philosophy has been predominantly objectivist, and has been marked throughout its history by a strong tendency to restrict and depreciate world facts as relative and distorted versions of reality, and finally to absorb them into a purely objective perspective. I shall not try here to review the manifold phases of this prolonged attempt to discredit ordinary language and its world. I shall single out two recent versions of this attempt, now widely familiar, for a brief concluding comment. One of these uses the distinction "private vs. public," the other that of "subjective vs. objective." Both distinctions are now commonly employed as ways of restricting the world horizon of everyday speech to a very limited perspective which, in this reduced form, can be more readily fitted into the scientific universe — the last framework into which objectivist thought has crystallized.

Those who make the former distinction arbitrarily cut off the human person from his world horizon and enclose him within a private world of his own. Since the sensory equipment of each individual is different from that of every other, we can understand why the sensations that arise in him must be different from their objective causes, and also different from those of another. Each individual lives in a private world of his own which he directly experiences within himself. These private worlds, though different in quality, vary in correlation with objective stimuli. Hence, if properly interpreted, they may be biologically useful and may justify the inferences of science. They appear with the human organism as a late phase of biological evolution and, as such, they may be fitted into the great public world of objects, which includes them spatially as well as temporally, and which is always the same for all observers. Just as the private dwellings of individuals are tiny parts of the public town, so the private worlds of individual organisms are tiny parts of the public universe of science. Both Russell and Broad have used the terms "public" and "private" in a reductive argument of this kind.

Of this argument we need only note that, while every experience arises from a private center, it always opens into a public world horizon, from which it cannot be separated except by arbitrary abstraction. My world is never exclusively private. It is my private way of relating myself and my experiences to an ultimate horizon which is shared. In its very constitution it is a union of the private and the public, and, therefore, has room within it for both. As a matter of fact, both factors are always found, as is clearly witnessed by ordinary language; for do we not only say that I myself, my body, my innermost thoughts and desires are in the world, but that the public streets, the fields, the mountains, and the stars are in the world as well? Both public and private are factually in the world. As the British philosopher W. H. F. Barnes remarks at the close of his interesting essay "On Seeing and Hearing" : "I have merely tried to bring out the simple and obvious feature about the senses which makes us feel rightly that each person is, by having senses, at once given access to a common world, and at the same time possessed of a private one." [7]

The distinction between subjective and objective has also been used to break down the integral structure of human existence in the world, and to discredit ordinary language for the sake of artificial constructions. Such attempts are subject to a similar criticism. Consciousness has a subjective center, but it is found to be always stretched out toward objects of some kind. These objects, and the way in which they are ordered, may differ from individual to individual and from culture to culture, but no self has ever been found in an objectless state. As a matter of fact, our experience is neither exclusively subjective nor exclusively objective but a relational structure to which neither term alone does justice.

[7] *Contemporary British Philosophy*, Third Series (New York : Macmillan, 1956), pp. 63-83.

Concrete experience is private as well as public, subjective as well as objective. Neither can be separated from the other and reified without distorting the facts, for human existence is open to a world horizon. Man carries this "field" with him wherever he goes, and it is now clear that this is a necessary aspect of his existence. Without a world there can be no man, and without man there can be no world. Far from containing us within a special, mental region, it is precisely our lived subjectivity that opens us to an ultimate world horizon, and it is precisely this last objective horizon that requires a subjective center. In the light of these remarks, I shall now venture to suggest that the distinction of private vs. public, and subjective vs. objective, as they have been commonly used in traditional philosophy, are phases of an age-old effort to depreciate the world of lived experience as subjective and relative, and to discredit ordinary language as hopelessly vague and confused.

A Final Question Addressed to Analytic Philosophers

I began this chapter by noting the present sharp separation of those phenomenological studies of the world of direct experience which have had a revolutionary effect on the continent of Europe, from the method of linguistic analysis which is now exerting a marked effect on Anglo-Saxon thought. In the light of the close correlation between ordinary language and the empirical world, this mutual separation and distrust seems strange, and I suggested that a study of the reasons for this mistrust of philosophy on the Anglo-Saxon side, as in any sense an empirical discipline, might have something to do with the traditional tendency to disparage or at least to restrict, the immediate data of experience as unstable and subjective.

I then examined a recent account of analytic philosophy, and showed that it was characterized by a certain ambiguity in its use of the term *fact* which easily leads to a reduction of world fact to scientific fact, and to a denial that philosophy has any empirical function to perform. After this, I made some comments directed toward the clarification of the notion of the human life-world, one of the most important discoveries of recent phenomenology. Then I offered four kinds of evidence to show that there are cogent reasons for making the distinction between world facts and scientific facts. Finally, I chose two types of argument, based on the distinctions private vs. public and subjective vs. objective, which have recently been used to restrict and discredit immediate experience as purely private and subjective. I showed that these arguments are subject to certain criticisms, and that our subjective experience, far from being reducible to a set of impressions, or inner sense data, actually opens into a world horizon which is markedly distinct from the objective perspectives of science and traditional philosophy. In the light of these observations, I should now like to raise the following questions which, it seems to me, are important for analytic philosophers.

Is it not true that ordinary language is concerned with facts of a different order from those of science? Is there not a world of ordinary language? Is it not likely that this world has a certain structure which is not the concern of any special science but is worthy of disciplined attention? Such a study has been inaugurated on the continent of Europe by the so-called phenomenologists. Is not such a study closely correlated with that of everyday discourse? Instead of being essentially opposed, are not these two approaches mutually supplementary and fructifying? In short, is there not a world of ordinary language, and is not the disciplined study of this world of interest to the analytic philosopher?

A number of analytic philosophers have shown an interest in these questions. But while we wait for a considered answer from them, let us now return to the life-world, and the new concepts and new methods that will be required for its disciplined exploration.

HARE, HUSSERL, AND PHILOSOPHIC DISCOVERY

by

J. COMPTON

The question whether linguistic philosophy and phenomenology have any significant common ground has been raised increasingly in recent years. It seems to me that one useful means of exploring this question is to examine descriptions of the very concept of philosophical analysis which each involves so as to suggest relevant similarities in aims and methods. There *are* many such affinities — and I shall want to mention some, ones which are important for establishing communication between these traditions customarily considered so disparate. There are also fundamental differences not only in techniques and doctrines but in style and, one might say, in cultural temper. This is to say nothing of the extensive variation and bitter disagreements internal to each tradition itself — among the proponents of early and late Wittgenstein, among followers of the early and late Husserl, and of course, within the personal evolution of these formative giants themselves.

If the detailed relationship of these philosophical styles is to become clear, it will take many books. In advance of this happy day, however, it is possible to suggest that the community of language and phenomenological analysis is to be found in the *problem* each finds central to its work — the problem of the future and function of philosophy itself — and that other comparable aims, methods, and conclusions result from this. At any rate, this is my contention. Certainly, the literature evidencing anxiety of this subject within each movement is enormous. But I cannot leave it at this. What I want to suggest specifically is that each movement falls (and recognizes that it falls) into embarrassment in its attempt to characterize what it means by genuinely philosophical statements, that these embarrassments are in principle the same, and that they result from preoccupation with essentially the same philosophical task, namely the clarification of meaning and that to undertake this task is their common resolution for the problem of the function of philosophy. Such a contention, justified, leads further to some conclusions about the nature of philosophic discovery. For convenience, I will refer chiefly to a paper by R. M. Hare [1] and to passages from Edmund Husserl as typical.

I

In his article, Hare examines the peculiar status of statements expressing the fruits of philosophical analysis, statements in which philosophers proclaim their "discoveries" such as that an object cannot both have and not have the same property or (my examples) that mind is a dispositional property of human behavior, or that perception cannot yield conclusive evidence, or that goodness is not a property. Such statements, made at the conclusion of an analysis of a linguistic sort, are usually termed analytic truths, that is, their truth is said to follow from the meaning or use which we give to the words used to express them and nothing else. We are said to discover these philosophic truths when we see the relevant use of "object," "property," "mind," "goodness," "perception," "evidence," and so on, in our language.

Now according to Hare the dilemma that faces the analytical philosopher is this : (1) Either these statements are indeed analytic, in which case they are, on the usual view, conventions or recommendations as to how words shall be used and thus are not discoveries; they are not informative, nor do they constitute any set of knowledge, for it would seem inappropriate to say that we "know" that a "rule" is "true." (2) Or else, these statements are contingent descriptions of the way in which certain groups (e.g. Oxford dons) actually employ language, in which case they are empirical propositions, properly parts of some statistical branch of descriptive linguistics, and not philosophical statements after all.

The real question at stake, as Hare points out, is whether statements expressing philosophic discoveries do not constitute a class of statements *neither* clearly analytic *nor* clearly empirical and if so how they are to be described. Certainly, there will be both decisional and empirical elements included in any complete account of such statements.[2] But the very

[1] "Philosophical Discoveries," *Mind*, LXIX, 1960, pp. 145-62; published also in part in a symposium on the "Nature of Analysis" in the *Journal of Philosophy* LIV (1957), 741-758. Further references on my part will be to the version in *Mind*.

[2] Professors Henle and Körner, commentators in the symposium (*op. cit.*) show reasons to consider statements in analysis analogous to "decisions" (753 ff.) and "rules" (761 ff.) concerning word usage, respectively, but clearly in an extended sense, since these decisions or rules must, it is admitted, formulate and "accord" (in some

divergence of proposals to explain them underlines their descriptively given, paradoxical characteristics : we are genuinely tempted to call them both necessary (normative) and synthetic. Statements in philosophical analysis do seem necessary and universal : For example, were we to find a speaker or speakers predicating of "an object" contradictory properties, we should be certain that either we did not understand what was the point of this special use or that it was a misleading and erroneous one. What we would surely *not* do, as philosophic investigators, is to modify our statement that "an object" (in the present sense) cannot both have and not have the same property. On the other hand, while such a statement is not empirical, there is a temptation to consider it synthetic : For it is in some sense (yet to be defined) a claim about the meaning or use of certain words, meaning which might be otherwise than it is, and which we have had to discover by a process not of decision but of dialectical investigation using paradigm cases of actual usage.

Hare's own proposal is that we consider the analogy between philosophical discovery and remembering. And he draws both upon the concrete example of remembering a dance such as the "Eightsome Reel" when it is danced, and upon Socrates' discussion of *anamnesis* in the *Meno*, to make the point that philosophical analysis formulates explicitly what "we learnt at our mother's knees and cannot remember learning," namely the appropriate use of the terms analyzed. He continues :

> Logic, in one of the many senses of that word, is learning to formulate the rules that enable us to make something of what people say. Its method is to identify and describe the various sorts of things that people say (the various dances and their steps) such as predication, conjunction, disjunction, negation, counting, adding, promising, commanding, commending, — need I ever stop? In doing this it has to rely on our knowledge, as yet unformulated, of how to do these things — things of which we may not even know the names, and which indeed may not *have* names till the logician invents them; but which are, nevertheless, distinct and waiting to be given names. Since this knowledge is knowledge of something that we have learnt, it has, as I have said, many of the characteristics of memory — though it would be incorrect, strictly speaking, to say that we *remember* how to use a certain word; Plato's term 'recall' (ἀναμιμνήσκεσθαι) is perhaps more apt.[3]

---

manner) with the philosopher's (or some one's) actual usage. Apparently, R. B. Braithwaite, on the other hand, in *An Empiricist's View of the Nature of Religious Belief*, (Cambridge : University Press, 1955) p. 11, is willing to consider these statements as plainly empirical.

[3] *Ibid.*, p. 159.

Hare's treatment of philosophic discovery, however tentative and incomplete, is especially valuable for the following reasons :

(1) Following recent uneasiness about this "dogma," Hare shows that it is impossible to insist that all statements must be (exclusively) either *a priori* or synthetic without begging the question whether *this* contention itself is a "discovery" or rather a stipulation. It is an open question, then, which further discovery must determine, whether there are any synthetic *a priori* statements, specifically whether statements in philosophical analysis are such, and, most importantly, whether it is philosophically instructive so to label them.[4] Thus, by his own *example* of philosophic discovery he confirms his own *analysis* of philosophic discovery — that is, by being unwilling merely to pigeonhole or explain away statements in philosophic analysis, Hare demonstrates that philosophical analysis (even *of* philosophical analysis) *does* proceed by a kind of description towards a kind of seeing, precisely as his conclusion requires.

(2) What we can see, both through his description and doing of analysis, is that statements in philosophical analysis *are* unique in type and that the kind of seeing which they claim to express is not empirical but, rather, resembles recall. The word "resembles" must be underscored here. Hare virtually forgets that the truth of a recollection lies in its accord with what occurred (in this case, the use that was learnt), the discovery and demonstration of which is an empirical matter. If such demonstration were literally considered to be the basis of philosophical analysis, then such analysis and the statements which are its fruit would form a part of history or genetic psychology.

(3) Remembering this *caveat*, we can see that the kind of "recollecting-seeing" expressed by statements in philosophical analysis is more nearly what Plato meant than Hare thinks : precisely what makes discoveries in philosophical analysis unique is that they are *not* about words or even the learning and recollecting of word usage, but about what is expressed or meant by those words and through that usage. Flew [5] and others have pointed out that post-war language analysis avails itself of paradigm-case

[4] Oliver A. Johnson has boldy carried the argument one step further. Not only is the statement, "No synthetic statements are *a priori*" false, it is necessarily false — for it itself is synthetic *a priori* and, therefore, self-contradictory. From this, he concludes that the statement "Some synthetic statements are *a priori*" is necessarily true and is itself an example of one. See his "Denial of the Synthetic A Priori," *Philosophy*, XXXV, July, 1960.

[5] Antony Flew, "Philosophy and Language," in *Essays in Conceptual Analysis*, (London : Macmillan, 1956).

reasoning — dancing through the examplary use — but its conclusions formulate, at least hopefully, a recognition of common meanings and meaning relations of concepts. Analysis, then, is conceptual analysis. It aims at a seeing which is understanding through description of meaning which is conceptual clarification.

(4) It is worth remarking, as Hare himself suggests, that the danger besetting any analysis of meaning, namely that it fall into either the issuance of verbal edicts or the reporting of philological or other factual data, reflects the historical context within which the ideal of analysis has developed. It is a context marked by the progressive occupation of all factual territory by the empirical sciences. It is a period of reaction against (largely idealistic) metaphysical recommendations on the one hand and various reductions of philosophy (particularly logic) to psychology and history on the other. The problem was and is to secure philosophy as responsibly scientific, yet independent both of metaphysical invention and empirical encroachment. Philosophy has been seen to require a method and subject matter of its own.

II

Now this is all well recognized. What is not so well recognized is that phenomenology was born in just this same historical context and with the same regulative idea leading it on. From his earliest critique of psychologism in *Logical Studies* to the final, partly published work on the *Crisis in European Science*, Edmund Husserl struggled, as he put it, to develop "philosophy as a rigorous science," if not as an exact or empirical one. By this he clearly meant to avoid both the sterility of analytic reasoning *more geometrico* and the assimilation of philosophy to empirical science. He saw that both formal reasoning and science, in fact, rest upon fundamental concepts which require clarification and justification and that philosophy needed, therefore, to become radical reflection upon all forms of meaning. But in what does such reflection consist and how is it to be carried out? These questions led Husserl to the notion of the reduction.

Phenomenological analysis, according to Husserl, is inseparable from the phenomenological and eidetic reductions. The theory of the reduction [6] is that a wrench is required, a conversion if you please, in order

[6] Edmund Husserl, *Ideas* (New York : Macmillan, 1931), sections 27-32, 88-90. See the Introduction and notes by Paul Ricœur to his edition and translation, *Idées directrices pour une phénoménologie*, (Paris : Gallimard, 1950).

to turn our attention from routinely living and working and speaking *in* the world to apprehend the meaning of that world simply as such. The purpose of the famous "bracketing of existence" is not to remove anything from philosophical consideration but only, as Husserl puts it, to "alter its sign," to neutralize our commitments and prejudices — metaphysical, scientific, practical — so as to allow the fulness of the world to appear to us as it is. The phenomena which are to be rendered apparent in such a purified or transcendental experience are the meanings of such concepts as "physical object," "mind," "perception," "evidence," "decision," "goodness," and the like. The reduction, as the method of phenomenology, then, involves (1) reflection, (2) which is disinterested, (3) directed from particular facts to the universal, the typical, the essence, (4) which is essence, not in the sense of natural type, such as is the object of natural history or natural science (sheep, granite, atom), but essence in the sense of meaning, which is to say, for Husserl, "signification for the subject." Meaning in this sense is "intentionality," a *way* (usually, the *ways*) in which some aspect of the world, designated by the concept, functions in the subject's experiencing. No more for Husserl than for Wittgenstein do meanings "exist" in some "domain" or is meaning confined to referring. Meaning is the feature of a world constituted in the living experience of man. But man "intends" his world in many ways. And on this view there are as many modes of intentionality, modes of meaning, as there are ways in which language functions to express them — describing, counting, defining, deciding, appraising, committing, feeling, commending, and so on.[7]

Within the reduction, the technique for bringing meanings to explicit or thematic formulation is described by Husserl as "free-variation."[8] Whatever is essentially involved in the meaning, say, of perception, will remain constant while particular features of a perceptual experience are varied in imagination or through a consideration of differing cases. Descartes' examination of the bit of wax is a classic example. And, I suggest, any attempt to prepare for analysis of a concept, such as perception, by imaginative linguistic performance — for example, by asking whether, if an object changed colour or turned out not to have another

[7] On the modes of intentionality : *Ideas*, sections 93-95; on meaning as function : *Ideas*, section 86; on language and meaning : *Logische Untersuchungen* (Halle : Niemeyer, 3rd Ed., 1922) Vol. II, part I, and *Formale und Transzendentale Logik*, (Halle : Niemeyer, 1929) sections 1-5.

[8] *Ideas*, section 70.

side, one would still *say* he had perceived it — is a rigorous analogue of this same procedure of free-variation.

It should be obvious that my sketch of phenomenological method is drawn to direct attention to the fact that its aim and techniques for descriptive meaning analysis are logically similar to those employed in linguistic analysis, the chief difference being that in the latter it is word-function which is the vehicle of study while in the former it is experience-function which is considered primary. The shift of philosophic attention from fact to meaning in language analysis is what Husserl terms the reduction, the use of the exemplary case corresponds to the method of free-variation, the "rule extracted" functions as does the "essence intuited" in phenomenological terminology. And these are but the more obvious correlations. The more deeply this relationship is meditated, I am convinced, the more clearly it appears that these two are species of a common philosophic enterprise.

Now the pitfalls facing phenomenology are notorious. It is to these that I will next turn for further evidence. Meaning analysis, considered as description of signification for the subject, threatens either to become introspective, individual psychology, or, through modification of the experience by impure reflection, tends to yield constructions of meaning which are invented for special purposes or which reflect unannounced presuppositions. These two spectres of philosophy, pseudo-psychology and metaphysical construction, have to be exorcised by Husserl again and again in the pages of his writings. Husserl in his famous *Nachwort* laments bitterly that his view of phenomenological description has been misinterpreted to mean introspection.[9] To the charge of psychologism, in *Ideas I* for example, he reiterates the requirement of the reduction — that there be a change in point of view which attends not to particular perceptions or joys, say, as if they were inner states of a particular man, but to the universal meaning or function of perception or joy implicit in their awareness as such.[10] To meet the danger of interference of alien categories with reflection, he restates the descriptive goal of phenomenology. At the conclusion of the fifth of the *Cartesian Meditations*, Husserl writes :

> Actually, phenomenological explication is nothing like metaphysical construction; and it is neither overtly nor covertly a theorizing with adopted presuppositions or helpful thoughts drawn from the historical metaphysical tradition. It stands in the sharpest contrast to all that, because it proceeds

[9] *Ibid.*, Author's preface to the English edition, pp. 11-16.

[10] *Ibid.*, section 53.

within the limits of pure "intuition" or rather of pure meaning-explication ... phenomenological explication does nothing but explicate the sense this world has for us all, prior to any philosophizing ... a sense which philosophy can uncover but never alter.[11]

In short, Husserl's response to the charge of confusing philosophical statement with factual ones is to remind us of the *a priori* character of the former; while his response to the charge of confusing philosophical statements with new rules for usage is to remind us that philosophical statements are descriptive. If this sounds familiar, having followed Hare's discussion, it should!

III

I do not intend to *judge* these claims here. I will have made my point if I have shown that such claims, or rather, such declarations of intent, with their attendant perils, are implicit in philosophical analysis of either sort and, very likely therefore, in the notion of philosophic discovery itself. Let me express my discoveries, if such they be, about philosophic discovery, in the following way :

(1) Phenomenological and linguistic analysis seem to be occupied with a common task, namely descriptive meaning analysis and reveal common features of analytic method and common embarrassments in employing and justifying that method.

(2) These commonalities in divergent traditions make apparent the paradoxical but irreducible characteristics of philosophic discoveries which have the form of statements expressing the meaning of a concept. Any philosophical statement asserting what a word or concept or experience "means" is at once necessary and corrigible, at once empirical in being drawn from cases but also *a priori* in presupposing the cases as typical, at once liable to present only *de facto* usage or individual impression and yet claiming transcendental validity. (And, of course, this holds of the philosophic description just made).[12]

[11] Edmund Husserl, *Cartesian Meditations*, (The Hague : Nijhoff, 1960) pp. 150-151.

[12] It further follows that these modern forms of philosophical analysis are continuous with more ancient (and "metaphysical") ones, notwithstanding their obviously different account of its import and foundations. Classical metaphysical statements can no longer be dismissed as either tautologies or proto-scientific hypotheses. Or, if one prefers, statements expressing conclusions in philosophical analysis and in metaphysics are of the same logical type. For statements of the type "If there are composites there must be simples" (Leibniz) or "To be is to be one" (Aristotle) are proposed as both necessary and factual, if true then true on pain of self-contradiction

(3) Finally, it is plain from this that philosophical analysis is not a mechanical matter of observation or remembering, but a matter of reflective or logical insight into meaning, dependent for its preparation upon the collection, arrangement, comparison, and criticism of examples, but never produced or fully justified by these activities alone. As Husserl and Hare both agree, recognition of meaning is, in the last analysis, its own and only evidence.

when denied, yet possibly false and requiring argument; in short, they show, on examination, precisely the characteristics above described of statements expressing (alleged) philosophic discoveries. See the extended defense of this point by Henry Veatch, "Matrix, Matter, and Method in Metaphysics," *Review of Metaphysics*, XIV, June, 1961, p. 592 ff.

PHENOMENOLOGY AND LINGUISTIC ANALYSIS : I

by

C. Taylor

In this paper I have tried to find some points of comparison between the methods respectively of phenomenology and linguistic analysis. I have tried to show that they are more alike than they appear at first sight, and that in their extreme forms they are as it were "symmetrical" deviations from what may come to be an agreed norm.

I have had to devote more time to phenomenology than to linguistic analysis for the obvious reason that it is the less familiar. Long as the exposé of phenomenology is it is still very summary and one-sided. I would rather apologize for its brevity than its length.

I. One of the key concepts of phenomenology is that of "intentionality," which Husserl took over from Brentano. In adopting it, Husserl altered its meaning quite radically, so that from being a refinement of empiricism in Brentano, it came to constitute for Husserl his point of rupture with empiricism.

The modern thesis of intentionality can be expressed as the thesis that whatever is an object of consciousness has "significance." [1]

In order to make this term clearer it would be best to concentrate on the sphere of perception. This is particularly justified, in that phenomenology, growing out of the empiricist tradition, has concentrated largely on perception, and has even, at times illegitimately, made it the model for all the operations of mind. The thesis in its restricted form can be put : that anything which is an object of perception has significance.

This is meant first of all to rule out any view that would construe perception on the model of a contact between material objects. In this context the thesis means that an object perceived plays a role in the life of the mind of organism in virtue or more than its material properties,

[1] This is the translation I have adopted for Husserl's word "*Sinn*." "Meaning," the normal translation, would lead to confusion.

these latter being delimitable roughly as the sum of the primary or secondary qualities of classical empiricism, or the sum of those properties which can make a physical impression on the organism. In this form it is a rejection of some of the theories current in modern psychology which try to account for behaviour and perception in terms of "colourless movements and mere receptor impulses as such" [2] and is similar for instance to a point made by Mr. R. S. Peters in his *Concept of Motivation*. These theories, as Peters shows, break down because they cannot account for intelligent behaviour. The terms they use for instance to designate the responses of animals in experimental situations, designate actions like "biting the floor boards" and "leaping the barrier" which are movements classified in terms of their end results.[3] The responses in question, therefore, cannot be characterized or classified without using such terms as "purpose" or "intelligence".

Now in the learning situation (the examples above are taken from experiments on learning) a given stimulus acquires the capacity to bring about a certain response. But we cannot speak of the same stimulus acquiring links with different "colourless" movements in the organism. We have to see this as the acquisition of a "discriminating" or "intelligent" response to the stimulus. But this means that the object of perception can alter while the stimulus remains the same — intelligence can be understood in terms of how much is "seen" in a given situation by different organisms when the stimulation is more or less the same.

This alteration in the object of perception or "phenomenal object" is a change in its significance. In so far as it has significance, therefore, we can speak of the phenomenal object not only as having a certain size, shape or colour, properties which could make a physical impression on the organism, but also as "being a means to" a desired end, as "hiding" or "bringing" something "into view", as "being the front of" or "the beginning of" an object or event. The phenomenal object is not just "present to consciousness", it plays a certain role in the life of the perceiver, *i.e.*, is relevant to his purposes, and is linked with events and objects which are not actual or perceived, or as phenomenologist authors put it : it "refers us" to these objects or events — *e.g.*, the further side of the mountain, or release from the cage. To quote Merleau-Ponty : "Each part (of the phenomenal field) announces more than it contains and ... thus is already laden with significance." [4]

[2] Clark L. Hull : *Principles of Behaviour*, Chap. I.

[3] *Ibid.*, p. 114.

[4] M. Merleau-Ponty : *Phénoménologie de la Perception*, p. 9.

The thesis of intentionality (still restricted for the purposes of this discussion to the field of perception) in its modern guise is, therefore, the doctrine that all perception has significance, which means at once that certain terms used to describe speech-acts, such as "announce", "refer to", can be applied to it in a transferred sense (a sense often used in describing music — a parallel frequently drawn by phenomenologues), and that each percept "announces" more than it contains. But thirdly — something that will have become evident from the discussion above — it means that perception is not to be seen as externally related to behaviour, that perceptual and behavioural space are one, that our behavioural know-how enters into what we see, and that this is what invests the phenomenal field with significance. It can be seen that unlike the Brentanian account of intentionality, this is a thesis about the correct application of the concept perception, and one which reposes on a model very different from the classical empiricist one. Behind such terms as "impression", "sensation", or "sense-datum", the classical theory was putting forward a model based roughly on the *camera obscura.* No matter how deeply this original image was buried in later more sophisticated theories of sense-data, the root idea remained, *viz.* that our perception was not action but passion, something that happened to us. In construing perception as a kind of behaviour, phenomenology has broken decisively with this tradition. If the animal's perception of the lever is "saturated" with his behavioural know-how about escaping from the cage, then it is comprehensible that the lever should "announce" something more than itself. If, on the other hand, we see it as an impression, then the significance it has must be something extrinsic, something 'inferred" or else acquired as a causal property by "association".[5]

In fact traditional empiricism has always considered the original layer of perception as "mute", and explained the acquiring of significance in one or other of the two (incompatible) ways just mentioned. In so far as the second way was adopted — explanation by association in the sense of a reinforcement of a physiologically-defined stimulus, then a theory like that of, say, Hull is the fulfilment of the promise of classical empiricism. We have seen that this theory cannot account for behaviour which can be described as intelligent. There is, however, another intellectualist strand in empiricism which construes learning as a kind of reasoning

[5] For detailed exposition of phenomenologist arguments against traditional empiricism and "intellectualism" see M. Merleau-Ponty : *Phénoménologie de la Perception,* Introduction.

on the basis of sense-data, which therefore tries to account for intelligence while maintaining that perception itself, or "immediate perception" is devoid of significance. Typical of this strand, for instance, is the characterizing of our beliefs about material objects as a "theory" to explain the occurrence of sense-data or as an inference from sense-data.

But this original mute layer of perception can only be made sense of, if we conceive the objects it contains as being radically separate from the world of things which we infer from them, for in so far as sense data announce no more than they contain, there is nothing more to be found out about them which is not known by the very fact of their existence. We cannot build a world out of them, we can only project one behind them, as it were. The plausibility of the view that we identify disparate sense-data and then begin to notice an order in their appearance which we project into the future stems from the fact that we can perform this kind of operation with objects. We can infer a connexion between two things. For instance we can see on separate occasions, either side of a mountain, and we can "infer" that they are in fact the sides of one mountain, and not two separate ones. But the validity of this kind of reasoning depends on our being able, at least in some cases, to verify this by "seeing" what we earlier "inferred" — in this case, by walking around the mountain. But this walking around only counts as seeing because each perspective of the mountain "refers beyond itself" to the next one, because each side "announces" the other side. This kind of "inference" therefore makes sense as between things or sides of things in the world. They are, in a sense, already combinable and they prescribe to us what is to count as a privileged moment of perception when the combination can be seen. Sense-data notoriously cannot be dealt with in this way. They are not part of the world and their connexions cannot be verified.

There are notorious difficulties connected with this view, which it is probably unnecessary to go into at this moment. The point I wish to make here is simply that the fact that our perception has significance is linked to the fact that it is of the world, that a layer of "immediate perception" which was mute would have to have as objects not things in the world, but the reflections of these things in the mind. It is this link which has led in phenomenology to the development of the thesis of intentionality from its general form "that consciousness is consciousness of ..." to the particular form that whatever is an object of perception has significance. For the latter not to be true, the "objects" of perception would have to be in some sense "in the mind". And this in a very peculiar sense, in which, say, feelings and emotions are not "in the mind". For these too are not all that they appear, we can explore them further, find out more about them, clarify them, and so on. Sense-data must be in a sense "parts of" the mind having as yet no reference beyond themselves; they must be, to use a traditional word, immanent. The thesis that perception may not have significance is the thesis that one can separate the immanent from the transcendent in perception, which is in turn the thesis that not all consciousness is consciousness of ...

Thus intentionality which was first considered a property of some immanent phenomena by Brentano, and later extended to all such phenomena by Husserl, eventually undermined the distinction between the immanent and the transcendent itself. The current distinction in phenomenology between object and phenomenal object is seen more on the model of that between vocable and word, or body and organism than of that between evidence and conclusion, or sign and significate. But the development took place over the whole span of Husserl's life-time, and many intermediate and ultimately untenable positions were adopted in the course of it, and many misunderstandings arose which marked the future course of phenomenology.

We are now in a position to understand another key concept of phenomenology, that of "essence". The essence of a Φ is the sum of those properties which it must have to be called a Φ. This use of the term is not particularly new. What was peculiar to the phenomenological doctrine of essences, at least in its early stages, was that these were to be discovered by a pure intuition of the way the different kinds of things were "constituted" in consciousness. There is no space at the present time to go into all the equivocation connected with the term "constitution" which bred so much confusion not only between Husserl and his opponents but in the work of Husserl himself. For our present purposes we can understand "the way things are constituted" as the facts about the significance of the corresponding phenomenal objects which contribute to our concept of a thing. Thus in Husserl's terminology, material objects were said to be "constituted" out of the series of perspectival views or "sketches" (*Abschattungen*) which we can have of them. If we try to set aside the misleading use of the term "constitution" which implies that we can somehow separate off the perception of the immanent sketches from our perception of the thing itself, we can translate this as a doctrine about the significance of the perspectival views which "announce" the other unseen sides of the thing.

But why are these facts about the significance of the corresponding phenomenal objects seen as relevant to the essence of a thing? One reason was connected with the rejection of the kind of nominalism which was a feature of some of the forerunners of modern-day linguistic analysis, logical atomism and logical positivism. Here the essence of anything was seen as a matter of arbitrary definitions. Those properties which a Φ must have to be a Φ were spelled out in tautologies which told us nothing new about the world, but merely clarified to us the decisions we had already made to use this vocable as the name of this thing, or the decision made for us in this sense by our linguistic ancestors. There is room therefore for only two kinds of study : one a factual one into the nature of the thing itself with the methods of some specialized science, the other a conceptual one into the relations between the words, but which could give us no information whatever about the nature of the thing. Now the whole of phenomenology is supposed to result from a third kind of study, the *Wesensschau* or intuition of essences, something literally incomprehensible from a logical atomist or logical positivist point of view.

The propriety of this third kind of study is justified in phenomenology by the thesis of intentionality. For what we can call for short the positivist view, *viz.*, that there are two and only two kinds of knowledge, is dependent on their doctrine of what it is to learn an empirical concept. And here the traditional empiricist epistemology plays a sinister rôle. For the positivists, empirical concepts were ultimately learned by ostensive definition, which was in turn seen as learning to apply a vocable to a quality or thing. There was always a certain ambiguity as to whether the quality or thing in question was immanent or transcendent, but in either case the class of things which fell under a given concept was always defined purely in terms of their material properties. The ostensive definition story couldn't make sense of the distinction between sense and reference in this context, for it construed the "sense" as some materially identifiable property or thing. But then the positivist view becomes plausible, for any attempt to define the sense of a word must either be telling us something we know already, the mere giving of equivalents such as "unmarried man" for "bachelor", and hence vacuous, or an arbitrary addition to it, a tightening up of the criteria, for all we know restricting its range of application. New knowledge about a concept either tells us nothing (hence is not knowledge) or constitutes an arbitrary alteration in the sense, whose repercussions on its extension could not be known *a priori* (hence is not knowledge either but legislation). Thus we are left only with two kinds of "knowledge", one (vacuous) kind about concepts, the other (contingent) of everyday scientific facts about things.

According to the phenomenologist view, on the other hand, learning an empirical concept is making explicit a certain unity of significance by the learning of a new piece of behaviour, or the acquiring of a new capacity, *viz.*, the use of the word. Now it is clear that this view of ostensive definition is much more plausible than the logical positivist one for whole ranges of our empirical concepts. We have seen above that our action-concepts like *e.g.*, "pushing the lever" cannot be seen as classifying movements, but are differentiated by an element of purpose. That is, to see the leftward movement of the right paw and the rightward movement of the left as both instances of "pushing the lever" we have to grasp the unity of significance between these two acts. A similar account is obviously required for all our so-called functional words, *i.e.*, where the function of the object in question enters somehow into the definition *e.g.*, "hammer", "chain", "constitution". But it is very doubtful if the logical positivist account applies to anything at all. In this connexion I should like to refer to an argument put forward by Mr. Geach in his book *Mental Acts*[6] where he shows that this doctrine which he calls "abstractionism" cannot even account for such simple concepts as "red", hitherto considered paragons of ostensive teachability. Geach shows that the abstractionist account cannot explain how we can learn to apply both the concept "red" and the concept "chromatic colour" to the same things. Chromatic colour can never be isolated in the visual field from red, blue, green and so on. Abstractionism cannot show how we can learn both "red" and "chromatic colour" from being shown the same object, and yet not apply them to the same objects later, as we would "triangular" and "trilateral". But if we see learning a concept as grasping a unity of significance, then the learning of a category word or a concept of more general application can be seen as the making explicit of a wider unity.

If this is our view on the learning of empirical concepts, the doctrine that there are two and only two types of knowledge begins to appear less plausible. For if learning a concept is grasping a unity of significance, then there is something which we can discover which is at once about the concept, and is not "compatible with all state of affairs". For although we know how to use the concept, we may not be clear about the elements of significance which the objects which fall under it share. To clarify these is to analyse the concept, to discover what properties things which

[6] P. T. Geach : *Mental Acts.* Sections 10 and 11.

fall under it must (logically) have, and at the same time to discover something about the things. For on this account we can know what things fall under a concept before this concept is fully clear. Whereas if we follow the positivist view of ostensive definition, making a concept clear, just *is* discovering what things fall under it. If a word is unclear, we simply keep on pointing.

The classical doctrine that all bodies are solid, in the sense that two cannot occupy the same place at once, is a case in point. The concept "body" is born once the broader unity of significance underlying our concepts "stick", "stone", "house", "mountain" and so on is made explicit. But men had this concept before they had made clear what the unity of significance consisted in. They did not make it clear simply by finding an existing property-concept which applied to all the things hitherto identified as bodies : the technical term "solid" is significantly different from the ordinary language concept. They uncovered an element of the unity of significance which underlay the concept in the first place : the impossibility of mutual penetration. They thus discovered a new concept which necessarily applied to all bodies, and yet the discovery was not vacuous; it was not necessary to examine all previously known bodies to ensure that they lived up to a new stricter criterion. They had hold of a genuine *a priori*, a truth both necessary and which tells us something about the world, a truth, as Husserl would say, of eidetic science.[7]

II. Husserl made the study of essences *the* method of philosophy. The whole of phenomenology is supposed to result from a study of essences. Parallels begin to suggest themselves between this philosophy and the school of linguistic analysis. In fact the parallels go very deep and extend to the very vices which both methods tend to generate. But before making the comparison directly, it would be advisable to consider an objection to the Husserlian *Wesensschau* or "intuition of essences."

The purity of the *Wesensschau* as a method of philosophy was in fact challenged by the question : What guarantees that our description is "free from presuppositions"? Husserl's claim in this sense depended on the extraordinary view that we can somehow stand back from the essences, fix them with our gaze and describe them accurately, as though we could somehow prise our language off the world, and, as it were, throw it behind us, and return to a pure intuition of the unities of signification

[7] *Cf.* M. Merleau-Ponty : *Les Sciences de l'Homme et la Phénoménologie*, pp. 26-27. "They (the classical physicists) contributed to develop an eidetic science of physical things."

which underlie our concepts. But this is clearly impossible. Reflection on our concepts, on the unities of signification underlying them is much too sophisticated an activity to be undertaken without the use of concepts. The Husserlian *epoché* — the great watershed of his philosophy — demands the suspension or the "putting in brackets" of all our concepts, and hence of all the models we have, to account for the things, animals, people we meet in the world. Once this is accomplished we can start from scratch, we have reached the real beginning point from which our entire conceptual scheme can be rebuilt, each essence being unequivocally clarified. But if it were possible to reach such a state — which fortunately it is not — no return would be possible. For we can only send in our concepts for overhaul, as it were, in small groups. To "suspend" one concept for re-examination requires that others are taken for granted in order to carry out this examination. Our entire conceptual machinery cannot be repaired in one fell swoop, any more than every bit of machinery in Great Britain can be repaired at one and the same time. The plea that the *epoché* "leaves everything as it is" without "taking it into account" has no force here, because to use a concept seriously in a description is to "take it into account" *i.e.*, to accept the interpretations it carries with it.

But if this is the case, then a philosophy without presupposition is impossible. We must always take some concepts for granted in examining others, accept some assumptions in order to call others into question. The history of philosophy is full of testimonies to this truth. The classical empiricist account of perception arose in just this way : one of the supporting considerations was surely something like this : that it was felt obscurely that all occurrences must somehow be fitted into the categories of contemporary natural science or reasonable facsimile thereof. Perception was therefore inevitably seen as an affect of the organism (or mind). These concepts were assumed as the starting point, and even Hume, whom Husserl admired as a kind of *phénoménologue avant la lettre*, did not challenge them.

Husserl in his later work and some of his successors, notably Merleau-Ponty, have come to the view that there is no absolute beginning in philosophy. As Merleau-Ponty puts it : "as it (philosophy) is also history, it also makes use of the world and reason as already constituted. It must therefore ask of itself the question it asks of all other kinds of knowledge, it will double back on itself to infinity, it will be as Husserl said, a dialogue or meditation without end..." [8] But in a curiously inconsistent

[8] *Phénoménologie de la Perception*, Preface, xvi.

way the language of the *epoché* is still used, and the call to a pure description is still uttered. The magic of a philosophy without presupposition is easier to deny than to exorcise.

III. The claim which has just been disputed to Husserl's phenomenology is also made in the name of linguistic analysis, and this provides an interesting point of comparison between the two philosophies. It is often said of modern British philosophy that it is free from all metaphysical presuppositions, indeed it is often explicitly anti-metaphysical.

What can be said about the claim to independence from metaphysics? In fact it takes two related forms. First it is sometimes said that metaphysical problems arise from misconstructions of certain expressions, and that they can be dissolved by clarifying the uses of these expressions. This is the rationale of the destructive, negative, or, as an extremist would put it, therapeutic, side of linguistic analysis. Then secondly it is claimed that we can solve problems, including perhaps eventually metaphysical problems, by a careful attention to ordinary language and to the "distinctions and connexions" reflected in it. This is the rationale for the positive constructive side of linguistic analysis. The first thesis announces the end of metaphysics : the second, what might amount to its reconstitution, but from a starting point free from presuppositions. Whatever we decide ultimately on the compatibility of these two views, it is clear that both are alike in denying any dependence on any metaphysical doctrines whatever.

Both views are often held by the same people, but it is possible to classify arguments as exemplifying one or the other. I shall therefore choose, somewhat arbitrarily, examples from the work of Professor Ryle and Professor Austin respectively to illustrate these two rationales of linguistic analysis.

In *The Concept of Mind*, Professor Ryle is arguing against what he believes to be a "category-mistake" which has generated the Cartesian theory of mind as an extra entity somehow "inside" the visible human person. Thus by "rectifying the logical geography" of the concepts involved he hopes to dispel the perplexity and with it the myth. We must ask of this programme as we did of Husserl's : can it really be carried through without presupposing any doctrine of the kind that it is attacking?

Ryle uses, for instance, the distinction between semi-hypothetical and categorial to combat the view *e.g.*, that a statement ascribing a motive to some person for some action is "really" compound in that it reports both an "inner" and an "outer" action. The compound report view arises because there seems to be no other answer to the question : what do we add to the simple report on the action when we ascribe a motive to the agent? The wrong answer, which Ryle refutes in a reductive argument, is of course that we tell about another "mental" event. The answer which Ryle adopts is : we add nothing about the event, we simply cast the report in more "law-impregnated" terms. Now why should we accept this answer? Presumably because the only alternative is the discredited "Cartesian" one. But this is not true, or rather it is only true if we hold some kind of behaviourist thesis, or *e.g.*, the epistemological view that the event : A doing X from motive M, is not wholly perceptible, only the action itself (A doing X) being seen. On either the first hypothesis, or the second together with some additional views on the possibility of talking about imperceptibles, our choice is indeed restricted to these two alternatives, and if we reject the one, we must accept the other. But this constitutes a pretty formidable set of presuppositions. Whether they should be called "metaphysical" or not is beside the point, they have certainly as much right to be so called as the "Cartesian myth" they replace.

This leads us to call into question the view that the error was generated by a category-mistake in the first place. For this thesis must not be understood as a diagnosis of the motives people had to fall into this error. It is meant in some sense as a definition of the error itself. For once it is exposed, not only the erroneous answer but the problem itself is to be dispelled. Now this meta-doctrine itself has doctrinal presuppositions. It assumes either that our everyday language, once this is properly understood, suggests a consistent view of the world which does not itself generate any problems, or that it only generates problems if we try to examine it too closely, trace the inter-connexions too clearly — each expression has validity in its place, but we cannot draw a precise map of their inter-connexions. The first is an assumption about the world, the second about the limits of language. According to the first view, metaphysical counter-commonsensical views are just confusion; according to the second they may also be "illuminating paradoxes".

If philosophy could fight itself through the thickets of misconstruction to the point where there were no more problems, then the case could be made that it was indeed without pre-suppositions. But it is very doubtful that such a point has been reached. Certainly *The Concept of Mind* does not show us where to reach this resting place, for it contains its own share of doctrines, such as the one quoted above, which are shocking to common sense.

The second rationale for linguistic analysis is represented by Professor Austin in his Presidential Address to the Aristotelian Society : "A Plea for Excuses". Here we are promised a set of positive doctrines about, in this case, human action if we take pains to study the ways people excuse themselves for their failures. The method of gathering examples and seeing "what we would say if ..." is very reminiscent of the Husserlian *Wesensschau*, a parallel which Professor Austin seems to welcome in using the term phenomenology, and which the distinction between words as part of the furniture of the world and words as the medium in which we talk about the world, seems to invite. On this view ordinary language will not necessarily have the last word, but it must have the first.

In this case the study of ordinary language would, at least as a propaedeutic, be free from presupposition, and in so far as its results cast light on the problems of philosophy, it will allow us to intervene in the debate without taking on any metaphysical baggage ourselves.

But the plausibility of this claim rests on a certain ambiguity about what is involved in investigating usage. We can illustrate the distinction between doing something by accident and doing something by mistake as Professor Austin does in the tale of the two donkeys, and get to "see the point". But for purposes of philosophy we have first to go on to characterize this distinction, *i.e.*, adumbrate some kind of model, secondly to argue in its favour. Neither of these steps can be taken without accepting certain assumptions as given.

Thus Professor Austin in his article entitled "Other Minds" [9] uses some facts about our everyday language to great effect in combating the view that emotions can be considered as compounded of physical symptoms and feeling. He points out for instance that we do not classify some emotions as either "physical" or "mental". Now why is this point relevant? It is relevant because the ordinary use clashes here with a specialized "infected" use of these terms in the context of a metaphysical theory. But this is not all. It also suggests a new model to replace the old one, one that would allow for the fact that not all entities can be classified as either physical or mental. And it is a model of this kind that Professor Austin goes on to sketch. But, thirdly, it implies that we have an argument to show why the ordinary use is to be respected in this case, *i.e.*, why this fact does not simply show the imprecision of ordinary speech.

The reason why most philosophical problems can't be solved simply by the study of ordinary language is that they do not arise there. They

[9] *Logic and Language* Series II.

arise within such bodies of doctrine as theology, metaphysics or science or on the borderline between these and ordinary fact. Each of these bodies of doctrine for instance has been responsible for a problem about the freedom of the will. But the reason why the study of our language can be useful in solving these problems is that metaphysical, theological or scientific doctrines "infect" it, provide a clarification or explication of certain key concepts in it. Ordinary terms such as "cause" and "freedom", "physical" and "mental" are only involved in such problems as that about freedom of the will or about other minds, because they are metaphysically "infected" in this way, and they carry this infection to all related concepts.

But then the facts about usage will not suffice even as a first step. For the citing of usage will only be relevant if it is taken as illustrating or supporting some model, *i.e.*, some clarification or explication of the concepts involved (as in the case cited above with "physical" and "mental"). But then we are already engaged in a debate in which no party can be free of presuppositions; we are clarifying some concepts with the aid of others, and these must, for the moment at least, be taken on trust.

We can avoid this conclusion by holding that any use of a term which is in conflict with its everyday use is *ipso facto* confused. Then indeed the facts about ordinary use would be decisive. But what justifies this dogmatism? Only some assumptions about the world or the limits of language similar to those mentioned above. To hold that the study of usage can be the "first word" in philosophy is to presuppose therefore that it can also be the last word, that the theories which inhabit the "infected" concepts flee on being confronted with their ordinary everyday selves.

The belief in a radical new beginning in philosophy is thus dependent on the belief in its imminent demise. But this thesis is, to say the least, unproven — it is even difficult to state it coherently. We could call it a re-affirmation of the commonsense view of the world. But there is really no such thing. In so far as common sense ignores the problems of philosophy it is irrelevant, in so far as it touches on them it has found no more coherent answers than philosophy itself. We have to fall back on a thesis about the limits of language : the solutions to philosophical problems can "dawn" on us, but cannot be stated. And how can this be proved?

IV. Up to now I have not tried to distinguish between the study of essences and the study of concepts. This is not a masterpiece of evasion. Understood a certain way, they become very similar studies, the difference being mainly that one is carried out in the formal and one in the material mode. It is true that "the proper concern of philosophy is with concepts", and "that this implies a concern with the uses of words." [10] But when we refine our concepts we are at the same time projecting a model of the thing concerned, we are making clear its "essence". Correspondingly the only way to clarify an essence is to criticise the concepts we use to describe it, and one of the best ways to accomplish this is to study the many uses of the corresponding word which are unclear to us.

The method of phenomenology and that of linguistic analysis are, therefore, properly understood, quite compatible. They are separated only by the exaggerated claims made for one and the other — claims which are themselves very similar but whose rationale in each case differs so widely as to pull them apart. On one side there is the belief that we can do without our concepts, that all of these can be put in the dock at once; on the other the thesis that all philosophical problems arise from mistakes about language. Both justify a belief in a philosophy without presupposition.

But these views resemble each other in another way as well. For each, by suppressing one of the poles of tension in philosophy tends to generate a strange permissiveness and tolerance as to the content of belief.[11] If philosophy is at least partly an attempt to assess our most important concepts for their adequacy to the things they are used to talk about, then the suspension of all concepts and the flight into a pure description of experience tends to leave us without the means to distinguish between the valid and the invalid. Theoretically for instance one could make a phenomenology of religious experience without deciding its validity. And this is surely a sign that something has gone wrong. In the same way, the view that our ordinary language is ultimately above reproach tends to leave us similarly without weapons of criticism. Part of the reason for this permissiveness is the underestimation of the rôle of argument — a point that I have not been able to deal with at sufficient length above. In Phenomenology this arises from the belief in "intuition" as the principal method in philosophy. Even after this method has been shorn of its more radical claims, it tends still to predispose to adopting "pure description" as the final arbiter. Linguistic Analysis differs from this largely because of the destructive "therapeutic" element in its tradition. To the extent that this predominates, argument, usually of a reductive kind, has the last word. But in so far as we follow the "constructive" programme and study the varieties of use without trying to impose a

[10] Warnock : *British Philosophy Since 1900*, p. 158.

[11] I owe this point to Mr. Michael Kullmann.

model on them, debate on questions of belief becomes impossible. All weapons are likely to be dashed from our hands as soon as we take them up as violations of ordinary usage. What is wrong with the language of religious worship in its appropriate place in the proper "language game"? Theology of course can be debunked, as in the *epoché* it is suspended, but the practice and/or experience somehow remains not above, but beyond reproach. But in neither case does this amount to a justification. As in the later system of Hegel, everything has its own place and its own validity, but since this everything contains incompatible elements, this is hardly an interesting kind of validity.

PHENOMENOLOGY AND LINGUISTIC ANALYSIS : II

by

SIR A. J. AYER

I

I agree with Mr. Taylor that "one of the key concepts of phenomenology is that of 'intentionality'," but I am somewhat puzzled by the account that he gives of it. I had always understood that the concept of intentionality was associated by Brentano and Husserl with their theory of mental acts. The guiding principle of this theory, which Mr. Taylor cites without comment, is that consciousness is always consciousness *of* something; in other words that every cognitive state or process is to be analysed in terms of act and object. The object need not be real : one can imagine what does not exist, one can long for something that will never happen; but, whether it is real or not, even in the case where it is thought of as unreal, it is posited by consciousness as an independent entity. I am not entirely clear what this means, but I think the doctrine may best be understood by contrast with what it denies. It is a way of rejecting any analysis of cognition which invokes only the presence of mental contents, or actual and potential behaviour, or some combination of factors of these kinds. It implies, for example, that it is impossible to give an adequate account of belief which eliminates any reference to an object, such as a proposition, on which belief is directed; believing that such-and-such is the case cannot simply be a matter of assenting to a given form of words and being disposed to behave in certain ways. Or again, it implies that the difference between perceiving something and imagining it is not analysable in terms of the existence of different mental contents, a sense-datum in the one case, and an image in the other. The object which is perceived is the same as the object which is imagined. What distinguishes the two cases is a difference in the mode in which it is posited by the respective acts of consciousness.

As I understand it, the thesis of intentionality is just the thesis that any activity, or state, or process which contains a cognitive element does have an object in this sense; the objects, whether real or unreal, which consciousness sets before itself are said to be intentional. These objects are represented, so to speak, as posing for consciousness, and the aim of the phenomenological reduction, which is the salient feature of Husserl's philosophy, is to catch them in a characteristic pose. They are then to be examined and described. They are "put in brackets" in the sense that no questions are raised about their ontological status, nor any account taken of any contingent relations in which they may stand to one another; in the case of propositions, no assumptions are made about their truth. The objects are set in a frame, as typical specimens of their kind, and everything outside the frame is disregarded. It is to be noted that acts of consciousness can themselves be framed in this manner : they can be made the objects of further reflective acts. One may inspect the act of perceiving or believing, just as one may inspect the things which are perceived or the propositions which are believed. These objects are inspected as they appear to consciousness, and they are viewed, not in their individual, but in their universal aspect. It is assumed that inspection will reveal the essential nature of the object; it will show what properties are necessary and sufficient for it to be the sort of object that it is. It is for this reason that the application of Husserl's method is said to result in the intuition of essences.

I shall not here attempt to criticize this programme in detail. Apart from the space that this would need, I am not sure that I understand it well enough. But of the thesis of intentionality, which is fundamental to it, I must say that I find it obscurantist. The notion of an object of consciousness seems to me to be one of those notions that call most loudly for an attempt at reductive analysis. To take it as primitive is simply to put a number of interesting and difficult problems on one side. This is not to say, however, that botanizing among these so-called objects may not yield fruitful results. To what extent the techniques by which these results are obtained resemble the techniques of linguistic analysis is a question which, following Mr. Taylor, I shall discuss at a later stage.

Mr. Taylor agrees that the general form of the thesis of intentionality is "that consciousness is consciousness of ...". But he thinks that this has developed into the special thesis that "whatever is an object of consciousness has 'significance' ". This might be taken to mean no more than that to be an object of consciousness is to be conceptualized, a revival of the Kantian dictum that intuitions without concepts are blind. In that case Mr. Taylor's formulation might be accepted at least as a rider to the thesis that acts of consciousness have intentional objects, though in the case where these objects were themselves concepts or propositions, it would be more accurate to say that they *were* "significances" than that they had them. But Mr. Taylor makes it clear that he is not thinking of anything so tame as this. His interpretation of the special or "modern" thesis of intentionality is that the objects of consciousness, and specifically the objects of perception, have significance in the sense that they refer beyond themselves; in short they are not *significata* but signs. As applied to all the possible objects of consciousness this thesis seems exceedingly implausible. C. S. Peirce held something like it, but he held it as part of a dynamic theory of meaning and truth, which, in spite of Peirce's declaring himself to be among other things a scholastic realist, is about as far removed as possible from Husserl's idea of consciousness as a magic lantern. I was not aware that it was held by modern phenomenologists, and indeed it would seem to be incompatible with the aims of their philosophy. It would be impossible that the essence of any object should be grasped by intuition if every object of consciousness referred to another which in its turn referred to another and so *ad infinitum*.

But even if it cannot be held that all intentional objects are significant, in Mr. Taylor's sense, important classes of them may be. And although Mr. Taylor does say that his thesis applies to every object of consciousness, he illustrates it only by reference to the objects of perception. A ground which he gives for this restriction is that phenomenologists have concentrated largely on perception, even to the extent of making it "the model for all the operations of mind". But he himself concedes that this could be a mistake.

Mr. Taylor's account of the way in which phenomenologists attribute significance to the objects of perception is drawn from the early chapters of Maurice Merleau-Ponty's *Phénoménologie de la Perception*. These chapters are regarded by Merleau-Ponty, and it would seem also by Mr. Taylor, as containing very strong arguments against empiricism, at least in so far as it is identified with a sense-datum theory of perception. Let us then try to see how strong they are.

We may begin with the statement, which Mr. Taylor quotes more than once, though incorrectly, that "every part (not, as Mr. Taylor says, of the phenomenal field, but of a figure within it) announces more than it contains and this elementary perception (for which Mr. Taylor substitutes 'every part of the phenomenal field') is therefore already laden with significance".[1] This statement occurs in a context where Merleau-

[1] *Phénoménologie de la Perception*, p. 19.

Ponty associates himself with the Gestalt psychologists in holding that the simplest visual datum that one can obtain is that of a figure against a ground, say a white spot on a homogeneous background of some other colour. The sense in which the parts of this datum refer beyond themselves is that they "have a common function which makes them into a figure." "The boundaries of the spot belong to it and are dissociated from the background with which they are nevertheless contiguous : the spot appears set on the background and does not interrupt it." In short, the sensible object, if we must not say "sense-datum", is part of a sense-field, and even the simplest sense-field has a structure. But why should it be thought that this is damaging to the sense-datum theory? The most it shows is that our sense-experience is not atomistic in the way that Locke and his successors may have thought it was. It does not imply even that individual sense-data cannot be picked out from their surroundings. On the contrary, this is what Merleau-Ponty does himself. For what else are these things that announce more than they contain?

Merleau-Ponty indeed admits that it is open to an empiricist to accept the results of Gestalt psychology. He can refer to stretches of space and time, and allow relations to be sensed as well as qualities. But then Merleau-Ponty poses a dilemma. "Either the spatial expanse is ranged over and inspected by a mind, in which case one has forsaken empiricism, since consciousness is no longer defined by impressions — or else it is itself given after the fashion of an impression, in which case it no more admits of a wider co-ordination than the atomic impression did." [2] In other words, whatever the empiricist takes as his phenomenal unit, whether it be a sensible point or an organised sense-field, he cannot, consistently with his principles, succeed in relating it to anything beyond.

The force of this argument depends on what one understands by something's being "ranged over and inspected by a mind". Certainly, if impressions merely bombarded us like hailstones rattling on a window-pane, the actual character of our perceptions would be inexplicable : neither would the position be improved if groups of these hailstones functioned as single units. The impressions must be brought under concepts, and they must at least arouse some expectation of further impressions to follow. But even so economical an empiricist as Hume allowed as much as this. He would, however, have claimed that bringing impressions under concepts was in the end a matter of associating them with one another, and also, wrongly, that forming expectations was just

[2] *Ibid.*, p. 21.

a matter of having images. What he did not see was that these images must function as signs, if they are to do the work required of them; so that there is here a *prima facie* case for saying that, even on Hume's principles, perception involves intentionality. How strong a case one thinks it is will depend on the theory one holds about the nature of signs. My own preference is for a behavioural theory, which would eliminate intentionality. It faces obvious difficulties, but I am not so easily persuaded as Mr. Taylor that they are insuperable.

Returning to Merleau-Ponty's argument, we find that the decisive question is whether our interpretation of our sense-experiences can be accounted for by the mechanism of association. Merleau-Ponty is convinced that it cannot be. His reasoning is not very easy to follow, but he seems mainly to rely upon the fact that association is selective. We pick out certain features of our present experience and interpret them in the light of corresponding features of our past experience. But this implies that we must already have organized our present data before we can bring to bear our memories of the past. "For the memories to come and complete the perception, the physiognomy of the given must make them possible. Before memory lends any assistance, what is seen must here and now be organized in such a way as to present me with a picture where I can recognize my previous experiences. Thus the approach to memory presupposes what it is meant to explain : the patterning of the given, the imposition of significance upon the sensible chaos." [3]

This may very well be true, if it is taken to mean that there never is a sensible chaos. It may be that from the very start of our lives, our sense-fields exhibit some kind of pattern, that there never is "a buzzing blooming confusion" from which the infant has to learn to pick things out. But this does not prove what Merleau-Ponty wants. It does not prove that the identification of objects within the pattern is not the work of association, nor does it prove that the pattern itself is in any degree a mental creation. The associations made by many machines are highly selective; but this is not a testimony to the activity of their minds.

Mr. Taylor gives a version of Merleau-Ponty's argument which is even less convincing. He says that it is only because each side of a mountain "announces" the other that we are able to perceive that it has two sides, and he implies that we could never do this if the sense-datum theory were true. But if he has any good reasons for making these assertions he does not give them. I suppose that what he means by saying that

[3] *Ibid.*, p. 27.

each side of his mountain announces the other is that, *independently of any previous experience*, an observer would be able to infer from the look of one side of the mountain that it has another side. I am not sure that this is true : but the point is that even if it were true it would be irrelevant. What we find out by walking round the mountain is not determined by what any other face of it suggests to us. There is no logical reason why the discovery that it has another side should not come as a surprise. It is not even necessary that we should start by assuming that we are seeing a real mountain at all. For all that these arguments prove, we may discover that it is real by sensing a suitable series of sense-data. Mr. Taylor asserts that the connexions of sense-data cannot be verified, apparently on the ground that they do not stay put. But their not staying put is not a bar to their being remembered, nor therefore to our discovering that they have a characteristic order. There may, indeed, be strong objections to the sense-datum theory, but the claim that what we see has an innate significance is not among them.

II

What Mr. Taylor has to say about essence, as the phenomenologists conceive it, is even more puzzling to me than what he has to say about perception. He starts with the innocent statement that "the essence of a Φ is the sum of those properties which it must have to be called a Φ", but he then goes on to deny that listing essences is a matter of giving arbitrary definitions. It would seem therefore that, on his view, to say that brothers are male, or that whatever is coloured is extended, or, to use his own example, that bodies are solid, is to make a statement which is both necessary and synthetic. But he does not try to explain how this is possible. The only clue that he gives is the statement, which he repeats several times, that to learn an empirical concept is to "grasp a unity of significance". But what sort of unity this is, or what our grasping it amounts to, he does not say.

In his attack on what he calls the positivist theory, Mr. Taylor makes two assumptions which seem to me to be false. The first is that analytic statements, like "bachelors are unmarried men", cannot be informative, and the second is that there is nothing more to giving a definition than an arbitrary decision to use one set of signs as a substitute for another. Now it is a matter of convention that certain sequences of letters have the meaning that they do, but once the usage of a word has been established then we cannot, consistently with this usage, make it mean anything that we please. Moreover, as has often been pointed out, the fact that one uses a word correctly is consistent with one's being unaware of all that it implies. That is why analytic statements, which explicate usage, can be informative. "Bachelors are unmarried men" is not a favourable example, just because the normal way to learn the meaning of the word "bachelor", in this usage, is to be told that it refers to an unmarried man. But a child who has gained the idea of whales from picture-books may learn something new when he is told that whales are mammals. I do not know whether he therein grasps a unity of significance, but what he learns, surely, is an analytic truth.

We are, of course, free to modify usage either, as Mr. Taylor says, by tightening up the criteria, or in other ways. For example, is it part of the essence of water that it is a chemical compound of two volumes of hydrogen and one of oxygen? We can make it so if we choose. But if we do, our decision will not be entirely arbitrary. It will be motivated by the belief that "the liquid of which seas, lakes and rivers are composed, and which falls as rain and issues from springs" [4] invariably has this chemical composition : and this belief is justified by experiment. So one can say, if one pleases, that such a definition rests upon a synthetic unity. But this is not a unity of significance. It is an empirical fact that the other "essential" properties of water and the property of being composed of H_2O are found together. Its discovery was not the fruit of *a priori* intuition but of chemical analysis.

The same considerations apply, so far as I can see, to Mr. Taylor's example of the essential properties of bodies. As it happens, the word "body" can correctly be used in English to refer to any physical substance, whether solid, liquid, or gaseous; one may also restrict its sense, as Mr. Taylor does, in such a way that the expression "solid body" becomes pleonastic. Now it is an empirical fact that things which look and feel solid seldom appear to fuse together, to merge into one. And if they do appear to coalesce, they do not appear to separate again and follow their independent paths in the same guise as before. The contrary is perfectly conceivable, but we do not find that it occurs. The result is that we adopt criteria of identity which make it logically impossible for two solid bodies to occupy exactly the same space, while still remaining two. If they did fuse together, we should say that one of them had been annihilated, or that some other single thing had replaced them both. At the same time, it is very easy to imagine circumstances in which we

[4] *O.E.D.*

should find it less natural to do this than to change our criteria of identity. Now I agree that it is a philosophical task to make these criteria explicit; but I still see no reason for holding that this results in the discovery of synthetic *a priori* truths.

Before I leave this question, I should like to say a few words about abstractionism. I do not know why Mr. Taylor thinks that logical positivists are committed to the view that empirical concepts are learned by abstraction. The view to which logical positivists are committed is that all empirical concepts are grounded in experience, in the sense that they apply, directly or indirectly, to what is, or could be, empirically given; and this entails no special theory about the way in which they have been acquired. Consideration of the ways in which we have in fact learned to use certain words is indeed a clue to their meaning, but it is no more than a clue. The concepts in question could fulfil exactly the same empirical functions, even though they were all innate ideas.

The fact is, however, that they are not : so that there is room for a psychological theory about the way in which we do acquire them; and this is what I take abstractionism to be. To try to make it account for the acquisition of logical, or numerical, or high-level scientific concepts would, I think, be a mistake, but this is not to say that it plays no rôle at all. Certainly Mr. Taylor's counter-examples do not convince me. I do not see why someone should not acquire "action-concepts" by classifying physical movements and noting that they had similar consequences; and I do not think it would be unreasonable to call this a process of abstraction. Neither am I so impressed as Mr. Taylor is by Mr. Geach's argument about chromatic colour. It rests on the fact that "in looking at a red window-pane I have not two sensations, one of redness, and one barely of chromatic colour; there are not, for that matter, two distinct sense-given features, one of them making my sensation to be barely a sensation of chromatic colour, the other making it a sensation of redness." [5] But the answer to this is that what makes one sense-given feature distinct from another is not that they are presented by different sensations but that the objects which exhibit them belong to different ranges : and this does apply to redness and chromatic colour. Two red objects resemble each other in a different way as being chromatic from the way in which they resemble each other as being red : and the difference is just that in considering them as chromatic one associates them with a wider range of objects than that with which one

[5] P. T. Geach, *Mental Acts*, p. 37.

associates them in considering them as red. Admittedly, I suppose that the normal way to learn the use of the expression "chromatic colour" is first to learn the use of colour words like "red", and then to be told that chromatic colour is that which is other than white or grey or black. But there might well be a child who naturally saw coloured objects as falling into two groups, one of them consisting of things which, as we should say, were either white or grey or black, and the other consisting of things which had a different colour from any of these. For him there would be initially just two sorts of colour, and if he had words for them, he would have acquired the concept of chromatic colour by abstraction. At a later stage, by further abstraction, he might break down the range of chromatic colour into sub-ranges of blue and red and yellow and so on. I say "by abstraction" because I take abstraction, in this context, just to be a matter of associating and dissociating sets of objects on the basis of observed resemblances or the lack of them. I am not claiming that any children do acquire the concept of chromatic colour in this way; only that they might. Whether any do is a matter for empirical investigation. Unlike Mr. Geach and Mr. Taylor I do not believe that such questions of child psychology can be settled *a priori.*

III

One point on which I do agree with Mr. Taylor is that if the intuition of essences consisted, as Husserl sometimes seems to imply, in gazing at concepts like stars in a planetarium, it would yield nothing at all. Whatever phenomenologists may think they ought to be doing, what the best of them in fact do is to study concepts at work. They try to discover what is essential to a given concept by seeing what is common to the situations to which it typically applies. But this, as Mr. Taylor rightly points out, brings them very close in practice to the linguistic analysts. For, however great the reverence that the linguistic analysts may think they ought to have for the Oxford English Dictionary, their most interesting results are obtained not by chasing synonyms but by reviewing the situations to which certain words apply. Sometimes grammatical points come in; for instance, an argument may be based on the fact that verbs of a certain type are never, or only very seldom, used in the continuous present tense; but most often what is said to be an analysis of the way in which words are ordinarily used might be more accurately represented as a phenomenological study of the facts which they are used to describe.

This comes out quite clearly in the work of Professor Ryle, to which

Mr. Taylor also refers. Professor Ryle's views might not be very acceptable to phenomenologists, who would be dissatisfied with their behaviouristic tendency, but they should have no reason to quarrel with his technique, at least as it is exercised in *The Concept of Mind.* For the principal feature of Ryle's method is to bring out the essence of willing, or knowing, or intelligence, or acting from a motive, or whatever it may be, by considering what actually happens in typical cases where someone knows something, or wills something, or acts from a motive, or behaves intelligently. In fact, Ryle is mainly concerned to show that an element which one might be tempted to think essential, the presence of some "inner" state or process, is really not so; and his way of proving this is just to exhibit cases of knowing, or willing, or displays of intelligence, or whatever is in question, in which no such inner states or processes occur. He uses other forms of argument, but this is the most effective and the one upon which he chiefly relies.

This method of looking at the facts without prejudice is characteristic also of Wittgenstein's later work. Wittgenstein differs from the phenomenologists in that he does not search for essences. On the contrary, one of his main theses is that the assumption that there must always be an essence is a typical philosopher's mistake : they take it for granted that the situations to which a given word applies must have a single quality in common, whereas in fact they may merely have a family resemblance. But this difference is much less important than one might think. Wittgenstein's analyses are more penetrating; he is not handicapped by the assumption that cognitive verbs must always stand for special mental acts : but the method of catching concepts at work by looking at examples of the situations which they cover is very much the same.

Mr. Taylor devotes the latter part of his paper to the claim, which he thinks is made both by phenomenologists and by logical analysts, that theirs is a philosophy without presuppositions; and on this point I have very little to add to what he says. It is obvious that a philosopher can neither get outside language nor "prise it off the world" : in analysing one concept he must make use of others, which he does not subject to criticism in that instance; there is of course no reason why he should not analyse them in their turn, but then he will be making use of some other concepts which he takes for granted, so that he presupposes at any stage whatever the concepts which he is employing in his analysis commit him to. This may, however, not be very much.

More serious presuppositions, which Mr. Taylor does not mention, are, on the part of the phenomenologists, the assumption that the being of things is identical with their being for consciousness, a principle which can be interpreted either realistically as implying that things are unaffected by our consciousness of them, or idealistically, as implying that they are the product of consciousness, or, as seems to be the case with Husserl, in both these ways at once; and, on the part of the linguistic analysts, the assumption of some form of the verification principle. This assumption is one that most of those who make it nowadays not only do not acknowledge but would explicitly repudiate; yet from what else does it follow that the analysis of an empirical statement is yielded by a description of the observable situations in which it holds?

It is true that this applies more to Ryle and Wittgenstein than it does to Professor Austin and his followers, whom Mr. Taylor perhaps has most in mind when he speaks of linguistic analysts. But they too have recourse to instances; nice shades of difference in our use of words are brought out by constructing specimen sentences and then distinguishing the situations which would verify what they express. Sometimes the points made are more strictly linguistic, as in the example, which Mr. Taylor gives, of there being emotions which we do not classify as either mental or physical. But remarks of this kind tell us very little, unless they are supported by an analysis of the facts. In the given case, we want to know what features these emotions have that would account for their not being classified as either mental or physical, if in fact they are not. I do not agree with Mr. Taylor that such an enquiry presupposes that one has "an argument to show why the ordinary use is to be respected", but it does at least assume that it deserves investigation.

This may not always be true. The important point, to my mind, is not that there cannot be a purely descriptive philosophy without presuppositions, but that the mere collecting of specimens, as a child collects seashells, is unlikely to be of philosophical interest. Description, whether it is said to be of essences or of the ordinary, or for that matter extraordinary, use of words, needs to be undertaken in the service of some theory or with the aim of elucidating some philosophical puzzle; otherwise it soon turns out to be a bore. As it happens, this rule is not very often broken by the members of either school. In this respect, their practice is better than their principles.

WHAT ARE THE GROUNDS OF EXPLICATION? A BASIC PROBLEM IN LINGUISTIC ANALYSIS AND IN PHENOMENOLOGY

by

E. T. GENDLIN

In this paper I will attempt to discuss linguistic analysis and phenomenology accurately so that the adherents of each can agree with what I say, and yet also the discussion of each method must be understandable to the adherents of the other. If I can really do that, the basic similarities will appear. I will attempt to state some propositions that apply to both frames of reference. The similarities which these propositions state are basic aspects of philosophic method, and they also pose a major problem.

The problem, as I see it, concerns the grounds of explication. In both methods the main assertions are founded neither on formal logic nor on observed relationships. They are based on an 'implicit' knowledge (if we call that 'knowledge') : on what is 'implicit' in experiencing, living, and acting in situations. How are philosophic statements founded on something 'implicit'? Such statements are called 'explications'. What is the basis for asserting and evaluating them? What criteria are possible for such statements?

The problem, as I will try to show, does not lead backward to a reassumption of 'external' criteria or constructs, but rather opens a new area of philosophic study.

I will not generalize away the differences between various linguistic analysts and between different phenomenological philosophers. (In fact, these differences bring home the problem of criteria.) I will limit myself to specific formulations from one philosopher in each mode. Generalizations of a lowest common denominator are not really usable without their detail. On the other hand, even one bit of detailed discussion, if closely examined, displays the method. I will use a few excerpts from the writings of Austin, and then from those of Sartre.

Propositions applicable to both methods will be formulated first as they arise from my excerpts of linguistic analysis. In this way the propositions will be connected to their detailed employment there, and yet phenomenologists will recognize them. Later, in my discussion of Sartre, I refer back to them. Thereby I may be able to show how the methods are similar and pose a similar problem of explication.

If indeed the methods are similar in the ways I try to show, then my later discussion of explication can be considered an instance of either method and should carry both methods forward into a new and central problem area. I realize that this is a considerable program, but if the methods are specifically similar in this respect, then the program is possible.

I

I turn first to that kind of philosophizing which proceeds from ordinary language. Austin approaches a question of moral philosophy as follows :

> ... a study of ... 'excuses' ... will contribute in special ways ... to moral philosophy in particular ... (p. 125) [1]
>
> When ... do we 'excuse' conduct ... In general, the situation is one where someone is *accused* of having done something ...
>
> Thereupon he, or someone on his behalf, will try to defend his conduct or to get him out of it.
>
> One way of going about this is to admit flatly that he, X, did do that very thing, A, but to argue that it was a good thing ... To take this line is to *justify* the action ...
>
> A different way of going about it is ... to argue that it is not quite fair or correct to say *baldly* 'X did A' ... perhaps he was under somebody's influence, or was nudged ... it may have been partly accidental, or an unintentional slip.
>
> ... briefly ... we admit that it was bad but don't accept full, or even any responsibility (PP, pp. 123-24).

In this excerpt Austin makes some discriminations : Defense by justification of an action is distinguished from defense by disclaiming responsibility. Then different kinds of disclaimers of responsibility are distinguished.

The excerpt shows that the question of responsibility (think of the traditional question of 'free will') is here discussed in a context. Linguistic analysis operates in the context of specific situations ("... perhaps he was under somebody's influence, or was nudged...").

[1] Unless otherwise indicated, page references in this section are to : Austin, J. L., *Philosophical Papers*. J. O. Urmson and G. J. Warnock, eds. (Oxford : Oxford U. Press, 1961). Hereafter cited as PP.

Proposition 1 : Philosophic terms are examined and used in the context of living and acting in the world. The use of each term marks a discrimination in that context.

What one cannot do (is advised not to do) in this mode of philosophy is to work with abstractions purely theoretically.

For example, 'responsibility' cannot be discussed in the manner of the 'free will problem' of some traditional philosophies : 'voluntarily' and 'involuntarily' are not 'contraries' such that one of them always applies to any action.

> ... given any adverb of excuse, such as 'unwittingly' or 'spontaneously' or 'impulsively', it will not be found that it makes good sense to attach it to any and every verb of 'action' in any and every context :
>
> For example, 'voluntarily' and 'involuntarily' : we may join the army or make a gift voluntarily, we may hiccough or make a small gesture involuntarily...
>
> 'Voluntarily' and 'involuntarily', then, are not opposed in the obvious sort of way ... The 'opposite', or rather 'opposites', of 'voluntarily' might be 'under constraint' of some sort, duress or obligation or influence : the opposite of 'involuntarily' might be 'deliberately' or 'on purpose' ... (PP, pp. 138-139).

If you ask about a phrase in this paper whether I wrote it 'voluntarily' you imply something rather unusual about my professional circumstances or about my editor. But, you don't imply the contrary (you imply something totally different) if you ask whether I wrote that phrase 'involuntarily' (perhaps it slipped out and went unnoticed).

If we examine each term as tied to the circumstances its use discriminates, then we are not examining the terms as constructs. *As constructs* these two terms above would be contraries. *As used*, they discriminate different and not directly related aspects possible in living.

But what of the vast main body of actions which involve neither of these special aspects? Are they done 'voluntarily' or not? Is one 'responsible' in general for actions (as per 'free will') or not? Obviously, the question is nonsense if one anchors the terms 'voluntarily' and 'involuntarily' each to their special contexts.

Does this mean that the famous and rich problem of human freedom has been avoided by a sleight of hand? Not at all. The problem has become many more specific problems, anchored to discriminations in the world in which we live and act. If we ground each term in the aspects it marks we can also discuss :

> ... the detail of the complicated internal machinery we use in 'acting' — the receipt of intelligence, the appreciation of the situation, the invocation of principles, the planning, the control of execution and the rest (PP, p. 127).

If we proceed in this way, nothing need be lost.

But, using such distinctions, can one *conclude* anything on a question, for example, a question of moral responsibility? Austin offers an example : Finney, an attendant in a mental hospital, ran scalding hot water into a bathtub while a patient was in the tub, killing the patient. Was Finney 'responsible'? Austin quotes his attorney :

> ...if the prisoner, knowing that the man was in the bath, had ... turned on the hot instead of the cold water, I should have said there was gross negligence; for he ought to have looked to see. But ... he had told the deceased to get out, and *thought he had got out.* If you think that indicates gross carelessness, then you should find the prisoner guilty of manslaughter. But if you think it *inadvertence* not amounting to culpability — i.e., what is properly termed an *accident* — then the prisoner is not liable (PP, p. 145).

For Austin the excerpt illustrates a "very free use of a large number of terms of excuse ... several as though they were ... equivalent when they are not," thus showing that 'ordinary use' in people we observe often needs sharper discriminating. But the excerpt also shows that discussion *and conclusions* are based *on the discriminations marked by our uses of terms.*

One could now argue that 'free will' is 'assumed' in this excerpt, since it concerns the fact that Finney didn't 'choose' the hot water tap knowing the patient was in the tub; we seem not to question here — but rather to assume — that, in general, a man can choose. Is there a general question of freedom 'above and beyond' (or 'underneath') the specific discriminations of various kinds of ordinary acting and responsibility?

By saying or asking about 'voluntarily' we imply aspects of coercion in the situation *within* the ordinary human world (not some 'underlying' constant coercion of 'determinism'). By saying 'deliberately', we discriminate something noticeable in an action (not some 'underlying' construct of 'freedom').

Proposition 2 : There are no entities, constructs or determinants assumed to be 'behind', or 'over and above' the world in which we live and act. There are no 'external' principles or criteria.

But if there are no more basic, underlying principles against which to evaluate language, must linguistic analysis simply accept the 'prisons of the grammarians', the assumptions in how language happens to slice and render the world? Not at all.

To examine and evaluate assumptions, constructs, 'models', is a main task of linguistic analysis. But this critique does not invoke superordinate principles. Rather, the critique leads models back to (and limits their use to) the specific circumstances which their use can mark. For example, take the assumption (the 'model') of 'free will' and of 'all actions'.

> ... 'doing an action', as used in philosophy, is a highly abstract expression — it is a stand-in used in place of any ... verb with a personal subject, in the same sort of way that 'thing' is a stand-in for any ... noun substantive, and 'quality' a stand-in for the adjective ... notoriously it is possible to arrive at ... an over-simplified meta-physics from the obsession with 'things' and their 'qualities'. In a similar way ... we fall for the myth of the verb (PP, p. 126).
>
> ... We take *some very simple action*, like shoving a stone, ... and use *this* ... as our model in terms of which to talk about other actions and events ... even when these other actions are ... much more interesting ... than the acts originally used in constructing the model ... (PP, p. 150).
>
> ... to say we acted 'freely' ... is to say only that we acted *not* unfreely, in one or another of the many heterogeneous ways of so acting (under duress, or what not) ... In examining all the ways in which each action may not be 'free', i.e., the cases in which it will not do to say simply 'X did A', we may hope to dispose of the problem of Freedom (PP, p. 128).

Proposition 3 : Arguments are not conducted or evaluated critically on general theoretical grounds. Instead, assumptions and models are critically evaluated in terms of what they discriminate in living and acting in the world.

An overextended use of an expression is called 'misleading' even when perfectly sound logical implications were drawn from it by logical necessity. To formulate what the use of an expression discriminates, we are not led by its logical implications, but rather by the 'implications' *of its use*. Not the expression as such, but its use, 'implies' the discriminated aspects in situations.

Let 'p' stand for an expression. We say 'p' only when facets A, B, C obtain. Therefore, *when we say* 'p', we imply facets A, B, C.

Austin writes : "not *p* ... but *asserting p* implies ... By asserting *p* I *give it to be understood* that ..." (*PP*, p. 32).

Thus the main assertions of linguistic analysis concern an 'implication' by an activity (*using* words).

Proposition 4 : The main philosophic assertions state 'implications' of a different sort than logical implications. They state 'implications' of an activity.

And now the question of criteria : When (as in most of its central assertions) linguistic analysis states what aspects of the world the use of a word marks, i.e., what the use 'implies', how may we tell when such statements have correctly (or adequately, or well) formulated these circumstantial aspects?

The question is illustrated by a celebrated [2] disagreement between Austin and Ryle in a case of this sort. Ryle said :

> In their most ordinary employment 'voluntary' and 'involuntary' are used ... as adjectives applying to actions which ought not to be done. We discuss whether someone's action was voluntary or not only when the action seems to have been his fault...

There is a contradiction in the fact that to "join the army or make a gift" (Austin's examples of when we use 'voluntarily') are not actions "which ought not to be done."

What criteria are there for statements that explicate such 'implications' as these?

Since not the word, but its use, does the 'implying', our question of criteria depends on what sort of 'implication' an activity like using can have. As we already said, it differs from logical 'implication' :

> ...'implies' must be given a special sense ... (PP, p. 32).

It is not an 'analytic' implication. If it were analytic, then whenever x is y,

> *y must* be either a part of *x or* not any part of it ... (as) *would* be the merest common sense if 'meanings' were things in some ordinary sense which contained parts in some ordinary sense (PP, p. 30).

The 'model' of 'analytic' implication is criticized by leading it back to just those situations it discriminates when used properly, situations where there are 'parts' which can be 'included'. Austin calls it a "shabby working model" which "*fails to fit the facts that we really* wish to talk about" (PP, p. 30). His italics in this sentence indicate that the circumstances of using a word do not have given 'parts'.

Proposition 5 : The activities whose 'implications' the philosophy states cannot be assumed to consist of parts or units in some ordinary sense.

But neither are these 'synthetic' statements. They are not based on a survey of how most people use a word, nor would such a survey be pertinent. Most people (like Finney's counsel) use language sloppily, or not as sharply as it can be used.

[2] Cited in B. Mates, "On the Verification of Statements about Ordinary Language," and S. Cavell, "Must We Mean What We Say?," in *Ordinary Language*, ed. V. C. Chappell (Englewood Cliffs, N. J. : Prentice-Hall, Inc., 1964).

Let us treat statements of 'implications' of use like any other expressions. We want to examine the use of such statements by philosophers, so let us see what they do, and when.

What do linguistic analysts do with such assertions? They formulate 'rules' for when we should use expressions. Who is entitled to formulate such rules? The answer is : the native speaker of a language. By 'native' is marked the sort of learning which doesn't occur from a book but rather, learning in a context of living. We have learned language (not as labels for rigid objects as might be pictured in a book, each with word below), but through living in contexts in which words are used. Thus, explication statements occur when 'native' speakers spell out specific aspects of the contexts in which they have learned to use words. Such statements spell out a learning (or 'knowing') which is not already cut up into the sort of 'parts', or units or variables we use in 'spelling out'. The learning and 'knowing' of language by a native speaker (his learning or 'knowing' the circumstances) is 'implicit' : Austin calls this a learning of "semantic conventions (implicit, of course), about the way we use words *in situations*" (PP, p. 32).

Thus the use of the word 'implicit' in this context marks several aspects :

Firstly, it marks a relation between an activity (like using) *and a statement*, such that what is called 'implicit' is 'in' the activity but not in the form of the spelled out units of statement.

Proposition 6 : The statements are 'implicit' in the activity, i.e., not in the sense that its verbal units, 'unit-meanings' or 'representations' are 'in' it.

Secondly, 'implicit' marks a relation between activity and *world* again in a sense other than as concrete or represented things 'in' it.

Proposition 7 : Aspects of the world (contexts) are 'implicit' in the activity, i.e., not in the sense that things (or images of them) are 'in' the activity.

Thirdly, our *knowing* when to use a word (our having learned to use it) is said to be 'implicit' in the activity of using the word (and in our habit or capacity to do so). This is the 'native' knowledge which entitles us to make assertions about 'when we should say ...'. If we did not call it 'implicit', then the 'knowledge' would be the sort we have after rules are formulated. But, we do not learn language by repeating explicit 'rules' to ourselves.

Proposition 8 : We know 'implicitly' what the main philosophic statements formulate, i.e., not in the sense of a knowledge separable from activity (or the capacity for the activity).

We now see that explication statements are neither 'analytic' nor 'synthetic' for the same reason : 'analytic' is used when there are already defined and separable units or parts (as in formal logic), and similarly, 'synthetic' is used when there are already defined observation units (as in observing two 'associated' traits). But we do not learn, know, or use language by knowing separate, defined, unitized 'variables' of circumstances.

The Linguistic Analyst has learned what the use of a word might mark, but not as separate 'synthetically' associated variables. He proposes exemplary sentences to himself in imagined contexts, and thereby he notices *newly specific* [3] variables standing out, which may convince him that the example is right or impossible.

Proposition 9 : Observation and experience cannot be assumed to be constituted of already given units, 'variables'.

Austin emphasizes that explicating the circumstances of 'use' is not merely a matter of observing already given variables. 'Situations', 'circumstances', 'actions', the contexts in which we 'use' language, are not given in already definite units (these would be reified verbal units). Austin says situations are capable of being "split up" along "various lines." For example, there is no hard-and-fast way of knowing what is 'an' action : "... what, indeed, are the rules for the use of 'the' action, 'an' action, a 'part' or 'phase' of an action, and the like?" (PP, p. 127). Austin indicates here that this problem must be dealt with by the same method as any other ("what are the rules for the use of 'the' ... or 'an' ... action"?). The criteria for unit actions would have to be found in the circumstances in which we use 'the' or 'a' or 'an action'. But circumstances of using do not come in already defined unit variables. Thus, to explicate the 'rules' (i.e., circumstances of use) for units of action involves the same difficulty. Austin points this out and urges us not to take as our model-cases only those simple and relatively dull

[3] See Shapere, D. "Philosophy and the Analysis of Language," *Inquiry*, 3 (1960) for an illuminating discussion : "... we seem forced to assume *both* that we know the facts, and so can discover the true meaning or real intention or true form of the proposition, *and* that we know the true meaning or real intention or true form of the proposition, and so can discover the facts" (p. 42). The author leads up to the realization that the method involves *newly* differentiating and explicating *both* language and facts.

circumstances in which variables are already definite units, plainly and easily given :

> ... is to think something, or to say something, or to try to do something, to do an action? ... All 'actions' are ... equal, composing a quarrel with striking a match, winning a war with sneezing... (PP, p. 127).
>
> ... what is *an* or *one* or *the* action? For we can generally split up what might be named as one action in several distinct ways, into different *stretches* or *phases* or *stages* ... we can dismantle the machinery of the act, and describe (and excuse) separately the intelligence, the appreciation, the planning, the decision, the execution and so forth (PP, p. 149).
>
> ... it is in principle always open to us, along various lines, to describe or refer to 'what I did' in so many different ways (PP, p. 148).

The method seems to offer no criteria to decide among those various 'lines' along which to split up.

Surely, we won't let it remain at this! Can it be that these philosophers uncritically use just whatever assumptions happen to creep into the 'lines along which' they 'split up' the circumstances of use and action?

Proposition 10 : The philosophical method has the problem that explications can be formulated along various lines. The explications depend partly on the given philosopher's mode of formulating, for which no justification is offered.

Philosophic questions, after all, are just those which deal with the problems of the variety of modes of conceptualizing. Are we to say that ordinary language philosophy cannot deal with just this most properly philosophic type of question?

The problem is rounded out since 'use' itself is *probably* an 'action' (it depends on how we split it up!). Austin's treatment of action here is therefore an inquiry into the fundamentals of how one explicates use. Austin formulates some parameters along which use or action can be split up in a variety of ways : "stretch," "phase," "stage." But he does not intend to make this into a scheme similar to the many schemes philosophy already has.

Proposition 11 : No one scheme can be given to analyze the various parameters along which possible explications may differ. Such a scheme would only again follow models or constructs. The activities in their contexts are always more basic than any system of constructs or parameters.

Austin wants us to notice that the context is not already "split up" into given, cut-and-dried variables.

> When we examine what we should say when, what words we should use in what situations, we are looking again not *merely* at words ... but also at the realities we use the words to talk about ... (PP, p. 130).
>
> We need therefore to prise them (words) off the world, to hold them apart from and against it, so that we can realize their inadequacies ... and can relook at the world without blinkers (PP, p. 130).

The world at which we 'relook' is thus not assumed to be already structured out for us in some hypothetical way, or as words have seemed to cut it. In the direct examination of the circumstances when we use words, we "relook" without being bound by the prisons, cooky forms, models of already given variables. Austin says we get "a sharpened perception" of phenomena "directly." The analysis of words' uses leads beyond the ways words *had* structured the world. We know the world 'directly' and we say of this knowing that it is "implicit." Words have no "handy appendages," "meaning" or "denotations" corresponding to them (PP, p. 29).

Proposition 12 : Since activities in context are more basic than constructs or pictures, the view of meaning and cognition differs from the traditional. No longer are contents, representations, denotations, pictures, objects as referents, considered basic. The representational view of meaning is overthrown. Neither world nor activities are assumed to be given already cut into 'handy denotations' or set given 'meanings'.

One can not argue that we simply note what is 'similar' in the different circumstances in which we use a word. Austin opposes the assumption that there is somewhere a denotation or 'respect' in which situations are 'similar' (PP, p. 38). "The different meanings of the word 'head' will be related to each other in all sorts of different ways at once" (PP, p. 43). And this is an argument not merely against real universals. It is an argument to show that the world of circumstances (in terms of which 'use' is explicated) is not already split up into handily packaged variables or denotations.

> A striking example is the case of 'pleasure' : pleasures ... *differ* precisely in the way in which they are pleasant. No greater mistake could be made than ... of thinking that pleasure is always a single similar feeling, somehow isolable from the various activities which 'give rise' to it (PP, p. 41).

There is no 'similarity' given such that we might simply look to see what is 'similar' when we use a certain word. For example, we must look 'directly' to see the circumstances in which pleasure is termed one, and those in which it is termed by various subtle specific words. Thus, while our formulations of circumstances are not arbitrary (they are systematically related to our 'looking directly') neither are these formulations governed by given 'similarities' or given variables of observation. The lesson is that the world cannot be assumed to consist of ready and waiting variables. Is Austin perhaps saying that our words and concepts do not necessarily conform to some *unknowable* nature of "things in themselves"? Just the opposite : he is saying that we may 'relook directly' and that we know 'implicitly'.

Proposition 13 : The method involves a direct access to an experienced world not yet split into word-like or thing-like units or traits. The method systematically relates formulations of philosophy to this direct access.

Is not this an attempt to leap out of the ancient problem of the variety of ways of construing anything? If we can 'relook directly' at the circumstances words mark, and if thereby we think ourselves freed of presuppositions, assumptions, constructs, variables already isolated, etc. — if we insist that circumstances are not given with 'intelligible essences' ('similarities') of their own, — are we not at the mercy of whatever assumptions and selections creep into our formulations of this direct, 'implicit' context?

How then can we evaluate a formulation (or worse : two differing ones)?

There is a seeming 'vicious circle' in evaluating all terms and propositions by what circumstances their uses implies, and then basing statements of use-implications on what? On direct looking. But we assert that the world looked-at 'directly', 'without blinkers' does not come marked out by heavy black lines into 'variables', 'kinds' of circumstance, 'similarities'. We assert thereby that direct looking cannot provide a foundation for the assumptions and varieties of formulations.

Proposition 14 : The ultimate statements of the philosophy are said to be 'direct descriptions', formulating what is already 'implicit' in certain human activities in the situational world. Yet, it is expressly denied that what we 'look at directly' has the structure various formulations employ. Thus one both asserts and denies that the structure and assumptions of descriptions inhere in the directly looked at.

But, if no ultimate structure is 'given' then why should we need for it to be? There must be a positive view of this seeming 'vicious circle'. We must accept that explication is not 'based on' something 'implicit', through a correspondence of structure, and must examine what the relationship is which is here called : 'based on'.

To do so we must examine what we do when we explicate.

II

Phenomenologists will have recognized that each of my 'propositions' is basic also to their method. But I have not yet presented phenomenology so that linguistic analysts could appreciate how these propositions apply in it. Also, I have not yet shown that the problem of explication statements is central also for phenomenology.

Linguistic analysts wish to limit discussions to precise formulations. Since the method (as, I hope, I have shown) centrally involves something 'implicit', i.e., something not formulated, they find it difficult to describe their method. Phenomenologists choose the opposite order : they begin by pointing to something unthematized, pre-objective, pre-conceptual, experienced and lived but not explicitly known.

This difference in where the two methods begin leads to characteristically different common misunderstandings of each : linguistic analysis can seem 'trivial', concerned only with extant words and linguistic conventions. Phenomenology can seem 'fuzzy', concerned only with unspeakable unknowables.

These characteristic misunderstandings point up that these methods involve a *relationship between* formulation and the not yet formulated. One mode is misunderstood as using *only* what is already formulated, the other as using *only* the inveterately unformulable.

It is well, therefore, to say of phenomenology first that it formulates, explicates, 'lifts out', renders in structures and discriminating description, aspects 'implicitly known' to us, but not known explicitly till formulated.

Phenomenologists too, like to claim that their formulations are 'direct descriptions'. They like to say that they are not 'explaining' (rendering in construct systems) but rather, 'only' describing. Heidegger considered *his* formulations as explicating *the* basic structure 'implicit' in living and acting, yet Husserl found them incorrect. Obviously not every aspect of these differing 'descriptions' is directly founded on phenomena directly viewed by all. (See Proposition 14.)

Phenomenologists (like linguistic analysts) do not argue from theoretical models. All terms, propositions and arguments are evaluated not by their theoretical structure but by what they 'lift out' directly for us. If, as a result of the 'description' we now notice something directly, the description has done its proper work.

Phenomenology depends upon our having, in addition to terms and constructs, something directly accessible ('phenomena') not assumed to be determined or patterned by assumed constructs. The method systematically relates philosophy to this directly accessible (Proposition 13).

What is the nature of directly accessible experience or phenomena? Husserl examined *only* 'experience' but experiences are always 'of' something. On phenomenological grounds Husserl rejected 'psychic entities' — he just never found them. They were never directly noticeable. They are mere constructs of a certain kind of psychology. Experiences are always of what is seen, noticed, heard, aimed at, wanted, expected, desired, etc. Husserl found more and more that the whole human world is involved when one examines 'only' experience.

It takes artificial constructs to say that our experiences are 'in' us, that they are 'subjective', that there is 'another' world out there, in addition to 'percepts' in us. Phenomenology is thus insistently not 'subjective'. The ordinary human world is 'implicit' in experience. Heidegger and Sartre begin where Husserl gradually arrived. Experience ('consciousness') is 'being in the world'.

Sartre begins where our discussion of linguistic analysis ended, namely, the refusal to assume that our activities (action, use, thinking) or the world are constituted of thing-like entities, meaning-constructs, or representations.

> (It is an error to) ... make the psychic event a thing and to qualify it with 'conscious' just as I can qualify this blotter with 'red' (liv) [4]
>
> We must renounce those neutral 'givens' which, according to the system of reference chosen, find their place either 'in the world' or 'in the psyche' (BN, p. li).
>
> Consciousness (of) pleasure is constitutive of the pleasure as the very mode of its existence ... and not as a form which is imposed by a blow upon a hedonistic material (BN, p. liv).

The point — even the choice of an example — is similar to Austin's, as already cited. There are not already given meanings, units or forms like 'pleasure'. Pleasure "is not a representation, it is a concrete event" (BN, p. liv). (Proposition 12.)

Sartre's emphasis is on the ongoing process, the activity. Representations ('objects of knowledge', 'objects of reflection') occur only as 'supported by' the concretely ongoing process. There can be conscious-

[4] Except where otherwise indicated, page references in this section are to J. P. Sartre, *Being and Nothingness*, trans. Hazel E. Barnes (New York : Philosophical Library, 1956). Hereafter cited as BN.

ness of representations, but not representations of consciousness. All structures, concepts, representations, schemes and laws are to be viewed as already involving a concretely ongoing activity, and thus they can never explain or picture it.

> It is futile to invoke pretended laws of consciousness ... a law is (an) object of knowledge; there can be consciousness of a law, not a law of consciousness (BN, p. lv).

Thus the concrete activity remains always more basic than any representations or laws (had only through it) and hence no ultimate laws of it can be given (Proposition 11).

Sartre's constructs ('for itself' and 'in itself', and various specific pairs of terms similar to this pair) stem from Hegel. They cannot be attributed to the very nature of consciousness or the world (except insofar as *with* these terms ... and with other terms, too ... we can 'lift out' and bring to notice aspects of living which we *then* can see directly, i.e., even without these terms).

You may therefore view Sartre somewhat as though he were a linguistic analyst who happened to like dialectical instead of British Empiricist types of terminology. Just as linguistic analysts are not party to British Empiricist assumptions although they often employ that philosophical tradition's terms, so Sartre is not fashioning an abstract dialectic although he uses dialectical terms.

But, is there any phenomenological foundation for this choice of terms? If there were, would we not have to assume that there is something inherently dialectical (or, if we oppose it positively, something inherently non-dialectical) in the phenomena and activities themselves? As we saw, no dialectical or other such "laws of consciousness" are possible. The concretely ongoing activities are always already involved even in the holding of such laws.

Thus there is no basis for the formulative assumptions and constructs with which the philosopher describes and discriminates (Proposition 10).

As we saw, Sartre rejects thing-like 'neutral givens', both 'in the psyche' and 'in the world'. Phenomenologists assume no static 'objects' or variables of observation 'out there' or representations of them 'in here'. Hence observation is no mere gaping at[5] already given entities, variables or perceptions which we need only 'associate' (Proposition 9).

Activity-in-context replaces the view of given entities. Why not, then, fashion philosophic terms that are not static representations?

[5] Heidegger's term : "gaping at."

We must not call Sartre's type of term 'ambiguous' if we are bothered only because it isn't a representational type of term. For this nonrepresentational character of human activity Sartre employs paired terms, designed for use in a movement from each to the other. Moving between these dialectically paired terms often has a paradoxical sound. Linguistic analysts should not miss their kinship to this mode of philosophizing because of a dislike for such terms. After all, linguistic analysts have not yet fashioned terms for this nonrepresentational aspect so central also to their method. Linguistic analysts bring home this same aspect, but they do it with examples — and these are also intentionally paradoxical, to point up the fact that activity in situations is not reducible to units, pictures, objects of knowledge, representations.

Both methods reject reasoning from constructs alone, and wish to evaluate constructs only in terms of what is done with them, how they are used, what they directly discriminate. It follows that we should not turn away from the type of constructs used before seeing what their use discriminates.

Sartre's dialectical terms do not make an abstract dialectical scheme. Traditional dialecticians object to Sartre's 'dialectic' because it remains on the 'first level' on which it starts. Sartre refuses to 'raise' his contradictory terms to a 'higher' (more abstract) synthesis. For Sartre, when Hegel's "being" and "nothingness" turn into each other and are then absorbed in a higher synthesis, they become "mere concepts" (BN, p. 16).

A pair of Sartre's terms are never absorbed. In moving from one to the other and back we discriminate an aspect of concrete living and moving, that cannot be represented by single static representations.

Such a pair of terms gets at something Sartre finds in a great many aspects of human living : "scissiparity" (a word reminiscent of scissors, borrowed from biology where it is used for amoeboid splitting of one organism into many). As Sartre uses it, 'scissiparity' names something he sees over and over again : some facet of human activity which is really one, and yet appears to have two poles. The traditional misrepresentation of the activity represents the two poles as though they were entities or things, and the activity is thereby misconstrued or lost. Thus consciousness (an activity) always seemingly involves "*something* present to *something*," and there you have the temptation to describe it all in terms of thing-like contents in a mirror-like consciousness.

For example : "reflected-reflecting." When we reflect on our own consciousness, to be conscious "of" always involves also our ongoing process or activity. We must not take one term as just itself ("it isn't identical with itself," Sartre will say). Nor can we simply put both terms together, as two representations tied together. That gives only the poles, not the movement. The wish to have the totality *represented* must fail. The movement, the activity, the process, is being discriminated.

In the following, a belief is used as an example to bring home the point that "a belief" is both a "content" and the activity, "the believing." But the activity of believing will be missed if it is equated to the belief we can reflect on.

> Thus by the sole fact that my belief is apprehended as belief, it is *no longer only belief* : that is, it is already no longer belief, it is troubled belief. Thus the ... judgment 'belief is consciousness (of) belief' can under no circumstances be taken as a statement of identity (BN, p. 75).

The phrase "no longer" illustrates the movement to which Sartre points with the pair "reflected-reflecting". These terms make no sense considered as separable somethings (as each "identical to itself") :

> On no account can we say that consciousness is consciousness or that belief is belief. Each of these terms refers to the other and passes into the other, and yet each term is different from the other. We have seen that neither belief nor pleasure nor joy can exist *before* being conscious... (BN, p. 75).

Sartre offers many other such pairs and with them he can characterize many detailed aspects of living, loving, smoking, doing, making, having, and so on. (Like linguistic analysis phenomenology seems unphilosophical to some because of its many new discriminations of life detail.)

The pairs of terms avoid the pitfall of a representational analysis. But are not these pairs themselves representations? No, they are not. Are they the proscribed "laws of consciousness"? No, they are not. Applying the method to our own use of it, we have to accept that we use not what the terms picture but our own ongoing activity. This activity is not being represented by the terms. They 'point to' this activity (much as examples in Linguistic Analysis do). Thus these philosophic terms are not 'the' structure of consciousness, but 'pointers' which newly discriminate concretely had aspects of what we do, have, notice. We ('implicitly') have and know what the terms get at, point to and explicate. (Otherwise they would be again just another set of constructs, "laws" or "representations" of consciousness.) (Proposition 8).

Our own concretely ongoing activity 'sustains' concepts or laws or representations or structures or terms. It is always more basic than they and not made up out of them.

> ... consciousness is not produced as a particular instance of an abstract

possibility but ... it creates and supports its essence — that is, the synthetic order of its possibilities (BN, p. lv).

These 'possibilities' of action constitute the 'self'. We seem to have a 'self' 'interrogate ourselves', 'refer to' ourselves inwardly, and 'aim' questions at ourselves. But Sartre denies that 'contents', 'entities' or 'meanings' characterize consciousness.

> ... some wrongly hold ... the 'I' ... to be the inhabitant of consciousness. ... through hypostasizing the being of the ... reflected-on ... these writers fix and destroy the movement of reflection upon the self ... We on the contrary, have shown that the *self* on principle cannot inhabit consciousness."
>
> It is an *absent-present* (note how this pair of terms operates) ... the existence of *reference* ... is clearly marked ... (Consciousness refers) *down there*, beyond its grasp, in the far reaches of its possibilities (BN, p. 103).

We refer not to something actually there but to something "absent," the "far reaches of its possibilities."

> But this possible ... is not present as an object ... for in that case it would be reflected-on (BN, p. 104).

Most often we talk of the 'self' as something unquestionably 'present' inside us — which misses the peculiar way in which we must interrogate, seemingly to find out what we are, feel, etc.

The Freudian 'ego' and 'id' come directly from this interrogating and digging. Again the poles of the activity are made into entities : the ego; the id. Sartre, phenomenologically, rejects both the constructs of a present and of an absent entity. It is the 'absent-present', not as a paradoxical sticking together of both constructs, but as a delineation of what we do : we seem to 'refer' to inward contents but — we find : for example, I am thirsty. What do I 'refer to'? My 'thirst' as a content, like 'pleasure', an object 'of' which I am conscious? Rather, it is the 'possible' of drinking.

Actions in situations are 'implicit' in the way consciousness "refers" to itself-qua "absent" :

> But this possible ... is non-thetically (not like an object is given) an absent-present ... The satisfied thirst which haunts my actual thirst (it "haunts" : it is not baldly here nor not here, it is my desire or possibility) is consciousness of itself-drinking-from-a-glass and a non-positional consciousness.

Rather than 'a thirst' as a 'content', when we 'refer' to and 'interrogate' our 'absent-present' self, we find the possibility of drinking from a glass — and this possibility of action in the situation is not given 'in there' as an object of reflection. Rather, there is this 'itself-drinking-from-a-glass' and a 'nonpositional consciousness' (the last phrase reminds us that it is *concrete activity*. If it were not, we would again interpret activity as representations, this time as representations of possible actions).

Actions in the situation (our possibilities) are 'implicit' in this activity of 'referring' to ourselves as 'down there' in our feelings. Indeed, every explication of feelings always reveals not entities like anger, fear, thirst, pleasure, etc., but anger at this and this situation, because it forces us to do so and so, and give up such and such, or fight with so and so. These are what we might do in the situation (Proposition 7).

How is it that we 'refer' to what we bodily feel and thereby 'make to be' such possibilities of situational action? The body is the "condition of possibility" (BN, p. 338). We are bodily in situations. The ongoing activity of consciousness is this bodily being in the world. This bodily feel Sartre calls "nausea" but he indicates that it needn't have just that specific quality. It is your ever present live sentient feel. He also calls it "coenesthetic affectivity." It is the body, again not as entities but as activity in context. That is what we 'interrogate' when we 'aim' questions 'at' our self 'down there'; the 'feeling' which isn't a content but the 'possibilities' of action :

> Coenesthetic affectivity ... provides the implicit matter of *all* the phenomena of the psyche ... it is this which we aim at ... and form into images ... in order to aim at absent feelings and make them present... (BN, p. 338).

And now, the problem of criteria : Granted that we are looking 'directly', without the 'blinkers' of words or constructs, and granting that a good 'description' leads us to notice newly discriminate aspects, nevertheless : do our descriptions not import a variety of assumption systems each with different consequences?

Consider that Merleau-Ponty — with similarly phenomenological intentions — argues strongly for a very different type of term and different assertions.

We have to grant that while philosophic statements 'lift out' what is 'implicit', 'already there', 'given' or 'noticeable' directly, it is not there in the structured units and patterns descriptions impose (Proposition 6).

These philosophers emphasize that 'phenomena' or activities ('consciousness', 'perception', 'being in the world') are not constituted of given units, things, representations, meanings, etc. Thus it is not the question whether Sartre's or Merleau-Ponty's descriptive terms represent the really 'given' units and structures. Both emphasize the 'pre-reflective' and 'prethematic' character of living activity (Proposition 5).

It follows that we must look more closely at how phenomenological descriptions are 'based on' our direct looking and living. Obviously, 'based on' here does not mark a correspondence of structure such that the formulation's structure corresponds to the structure of the given (although, why oh why is just that so often claimed?)

When a phenomenological philosopher offers his descriptions as 'ontology' he claims only that we already know 'pre-ontologically' everything he has to say. We know it in living, but without the explicit structure which he 'lifts out' with his description (Proposition 4).

But, if descriptions are not congruent with the pattern already there (because what is there isn't given so patterned), then are they arbitrarily imposed? Are phenomenological philosophies mere speculative assumption systems no different from other such systems? Is the claim to phenomenological grounding merely an unfounded claim to special privilege for one's assumptions?

Just as linguistic analysts feel you are missing the point when you question the constructs and assumptions in their "descriptions" (of circumstances), so phenomenologists feel that the point is being missed when the variety of construct systems is questioned. The point is that as a result of a description (no matter how wild its terms) you may directly notice something you had not previously noticed. Do not evaluate the description as a set of constructs, but as a set of pointers. All constructs are evaluated by what they discriminate directly (Proposition 3).

But suppose we do not miss the point. Suppose we call a description 'good' whenever it 'lifts out' something for us. Even then, we must ask : can two different descriptions lift out the 'same' aspect for our notice? If we say yes, we assume that the given activities come already cut up (such that there is a 'same' aspect waiting there apart from the differing descriptions). If we say no, we admit that the supposed directly discriminated aspects are really a function of our descriptive 'blinkers'.

We must view phenomenological *explicating* also as an activity. Then we will not assume that it is determined by some system of entities or constructs that lies beneath phenomena. Hence no 'same' aspects can be waiting for us there (Proposition 2).

But our activity (as much during explicating as any other time) doesn't only 'sustain' representations (it isn't reducible to representations). It also 'surpasses' them ... it reorganizes, reinterprets, creates new alternatives, new possibilities. For example, Sartre does not believe in an abstract 'freedom' such that I might be able to leap out of the situation I am in. (If I am a cafe waiter, this role doesn't define me. It is a representation which I sustain, but I cannot suddenly be a diplomat instead.) Activity surpasses representations in all sorts of ways, but not in just any old way : always in regard to the situation I am in : the 'facticity' of the situation (Proposition 1).

The pair of terms : 'facticity-surpassing' is another Sartrian pair. A situation's factual constraints cannot be described apart from my activity and possibilities. Its factual constraints are created by, posed for, and in terms of, my possible activities in the situation. Similarly, my activities always create new possibilities (and thereby aspects of the situation which it couldn't have been said to have, before and apart from me). Similarly, the world isn't given in just such and such a structure so that we might read it off. Rather, our activity creates, sustains and surpasses the patterns we explicate.

But it is clear, therefore, that we lack any way to examine the various explications, how they newly 'make be', 'surpass', 'split up', and describe, and their various unexamined assumption systems and consequences.

We cannot leave this problem in this shape : all claims of a phenomenologist's basis for description is in question. We must ask : what then *is* the way in which explication is 'based' the implicit pre-structured?

III

The 'implicit' factor is so central in these methods, that we have already had to say a good deal about it, and about 'explication'. The propositions I offered constitute a treatment of explication, provided we now continue.

(a) We said that a 'good' explication statement (we were asking for criteria for such statements) leads us to notice directly some aspect we had not previously noticed. That is actually a striking criterion (of a peculiar sort, to be sure) which sets successful 'explication statements' apart from the many statements one can always formulate which do *not* succeed in bringing something new to direct notice.

(b) Furthermore, we don't always call a statement an 'explication' when it leads us to a newly noticed aspect. One can always devise very many statements which (by objective criteria) state the many facts that were there and had not been noticed. One does not call these 'explications'. It is an 'explication' only if we are 'sure' that the new aspect 'was implicit' before (i.e., we now insist that it was 'known' to us, or 'there' for us). This retrospective assertion of the newly noticed aspect is also something only few special statements bring about.

The new aspect (once noticed) must have this special relationship to what we do remember noticing (or feeling, or knowing) so that we now 'insist' it 'was implicit' in what we knew, felt, or noticed, and not just another fact in the situation.

(c) Once an aspect is discriminated and newly noticed, it cannot be made unnoticeable again. Of course, one need not pay attention to it, one can forget it, consider something else, etc. But once discriminated, the aspect cannot directly be made to merge away again.

(d) These three powers of a newly discriminated aspect are not totally dependent on the explication statement. The statement leads us to the newly discriminated aspect, but once it has done so, the aspect is noticed 'directly'. Also its quality of 'having been implicit' in what we knew or did before doesn't come from the statement (usually cannot be reduced to formal relationships between statements of what we knew before and this statement). We may throw the statement out and still the newly discriminated aspect cannot thereby be made to disappear again.

Because of this partial 'independence' of the discriminated aspect we can say that there is 'direct' noticing and not *only* various statements. If what is directly noticed depended *entirely* on the statement (not only for its being noticed, but also for its quality and for its remaining noticeable) then all discussions would again become a matter of various formulations related to, or clashing with, each other.

(e) But, neither can we say that the newly discriminated aspect is *fully* independent of the variety of statements once we notice it. It would be convenient (though, in the long run it wouldn't be at all desirable) if we could say flatly that once we notice the aspect we can use various statements of it equivalently for this 'same' aspect. At a particular juncture of some discussion or task two very different statements might serve to discriminate the 'same' aspect, but the very next step of the discussion, or the next difficulty in the task, might require that we discriminate further aspects, and we may then note that the two statements are no longer equivalent (or, perhaps they still are — but we must look).

(f) Because the newly discriminated aspect is the function and purpose of the statement, we need not argue from the statement as from a model : we *can* but we *need not* be bound by the logical necessity with which all kinds of logical implications follow from the statement.

Yet, if we were to deny the statement all logical character it would cease to have any discriminating power. How do we decide what logical implications we use, as against those we ignore? We decide by noticing what the logical implication may further discriminate in the directly noticeable aspect.

This means that logically different explication statements with different models *can* always discriminate *different* further aspects of anything we directly notice. It is a decision, to consider these differing further aspects unimportant (for the present discussion, task, etc.) — a decision which has to be made at every step, since at each step these differing aspects may become important.

Thus the logical characters of different explications can neither be always accepted nor always ignored, but must be pursued to notice what is differently discriminated by them. Only so can we have explication statements that are not again mere formulative assumptions.

(g) I cannot go into it very far here, but because of the way one can neither drop, nor uncritically accept the logical structural aspects of explication statements, there is a whole field of such procedural choices we use and must examine.[6]

Either linguistic analysis and phenomenology are to be considered merely arbitrary play with arbitrarily chosen assumption systems, arbitrary ways of selecting and defining new distinctions, arbitrary imposition of formulative patterns, that is to say, either we consider these modes of philosophy to be no different (though less self-critical) than traditional philosophy, or we will have to grant the central role of directly had, not yet formulated experiencing.

Only because these methods involve the use, during philosophizing, of directly had, not yet formulated experiencing, is the appeal to phenomena or to 'direct looking' more than a circular and invalid claim to special privilege.

But this raises, as a central problem, the question of how formulations may be related to directly had, not yet formulated experiencing.

Sometimes this directly had, not yet formulated experiencing is called 'feeling'; (for example, in this common conversation : Question : "On what do you base your assertion that this rule explicates the use of this word?" Answer : "The use it states feels right to me. Doesn't it feel right to you also?"). Either we take such assertions of 'feeling' to be merely self-righteous claims, or we must really examine what sort of relationships a formulation may have to 'feeling'. (You might call it 'sensing' : "Ryle sensed trouble where trouble was" says Cavell [7]).

Notice also, that such 'feeling', 'sensing', or not yet formulated but

[6] E. T. Gendlin, *Experiencing and the Creation of Meaning* (New York : The Free Press of Glencoe, 1962).

[7] Cavell, *op. cit.*

directly had experiencing *is used as we formulate*. Similarly, the few criteria and procedural distinctions given above concern the use of direct feeling or sensing (We 'insist' ... we are 'sure' we have a direct sense that the newly discriminated aspect was involved in what we did notice earlier ...). We can further explicate and give a logical rendition of any such instance, but this still involves the direct use of the experiential discrimination so that we may explicate *it* and thereby set up logical explicit accounts of how we have already proceeded.

Philosophy is not the only discipline in which this relationship between the directly felt experiencing and conceptualization arises. Another such discipline is psychotherapy.[8] There, too, an individual freshly discriminates and conceptualizes directly felt, not yet formulated experiencing. There, too, the individual backs his formulations up with insistence that it 'feels right', and unless this be fatuous, much more is involved in this peculiar relationship between direct feeling and concepts.

And, does it not seem now that these philosophic approaches have after all fallen back on a 'private datum' or 'content', much as they eschew such a view? Again, this will be the case only if we leave the relation between feeling and concepts unexamined. If we examine it, we notice that we deny the assumption that the whole sequence of explication (or behavior) is somehow folded into the feeling, like an accordion. We deny that feeling, as such, needs to be 'checked' against, (as in the spurious problem of the 'private' supposed basis for first person statements). We have already seen that feelings or 'implicit' knowledge is not such as to permit checking its correspondence with what is said. Even if the feeling were not at all 'private', even if it were an object on the table, it would not contain in itself explicitly the whole sequence of explications or behaviors. Explication and behavior occur in the world. Feeling ('implicit' experiencing) is not fully behaved, not fully explicated. As *not* fully behaved it does *not* yet contain the objective sequence. But it functions centrally (we must see how) in behaving or explicating, and when it does, there is no problem of observing its bearing in the world. For example, my six year old daughter, just before getting the mumps, had a pain and told me about it in an explicated and behaved way which needed no 'checking' : "Daddy, right here under my ear (pointing) it feels like a black-and-blue mark, but I looked in the mirror and there isn't any black-and-blue mark there!'

[8] Gendlin, *op. cit.* See also "A Theory of Personality Change," in *Personality Change*, Worchel and Byrne, eds. (New York : Wiley, 1964).

When not-yet-formulated experiencing plays its role in formulating and behaving, the way it bears on aspects of the world becomes quite clear and observable. Before it plays such a role, it is not yet all that. The activity of explicating or behaving doesn't just play out steps fully contained in pre-formulated experiencing. Rather, it carries experiencing forward, formulates and creatively shapes it further; and yet a given feeling won't function to support just any and all formulative attempts (as our 'criteria' above show). Only *some* very fortunate formulations (often we fail to find *any*) obtain these characteristic responses from the directly felt.

Thus, on the one hand, the directly experienced 'implicit' knowledge we feel doesn't fully determine the formulations and hence leaves us open to assumptions and contradictory possibilities. On the other hand, it doesn't permit any and all arbitrary formulations. It is therefore essential that we specify the kinds of support which the directly used 'implicit' gives to formulations.

Such an examination must occur in terms of procedural choices which can be specified. The role of feeling in explicating can't be examined except in explicating. But, there it must be examined, otherwise very different procedures in regard to formulational models will be mixed together, our use of them will be arbitrary, our accepting some logical implications of some models will be arbitrary and our rejection of other logical implications of the same models will also be arbitrary, we will have no way of dealing with contradictions between seemingly applicable 'rules' or 'explications', and no systematic way of appealing beyond mere theoretical constructs to direct experience.

Elsewhere,[9] I have attempted this examination. Here I have been able to give only a few instances.

My main purpose in this paper has been to show that both phenomenology and linguistic analysis employ not yet formulated, directly had experiencing in their methods. I have tried to show that this is no abstract or ephemeral thing, but something the individual must directly have and use, otherwise the rules and explications he formulates are merely arbitrary.

I have tried to show that this type of philosophy indeed breaks out beyond mere theoretical assumptions and constructs, that it breaks out

[9] E. Gendlin, *Experiencing and the Creation of Meaning* (New York : Free Press of Glencoe, 1962).

toward directly had and used 'implicit' experience, not yet formulated or cut up into neatly packaged traits, variables, denotations, etc.

The vicious circle I pointed out was not intended to lead us back to the imposition (the reading in) of theoretical constructs as basic immutable assumptions. Instead, the problem leads forward to an examination of the relationships between the directly sensed 'implicit' experiencing we use, and the variety of formulations and procedural choices we make.

NOTES ON CONTRIBUTORS

Sir Alfred J. Ayer received his advanced degree from The University of Oxford, and is Wykeham Professor of Logic at The University of Oxford.

Professor John Compton received his advanced degree from Yale University, and is Professor of Philosophy at Vanderbilt University.

Professor Harold A. Durfee received his advanced degree from Columbia University, and is William Frazer McDowell Professor of Philosophy at The American University.

Professor Stephen A. Erickson received his advanced degree from Yale University, and is Professor of Philosophy at Pomona College.

Professor Eugene T. Gendlin received his advanced degree from The University of Chicago, and is Associate Professor of Psychology at The University of Chicago, as well as Editor of *Psychotherapy*.

Professor John M. Hems received his advanced degree from The University of Aberdeen, and is Professor of Philosophy at The University of Guelph.

Mr. Ingvar Horgby is "fil. lic." in philosophy, and is Lektor in Philosophy at Per Brahegymnasiet, Jönköping, Sweden.

Professor Don Ihde received his advanced degree from Boston University, and is Professor of Philosophy at The State University of New York at Stony Brook.

Professor James C. Morrison received his advanced degree from Pennsylvania State University, and is Associate Professor of Philosophy at The University of Toronto.

Professor Paul Ricœur received his advanced degree from The University of Paris, and is Professor of Philosophy at The Université de Paris à la Sorbonne, and John Nuveen Professor of Philosophy at The University of Chicago.

Professor Gilbert Ryle received his advanced degree from The University of Oxford, was Waynflete Professor of Metaphysical Philosophy at The University of Oxford where he is Professor of Philosophy Emeritus, as well as the former distinguished Editor of *Mind*.

Professor Robert C. Solomon received his advanced degree from The University of Michigan, and is Associate Professor of Philosophy at The University of Texas.

Professor Charles Taylor received his advanced degree from The University of Oxford, and is Professor of Philosophy and Political Science at McGill University.

Professor John Wild received his advanced degree from The University of Chicago, and was Professor of Philosophy at Yale University.

SOURCES

I wish to thank the authors and publishers of these essays for their kind permission to reprint the articles in this anthology, which originally appeared as indicated below.

Ayer, Sir A. J., "Phenomenology and Linguistic Analysis," in *Proceedings of the Aristotelian Society, Supplementary Volume 33* (London : Harrison, 1959), by courtesy of the Editor of The Aristotelian Society, (c) 1959 The Aristotelian Society.

Compton, J., "Hare, Husserl, and Philosophic Discovery," *Dialogue*, 3 (1964).

Durfee, H. A., "Austin and Phenomenology," *Journal of the British Society for Phenomenology*, 2 (1971).

Erickson, S. A., "Meaning and Language," *Man and World*, I (1968).

Gendlin, E. T., "What are the Grounds of Explication? A Basic Problem in Linguistic Analysis and Phenomenology," reprinted from *The Monist*, Vol. 49, No. I (1965), La Salle, Illinois, with permission of the author and publisher.

Hems, J. M., "Husserl and/or Wittgenstein," reprinted with permission from *International Philosophical Quarterly*, 8 (1968).

Horgby, I., "The Double Awareness in Heidegger and Wittgenstein," *Inquiry*, 2 (1959), by courtesy of Universitetsforlaget, Oslo, publishers.

Ihde, D., "Some Parallels Between Analysis and Phenomenology," *Philosophy and Phenomenological Research*, Vol. 27, No. 4 (June, 1967).

Morrison, J., "Heidegger's Criticism of Wittgenstein's Conception of Truth," *Man and World*, 2 (1969).

Ricœur, P., "Husserl and Wittgenstein on Language," in Lee, E.N. and Mandelbaum, M., *Phenomenology and Existentialism* (Baltimore : Johns Hopkins University Press, 1967).

Ryle, G., "Phenomenology," in *Phenomenology, Goodness and Beauty, Aristotelian Society Supplementary Volume XI* (London : Harrison, 1932), by courtesy of the Editor of The Aristotelian Society, (c) 1932 The Aristotelian Society.

Solomon, R. C., "Sense and Essence : Frege and Husserl," reprinted with permission from *International Philosophical Quarterly*, II (1970).

Taylor, C., "Phenomenology and Linguistic Analysis," in *Proceedings of the Aristotelian Society, Supplementary Volume 33* (London : Harrison, 1959), by courtesy of the Editor of The Aristotelian Society, (c) 1959 The Aristotelian Society.

Wild, J., "Is There a World of Ordinary Language?" in Wild, J. *Existence and the World of Freedom* (Englewood Cliffs : Prentice-Hall, 1963), reprinted with permission of Prentice-Hall, Inc., *The Philosophical Review*, and Mrs. John Wild.

BIBLIOGRAPHY

In addition to the essays presented in this volume the following books and articles are especially relevant to the concerns of this anthology.

BOOKS

Acton, H. B., "Phenomenology," in *Phenomenology, Goodness and Beauty, Aristotelian Society Supplementary Volume XI* (London : Harrison, 1932).

Apel, K-O., *Analytic Philosophy of Language and the Geisteswissenschaften* (Dordrecht : D. Reidel, 1967).

Caton, C. E., *Philosophy and Ordinary Language* (Urbana : University of Illinois, 1963).

Cowley, F., *A Critique of British Empiricism* (London : Macmillan, 1968).

Crosson, F. J., "The Concept of Mind and the Concept of Consciousness," in Edie, J. M., *Phenomenology in America* (Chicago : Quadrangle, 1967).

Dufrenne, M., *Language and Philosophy* (Bloomington : Indiana University Press, 1963).

Dufrenne, M., "Wittgenstein et Husserl," in *Jalons* (The Hague : M. Nijhoff, 1966).

Durfee, H. A., "Emmanuel Levinas' Philosophy of Language," in Blose, B., Durfee, H. A., Rodier, D. F. T., *Explanation : New Directions in Philosophy* (The Hague : M. Nijhoff, 1973).

Edie, J. M., "Can Grammar Be Thought," in Edie, J. M., Parker, F. H., Schrag, C. O., *Patterns of the Life World* (Evanston : Northwestern University Press, 1970).

Ehrlich, L. H., "Mysticism or Metaphysics? A Juxtaposition of Wittgenstein, Thomas Aquinas, and Jaspers," *Akten des XIV. Internationalen Kongresses für Philosophie, Vol. III* (Wien : Herder, 1969).

Erickson, S. A., *Language and Being : An Analytic Phenomenology* (New Haven : Yale University Press, 1970).

Hodges, H. A., "Phenomenology," in *Phenomenology, Goodness and Beauty, Aristotelian Society Supplementary Volume XI* (London : Harrison, 1932).

Küng, G., "Ingarden on Language and Ontology," in Tymieniecka, A-T., *The Later Husserl and the Idea of Phenomenology* (Dordrecht : D. Reidel, 1972).

Küng, G., "Language Analysis and Phenomenological Analysis," *Akten des XIV. Internationalen Kongresses für Philosophie, Vol. II* (Wien : Herder, 1968).

Kurtz, P., *Language and Human Nature* (St. Louis : W. H. Green, 1971).

La Philosophie Analytique (Paris, 1962).

Manser, A., *Sartre* (New York : Oxford, 1966).

Mays, W., Brown, S. C., *Linguistic Analysis and Phenomenology* (London : Macmillan, 1972).

Mohanty, J. N., *Edmund Husserl's Theory of Meaning* (The Hague : M. Nijhoff, 1964).

Montefiore, A., *Philosophy and Personal Relations* (Montreal : McGill-Queens, 1973).

Montefiore, A., *Philosophie et Rapports Inter-Personnels* (Montreal : Les Presses Universitaires, 1973).

Olafson, F., *Principles and Persons* (Baltimore : Johns Hopkins University Press, 1967).

Peursen, C. A. van, *Phenomenology and Analytic Philosophy* (Pittsburgh : Duquesne University Press, 1972).

Pivcevic, E. *Phenomenology and Philosophical Understanding* (New York : Cambridge University Press, 1975).

Rorty, R., *The Linguistic Turn* (Chicago : University of Chicago Press, 1967).

Rosen, S., *Nihilism* (New Haven : Yale University Press, 1969).

Schmitt, R., *Martin Heidegger on Being Human* (New York : Random House, 1969).

Spiegelberg, H., *The Phenomenological Movement, Vol. I & II* (The Hague : M. Nijhoff, 1960).

Spiegelberg, H., " 'Linguistic Phenomenology' : John L. Austin and Alexander Pfänder," *Memorias del XIII Congreso de Filosofía*, 19 (1964).

Spiegelberg, H., "On the Right to Say 'We' : A Linguistic and Phenomenological Analysis," in Psathas, G., *Phenomenological Sociology : Issues and Applications* (Somerset : J. Wiley, 1973).

Te Hempe, E., "The Life-World and the World of Ordinary Language," in Edie, J. M., *An Invitation to Phenomenology* (Chicago : Quadrangle, 1965).

Warnock, M., *Existentialism* (New York, 1970).

ARTICLES

Apel, K-O., "Wittgenstein und das Problem des hermeneutischen Verstehens," *Zeitschrift Für Theologie Und Kirche*, 63 (1966).

Apel, K-O., "Wittgenstein und Heidegger : Die Frage nach dem Sinn von Sein und der Sinnlosigkeitsverdacht gegen alle Metaphysik," *Philosophisches Jahrbuch*, 75 (1967).

Bar-Hillel, Y., "Husserl's Conception of a Purely Logical Grammar," *Philosophy and Phenomenological Research*, 17 (1967).

Cavell, S., "Existentialism and Analytic Philosophy," *Daedalus*, 93 (1964).

Chappell, V. C., "Ego and Person : Phenomenology or Analysis," *The Monist*, 49 (1965).

Chappell, V. C., "Response to Professor Chisholm," *The Monist*, 49 (1965).

Chisholm, R. M., "Notes on the Analysis of the Self," *The Monist*, 49 (1965).
Downes, C., "On Husserl's Approach to Necessary Truth," *The Monist*, 49 (1965).
Durfee, H. A., "Austin and Phenomenology Revisited : A Reply to Professor Meyn," *Journal of the British Society for Phenomenology*, 3 (1972).
Edie, J. M., "Phenomenology as a Rigorous Science," *International Philosophical Quarterly*, 13 (1973).
Gill, J. H., "Linguistic Phenomenology," *International Philosophical Quarterly*, 13 (1973).
Goff, R. A., "Wittgenstein's Tools and Heidegger's Implements," *Man and World*, 1 (1968).
Gorner, P., "Husserl and Strawson," *Journal of the British Society for Phenomenology*, 2 (1971).
Gutting, G., "Husserl and Logical Empiricism," *Metaphilosophy*, 2 (1971).
Harries, K., "Wittgenstein and Heidegger : The Relationship of the Philosopher to Language," *The Journal of Value Inquiry*, 2 (1968).
Kuntz, P. G., "Order in Language, Phenomena, and Reality : Notes on Linguistic Analysis, Phenomenology, and Metaphysics," *The Monist*, 49 (1965).
Leiber, J., "Linguistic Analysis and Existentialism," *Philosophy and Phenomenological Research*, 32 (1971).
McCormick, P., Schaper, E., Heaton, J. M., "Symposium on Saying and Showing in Heidegger and Wittgenstein," *Journal of the British Society for Phenomenology*, 3 (1972).
Mickunas, A., Oastler, J., "Toward a Rapprochement," *Philosophy and Phenomenological Research*, 33 (1972).
Munson, T. N., "Wittgenstein's Phenomenology," *Philosophy and Phenomenological Research*, 23 (1962).
Murray, M., "Heidegger and Ryle : Two Versions of Phenomenology," *Review of Metaphysics*, 27 (1973).
Murray, M., "A Note on Wittgenstein and Heidegger," *Philosophical Review*, 83 (1974).
Natanson, M., "Phenomenology as a Rigorous Science," *International Philosophical Quarterly*, 7 (1967).
Natanson, M., "Reply to Edie and Tillman," *International Philosophical Quarterly*, 7 (1967).
Peursen, C. A. van, "Edmund Husserl and Ludwig Wittgenstein," *Philosophy and Phenomenological Research*, 20 (1959).
Schmitt, R., "Phenomenology and Analysis," *Philosophy and Phenomenological Research*, 23 (1962).
Skjervheim, H., "Objectivism and the Study of Man," *Inquiry*, 17 (1974).
Smith, D. W., McIntyre, R., "Intentionality Via Intentions," *Journal of Philosophy*, 68 (1971).
Spiegelberg, H., "The Puzzle of Ludwig Wittgenstein's Phänomenologie (1929-?)," *American Philosophical Quarterly*, 5 (1968).
Spiegelberg, H., "A Phenomenological Approach to the Ego," *The Monist*, 49 (1965).

Spiegelberg, H., "Rejoinder to Vere Chappell and Roderick Chisholm," *The Monist*, 49 (1965).

Tillman, F., "Transcendental Phenomenology and Analytic Philosophy," *International Philosophical Quarterly*, 7 (1967).

Tillman, F., "Phenomenology and Philosophical Analysis," *International Philosophical Quarterly*, 6 (1966).

Tranøy, K. E., "Contemporary Philosophy : The Analytic-The Continental," *Philosophy Today*, 8 (1964).

Turnbull, R. G., "Linguistic Analysis, Phenomenology and the Problems of Philosophy : An Essay in Metaphilosophy," *The Monist*, 49 (1965).

INDEX OF NAMES

AMERICAN UNIVERSITY PUBLICATIONS IN PHILOSOPHY

Volume I, 1973	EXPLANATION : NEW DIRECTIONS IN PHILOSOPHY by the Faculty of Philosophy at The American University
Volume II, 1976	ANALYTIC PHILOSOPHY AND PHENOMENOLOGY edited by Harold A. Durfee